HOUSES WITH NAMES

My grandmother was born in a house with a name. La Casella.

'HOUSES
WITH NAMES,

THE ITALIAN IMMIGRANTS OF HIGHWOOD, ILLINOIS

Adria Bernardi

UNIVERSITY OF ILLINOIS PRESS

Urbana and Chicago

Manufactured in the United States of America
C 5 4 3 2 1

All photographs in this book are by Adria Bernardi.

This book is printed on acid-free paper.

Library of Congress Cataloging-in-Publication Data

Bernardi, Adria, 1957-
    Houses with names : the Italian immigrants of Highwood, Illinois /
Adria Bernardi.
        p.   cm.
    Bibliography: p.
    Includes index.
    ISBN 0-252-01581-9 (alk paper)
    1. Italian-Americans—Illinois—Highwood—Social life and customs.
2. Highwood (Ill.)—Social life and customs.   3. Apennines (Italy)—
Emigration and immigration.   4. Highwood (Ill.)—Emigration and
immigration.   I. Title.
F549.H65B47   1990
977.3′21—dc19   89-30741
                                                                CIP

For my grandparents,
Massima and Tony Vanoni, and Mariuccia and Nello Piacentini

Contents

Preface

Before I could speak, I heard the stories of people whom I had never met. My grandmother spun out strings of names that meant nothing to me—the names of aunts and uncles, of great aunts and great uncles, and people long dead from across the valley. How many times I heard the story of her sister Ada:

A beautiful girl, she looked like a Madonna, with long, black hair. She was like an angel. And smart. She was smart enough to be a teacher, but we were too poor. Then she got sick, poor Ada, *povrina*, with polio, and she sat in a chair. Everybody came to see her. How many times, I carried her on my back because she could not walk up the mountains. On my back.

There is a villa in Groppo. It belonged to Signora Angeletta who came up to the mountains each summer from Modena. Your grandfather and his family were *contadini* for them, your *zia* Teresa and your *zia* Nilde, too. Their family had a piece of land and an *ara*, the place in front of the house where you beat the grain. And they cultivated the rest of the land for Signora Angeletta. One time, Signora Angeletta went to visit my sister Ada in the hospital in Modena. Ada went there to the clinic many, many times. All the *signori* would come to visit her at La Casella, our house. There was always a full house. One time Adolfetto Ferrari, the secretary of Modena, brought her back from the clinic. In fact, he paid the bill. The secretary of Modena.

If, in a family, one member refuses to release the past, it lingers on, an uninvited guest. An intruder in out-of-date shoes imposing his bad jokes and secrets on you. You are linked to me, this intruder says. I will not stop talking. You can't deny me. You are not interested? Too bad. You are involved. This is fact.

In my family, my grandmother Mariuccia's relentless grip led to an

xi

eternal dance with the past. Her emotions were different from those that inspire descendants to preserve (or invent) family crests. For her, the past was more alive than the present.

Three times, as a child, I was allowed to look in a trunk where she kept the sacred vessels of the past. Linens worked for betrothal. Photos of the funeral corteges of her sister and mother. And in her second-story bedroom, kneeling before the chest, on a floor whose boards mumbled, she showed me—her greatest, most awful, treasure: a plait of her sister Ada's hair. The hair of a woman dead twenty-five years, black as a raven, in a chest with mothballs.

My grandparents, Mariuccia and Nello Piacentini, and Massima and Tony Vanoni, joined other Italian immigrants who had started coming to Highwood, Illinois, before World War I, when it was a town of laborers on Chicago's affluent North Shore. This history of Highwood was born, in part, of my grandmother Mariuccia's obsession with the past, handed on to me in the form of an involuntary impulse that makes me constantly look back over my shoulder. My grandfathers, like so many immigrant men of their generation, rarely spoke of the past. When they closed the doors of their stone houses behind them, they slammed them tight. If part of the reason I started to record the recollections of Highwood's Italians was an imposed sense of duty to keep the past alive, another was the sense of loss after my grandfathers died.

Forty-four people speak in this history of Highwood's Italian immigrant community. They spoke with me in tape-recorded interviews about their lives in Italy, in Highwood, and in other places throughout the world. Eight chapters of the book are oral histories, based on these interviews. The other chapters are essays, and they attempt to take up various questions about ethnicity, identity, and memory.

How we eat, what we are called, and how we speak are three distinct ways in which our identities, our allegiances and personal boundaries, are revealed. The last two chapters, "The Smoke of the Train," "The Burden of a Name," and the epilogue, "*Belote* in a Foreign Tongue," deal with these themes. We are first shaped within the family—over the dinner table as mothers and fathers and grandmothers and aunts coax allegiances with their sauces, broths, and desserts. A name represents the hopes of the parents who chose it and the identity of the person who owns it. Over generations, even as food and language and other identifiers fade, a name is a sign that remains to mark cultural heritage. The epilogue, "*Belote* in a Foreign Tongue," examines language and identity. The language we speak is a badge; in an immigrant community, it shows where one stands in relation to the ethnic community and the society outside. This essay also discusses writing a narrative that recreates oral communications—that is, writing a story based on a spoken story.

The book's title, *Houses with Names,* refers not to a custom in Highwood, but to a custom in the Modenese Apennines, where houses have had names for longer than anyone can recall. It represents, in a sense, the beginning of a story, the place where a person began.

And before beginning, I would like to thank those who supported this project, first, the men and women who allowed me into their houses to interview them. I am grateful I will be able to carry with me their words and voices. Their names are listed at the end of the book.

Way back before I started five years ago, John Egerton, writer and friend, believed I had a worthy project. I thank him for his encouragement, advice, and generosity. Mary Powers, Sarah Nordgren, and Mark Wukas read drafts of the book from beginning to end, and I am deeply indebted to them. It would have been much harder to begin without the encouragement of friends Kevin and Daniela Gitlin, and Susan Glazer. Studs Terkel's kind words of encouragement were very important to me at a point when I was still fitting together the pieces that became this book.

Rudolph Vecoli and the Immigration History Research Center at the University of Minnesota supported my research early on. The American Italian Historical Association provided a forum to test out the work, and I especially thank Dominic Candeloro and Luciano Iorizzo of this group. I would also like to thank the United Mine Workers of America which gave me a grant to have Lawrence Santi's interview transcribed.

I'm grateful to the people who opened up their homes during the course of my travels: Helen and Emilio Cadamagnani, Ralph and Jean Stone, Phyllis and Robert Gitlin, Peter Swanson, and Will McDowell and Kimberly Bell. Gary Mormino, Fred Gardaphe, Stephanie Booth, Michael Ebner, and Leslie Orear of the Illinois Labor History Society made useful suggestions during the course of my research. Others shared published material and other information with me, including: Franco Marchioni, Adolfo Galli, Alberto Galli, Giacomo Cortesi, Guerrino Piacentini, Mario Fanti, Dr. Hugh Bernardi, John Mussatto, Steve Stout, Cesare and Mary Rose Bernardi, Anna Cavinato Wickman, and my sister-in-law, Beth Shackleford Bernardi.

While writing the book I had the privilege of collaborating with a longtime friend, sculptor Margot McMahon, on a documentary portrait of Highwood's Italian immigrants called "These Hands Have Done a Lot." I thank Eileen Mackevich of the Illinois Humanities Council;

Anthony Fornelli of Unico; and Mayor Fidel Ghini, Bruno Bertucci, and Debra Warren of Highwood.

I have been most fortunate to work with the University of Illinois Press and its director, Richard Wentworth. Carol Bolton Betts, my editor, made the work stronger with her insightful observations and a genuine understanding of it.

I thank the friends who watched over me, asking countless times, "So, how's the book coming?"—especially, my brother, Ron, and sisters, Michelle and Jennifer. My inlaws, Thomas and Virginia Stovall, could not have been more supportive had I been born to them. My parents, Edward and Mary Bernardi, have been most generous, and I thank them for trusting me with their pasts and the pasts of their parents.

And last, I thank my husband, Jeffrey Stovall, for walking beside me.

Introduction

In the winter in the Modenese Apennines, the snowfall was deep. During the growing season, the mountains of calcified soil and clay yielded little. People lived on a diet of the flour from chestnuts and *polenta*, cornmeal mush.

In the 1890s emigrants left the mountains to find seasonal work. They went to the plains and the big cities. The men went to work in the foundries of Germany, the coal mines of Luxembourg, and the factories of Switzerland. They went to Sardinia, Corsica, and North Africa. They went to France to work as farm laborers. They went to North, Central, and South America. They journeyed as merchants, shepherds, charcoal makers, woodcutters, stonecutters, and stonemasons—*scalpellini* in Italian, *scarplin'* in the dialect of the Frignano region of Modena.

The women, too, left the mountains to work. Young girls left their homes each winter to work as maids and nursemaids in the big cities of Livorno, Florence, and Pisa, and in southern France. By World War I the word "emigration" was synonymous with depopulation.

In their search for work, Domenica Mocogni said, the Italians were everywhere, "like the grace of God." Between 1901 and 1909, nearly 600,000 Italians emigrated yearly; nearly 2,000,000 entered the United States between 1899 and 1910. This pattern of emigration, so long inscribed throughout Italian society, prompted contemporary historian Robert Foerster to describe Italian emigration of this era as one of the "extraordinary movements of mankind."

Who was the first Italian to arrive in Highwood, Illinois? This is a matter of debate. This is what Adelmo Bertucci told me when he was ninety-eight: "Some, they say, 'twas the Mordini, and some, they say, it was the Ori. Enrico Mordini, he said, he was the first to come in Highwood. I don't know."

The Oris say they came in the early 1900s. The Mordinis say they

1

came in 1904. They came to Highwood from Chicago to work as ditchdiggers for plumbers. Then, the Mordinis say, other Italian families moved in. There were the Santi brothers who came in 1906. And there were the Muzzarelli, Lomoro, and Lorusso families who arrived here early. So did the Nustra family. Then, there is the account of Emilio Piacenza from Sant'Annapelago in the province of Modena. When Emilio worked in Highland Park in 1900, according to his cousin Aldo Piacenza, the only Italian there was a carpenter named Agosto de Bon, a Venetian.

Most of the Italians who settled in Highwood came from the Frignano, a region of the province of Modena in the north central part of Italy. If this book betrays a bias in favor of the Modenese, it is because this is my grandparents' region of origin. The tilt is not without merit, since the Modenese have dominated Highwood since the 1920s when they overwhelmed the Swedes, Irish, and Germans who preceded them. Other families came from the Apennines of Bologna and Tuscany, provinces that intersect Modena in the mountains. Immigrants from the *Piemonte*, in the north, and Naples, Rome, Bari, Sicily, Calabria, and the Abruzzi settled in Highwood.

The Italians came to Highwood to work for the wealthy of the surrounding communities. One man, working in Chicago during the 1920s, was told by a fellow immigrant: "You better go way north. Up to those rich towns. Plenty of work up there."

By the turn of the century, a transformation had begun along Lake Michigan. An area that had been farmland, countryside, and small villages where Chicago's elite had summer retreats was growing into suburbs where the wealthy were making their permanent homes. After World War I, the North Shore boomed. The populations of towns like Kenilworth, Lake Forest, Glencoe, Winnetka, and Highland Park doubled between 1920 and 1930. The creation of the North Shore suburbs was integrally tied to that razzle-dazzle, move-at-a-clip, buy low–sell high, commercial kinesis that made Chicago a great city.

These communities are among the wealthiest in the United States. The wealth is so pervasive, so casual, it is easy to convince oneself that this is the norm. In 1985, Kenilworth was the wealthiest town in the nation. Six others nearby, including Glencoe, Winnetka, and Lake Forest, ranked among the top fifty.

Historian Michael Ebner has written in his book on the North Shore that Highwood is a community "out of place." In a sense it is. It has been a town of laborers amidst towns of industrial barons, presidents of banks, and chairmen of boards. It is an ethnic town among communities whose inhabitants, either by generational distance or conscious decision, are removed from their ethnic origins.

Highwood has always been a tavern town, an aside on an otherwise sober shoreline. Highwood, Philip Pasquesi said, "has always had a very bad, bad, bad, bad reputation." During Prohibition, Italian women ran "blind pigs," houses where liquor was sold illegally. There was gambling and prostitution. Throughout the years, Highwood was a thorn in the side of its neighbors. Once, at the ballot box, Highland Park rejected a bid to annex Highwood. To its neighbors, Highwood has been an embarrassment, perhaps even a joke.

Highwood was incorporated in 1887, a year after the violent Haymarket massacre in Chicago. It grew up as a garrison town beside Fort Sheridan, a federal army base built on land donated by Chicago businessmen with ties to the North Shore who feared that potential uprisings by urban workers threatened their investment. As a North Shore community, Highwood has always been a minor shareholder in that investment.

Highwood was a community of laborers and craftsmen who worked in the jobs spawned by affluence. Country clubs and new roads were built. Schools, hospitals, and other public buildings were erected. Wealthy people needed chauffeurs, gardeners, maids, cooks, and laundresses. The Italians came to the North Shore, as I have heard time and time again, "to work for some rich people."

They worked on the railroad lines that helped transform the countryside into suburbs. They worked on the construction of country clubs, such as the Old Elm in Highland Park and the Lake Shore in Glencoe. They worked as gardeners and mechanics on the estates of powerful men like Harold and Cyrus McCormick, heirs to the International Harvester fortune. They served members of the Swift and Armour families of Lake Forest.

They worked for some of the most powerful men in the Chicago business world: General Robert E. Wood, head of Sears and Roebuck; Stanley Harris, chairman of the Harris Trust and Savings, and "dean" of Chicago bankers; members of the family of A. B. Dick, who founded the mimeograph corporation of the same name; Samuel Insull, whose empire, founded upon the distribution of electricity, made him the most powerful man in Chicago until the Depression; and Albert Lasker, the executive credited with having founded modern advertising.

The women worked as maids, laundresses, seamstresses, and cooks. Mary Baldi told me this: "That was the main thing—cleaning house and ironing and laundry. Most all the Italian women went out doing this. They were good, hardworking girls. At that time, it was hard to get anybody, and there were all these Italian immigrants from Italy, didn't know how to speak—but still they knew how to work."

For many Highwood families the first stopping point in the United States was Chicago. Immigrants from Sant'Annapelago worked as fruit vendors at Chicago's South Water Market. Sante Pasquesi worked in the Gonnella bakery in Chicago before bringing members of his clan to work in Highland Park at the Moraine Hotel, which then overlooked Lake Michigan. Women worked as seamstresses in the garment district west of downtown Chicago. Enea Cortesi worked as a construction laborer at a United States Steel plant in Gary, and Ciro Gibertini worked at a Chicago fish market.

A few families tried farming in Minnesota, Indiana, and on the North Shore, only to abandon the endeavors.

Many of the Italians who settled in Highwood, particularly those who emigrated from the southern provinces of Italy, worked on the railway before settling on the North Shore. Mike Lorusso worked as a railroad laborer, traveling between Chicago and Vancouver. "Just like a hobo," he said. "Today here, tomorrow over there."

Highwood families, especially those of Modenese, Bolognese, and Piemontese origin, first came to the United States to work in the coal mines of Colorado, Alabama, Illinois, and Texas. They lived in mining communities near Des Moines, Iowa, and Missouri. Many of the Italians who settled in Highwood faced layoffs, shutouts, and strikes in Midwestern mines during the 1920s and 1930s.

Other families came up to Highwood from the northern Illinois coal fields that included the towns of Dalzell, Cherry, Ladd, Mark, and Spring Valley. In 1908, the Chicago Italian Chamber of Commerce *Bulletin* reported more than two thousand emigrants from Modena and Bologna in this area. It attributed the start of this emigration chain to a man from Modena named only as "Fabiano of Fanano."

Highwood's Italians also have ties to the northern Illinois coal towns of Carbon Hill and Coal City. In an 1899 poster, the miners of Carbon Hill—where five hundred Italians lived in 1908—sent a message back to their "fellow workers" in their hometowns in Modena and Bologna, towns like Fanano, Sestola, and Grecchia. The message was posted on May 14, the feast day of the Madonna of the *Querciola* (the young oak), a day of both religious and proletarian significance. The devout pray to the Blessed Virgin for their loved ones. And they pray for the salvation of "all the workers, all the poor and all the oppressed." The children of these laborers were among those who settled in Highwood.

Many who came from the mines worked at golf courses and estates during the summer, returning to the mines in the winter. Adele Dinelli, who emigrated from near Fanano, told about the mines and coming to Highwood:

There was no work for women. There was no work for the men, neither. The mines, the coal mines, sometimes, they stopped. There was not work all the time because there was strikes and they don't work for so long. My husband came over here to work in the golf course. After we came in Highwood, he wanted to move from here, too. I say, "You can move, *ma*, I don't move anymore. Me, I stay here because if you don't work, I could make my living." Because I was work for five dollars a day. Washing floors, washing clothes, wash ceiling, wash windows, all over around here.

This influx of Italian immigrant mining families during the 1920s and 1930s coincided with a surge in Highwood's population. In 1910, Highwood had a population of 1,219. Between 1920 and 1930, it grew from 1,446 to 3,590. This parallels the doubling of population in other North Shore communities during the 1920s, suggesting the level of economic activity during the years following the war.

The arrival of Italian families to Highwood is reflected in the records of the graduating classes of Oak Terrace Elementary School. In 1923, there were no children with Italian surnames graduating. Four years later, 41 percent of the graduating class had Italian names. In the class of 1939, 66 percent of graduating eighth-graders were of Italian origin.

In paese, uptown, Highwood looked like a town of immigrants. On the street, people spoke Italian. There were Italian grocery stores and bakeries. When she arrived in the late 1920s, Domenica Mocogni had no trouble finding the foods to which she was accustomed. Though she spoke no English, she could get along as well uptown in Highwood as she could in Piandelagotti.

Today, the descendants of the original immigrants set the tone of Highwood. The mayor, Fidel Ghini, son of an immigrant from Piandelagotti, grew up in an Iowa coal town. The city council and public organizations are dominated by Italians. In 1980, Highwood's population was 5,452. Of that population, 31 percent claimed some Italian heritage. Twenty-five percent said they were exclusively of Italian origin.

Italians now share Highwood with more recently arrived ethnic groups of Hispanic origins. Workers from Mexico—many of them from the state of Guerrero—began coming to the North Shore in the years following World War II, to do much the same work as the Italian immigrants had earlier in this century. Others, who arrived more recently, have come from the war-torn countries of El Salvador and Nicaragua.

In Highwood, the Italians created a community that somehow managed to be solidly rooted, while constantly weaving between traditional ethnic ways and the ways of modern suburban living. They embraced this modern country which could give them what they had lacked. They fiercely loved the United States, which made — and kept — promises. Yet, they remained wary of its excesses. When someone says, 'n trova' America, "he has found America," it is neither lavish praise for America's wealth, nor a commendation of a person's success. It is a comment reserved for times of disapproval over luxury and excess.

No matter how much money they made (and there were millionaires to emerge from this immigrant community), never did the immigrants mistake themselves for *signori*. They considered themselves craftsmen, laborers, and servants, and were proud of their work. They maintained attitudes of "we" and "they," workers and rich people, yet, rarely did I hear that division expressed in proletarian language. Perhaps this apparent lack of militancy can be explained in part by the political legacy of the Apennines of northern Italy, as argued by Roland Sarti in his history of the region. The people were, he suggests, "cosmopolitan villagers" who had a long history of being able to adapt to changing economic conditions. They were simultaneously *contadini* and workers who had contact with the world outside. They came from small, independent towns with democratic histories. By and large, Sarti maintains in *Long Live the Strong*, they did not subscribe to the radical ideologies that took hold in the plains of Emilia and Tuscany.

Yet, many of Highwood's immigrants came from coal towns, militant communities where people believed in clear distinctions between those who work and those who own. In the northern Illinois coal fields of Spring Valley, Ladd, Dalzell, and Cherry, there were centers of radicalism and anarchism.

There are strains of both of these heritages in Highwood, that of the more moderate "cosmopolitan villager," and that of the militant worker who looks with distrust at *i capitalisti*. Politics is a dangerous thing, especially for immigrants settling in a bastion of Republicanism. Perhaps it was considered radical enough to be a New Deal Democrat on the North Shore.

In Highwood, the immigrants formed a particular and peculiar community where notions of the old world and the newest world met. They carried to the North Shore diverse ideas that meshed and collided. They carried the ideas of peasants capable of supporting enormous work loads, of enterprising merchants, of militant miners, of loyal servants, and of skilled artisans. In Highwood, there were immigrants who were fiercely antichurch and those who were devout Catholics. They brought from Italy notions of democratic socialism and rooted themselves in suburban capitalism. If this journey with Highwood's Italians has taught me anything, it is that it is possible to be simultaneously strongly rooted and steeped in ambiguity.

The Italians of Highwood say many things in this book: Highwood is a tiny semiprecious stone set in the middle of a dazzling diamond cluster. They are well traveled. There is coal dust under their nails. And when they call someone a big shot, it's not necessarily a compliment.

But their story begins, of course, in Italy. It starts in a time and place before electricity altered night and day, in a time and place of houses with names, names rich with meaning and names whose origins are unknown.

1

Houses with Names

MY GRANDMOTHER WAS born in a house with a name.

La Casella. A country house pressed into unyielding mountains. My ancestors could have called it nothing at all. Or they could have simply called it La Casa, standard Italian for "the house." But someone along the line had a flair, and added the diminutive like a flourish to an otherwise unadorned letter, as if the ending "ella" could transform a square concrete building into a palace, like the cinder girl who becomes Cinderella for one evening.

The house-namer was a woman. I am certain of that. Her husband and sons, gone six months to work in Tuscany, taking the sheep to warmer plains or cutting wood for charcoal makers, had come home to find the house christened. The winters are too long, the snow too deep, to live in a house that is only called "the house."

That *casella* means "pigeonhole," according to the modern diction-ary—or "a modest house" in a more antiquated usage—would have been met with an indignant toss of the head and a thrust of the chin by a house-namer who had no time to worry about the distinctions of professors. "This house, is better than a house, that's why it's called La Casella," she would say.

Although my grandmother lived in La Casella, she spent more time at her mother's birthplace, christened La Rimessa, which means "resting place." It was a stop on the Via Giardini, the major road that cuts through the mountains and connects Modena and northern Italy with Tuscany and the rest of central Italy. Dukes, cardinals, and emperors traveled this road. In June of 1796 Napoleon journeyed on the Via Giardini. Twice it was traveled by a pope. At La Rimessa, travelers of less regal standing rested themselves and their horses. This house, so dark and serious, was named by a calloused merchant with a mule and wagon, not by the woman who named La Casella.

My other grandmother's house also had a name: Tavernaro. Like La

Rimessa, Tavernaro edged the highway. Maybe in olden times it was a tavern, she says, but certainly not during her lifetime. After all, my grandmother from Tavernaro was raised by a strict, unmarried aunt who ironed altar linens of the church. Certainly, she was not a woman who would have tolerated the excesses of a roadhouse.

So, I want to know why my ancestors and their neighbors named their houses. An eager student with hand waving mid-air, I want explanations. "Why does a house have the name that it does?" I ask my grandmother. What does it mean? How does it translate? My grandmother cannot tell me why her house was called La Casella, instead of simply, "La Casa."

"A house has its name. Like you have a name. 'Adria.' I have a name. 'Mariuccia.' It doesn't mean anything. It's a title. It's a name," she says.

But some names can be explained, I reason with her. Cà d'Vento— House of Wind that grips the mountaintop when the wind blows. There's Mezzanotte, which means "midnight," and Il Casotto, named "the little house" by someone modest.

How long have these houses had names? How old is the house? Who named the house? I ask, as if by repeating the question, rephrased, I can coax a different answer. The answer is always the same.

"When your mother was a girl," I ask, "was the house named La Casella?"

"Yes, it was, it was. Always that name. Always, always it had that name. Who knows how many years? Who knows how it got that name?" she says, starting to list other houses with names.

There's Canova, literally "Casa Nuova," which means "new house." Exactly how old is this new house? I ask.

"Chi sa. Chi sa. Chi lo sa?" she says. "Who knows? Who knows? Who knows? As long as I've heard its name."

"A hundred years?" She scoffs at my question. "Never mind a hundred years! Many, many more, because you know, I always heard it called that, it always had that name."

The Apennine mountains of Modena were ungenerous, and starting in the 1890s the dwellers of houses with names emigrated to other countries. They came from well-named towns: Pievepelago, Sant'Andreapelago, Roccapelago, Sant'Annapelago, little islands beating back an unsympathetic sea. Two are named for saints—Sant'Anna and Sant'Andrea—and a third, Pieve, means "parish."

There are other well-named towns nearby. Riolunato, named for its river and a moonlit mountain called Monte Cimone. There is Groppo, a cluster of houses my grandfather decided was too small. "Why should I stay in a place that means 'lump'?" he might have said.

So, tell me, I ask my grandmothers and others, tell me about these houses and their names.

I remember Casolari, says this grandmother whose aunt ironed the priest's vestments. (It means "hovels.") Casa Guerri. ("Wars.") Casa Quattro. ("Four.") Because there were four houses? I ask. No, there were more, but that's what they called it. Perhaps, then, Casolari wasn't a hovel and the inhabitants of Casa Guerri got along with each other.

Actually, it was Casa Quattro that was born of war, says Viterbo Ponsi. "My mother was born there. I know. There were four people who escaped from the Romans. They didn't want to go to war anymore, and they passed into these mountains for safety."

Teodoro Sassorossi, who reminds you to put five *s*'s in his name, comes from Fontanini. Nearby were Ambrizana, La Borra, and Roncadiccio. We travel up the mountain. "Then there's Casa di Veneziano ('house of the Venetian'), Le Borelle, Casa Baroni ('house of the Baron') and Vaccarecce. These are all from *il comune*, the municipality, of Pievepelago. After that comes the parish of Sant'Anna. The other part is Roccapelago, and in the other direction, there's Sant'Andrea, which is a parish by itself and where your family comes from. And in the other direction is Modino—that's toward Fiumalbo—and the river comes from Tagliole, way up, near Lago Santo ('holy lake'). Those are really the last inhabitants in the mountains. I remember those places better than I remember a lot of people. I remember the places like it was today," says Sassorossi, whose name means "red stone."

Near Sassorossi's Fontanini perches Cadagnolo. "Casa di Angelo"— Angelo's House—becomes in dialect, "Cà d'Agnolo," shortened further to "Cadagnolo" by ejecting extravagant syllables. A thrifty title for this family known for its acumen in commercial affairs.

Calling a *casa* a *cà* is common in these parts. In Sant'Anna, there is Cà Rossa, "the red house." In Piandelagotti, there is Cà Rossi, named for a family.

There are Cà d'La and Cà d'Cia. The house over there and the house over here, both overshadowed by a craggy rock called Sasso Tignoso, which means "mean-spirited stone" because it offers nothing besides its ugly face.

In Venice, the palaces of patricians were called *ca'*. Ca' d'Oro— "House of Gold." In these mountains the houses are not of gold, and dukes did not inhabit them, although some houses with names claim noble origins. Enea Cortesi was born in Il Baronio, where a baron lived a hundred and fifty years ago. And what of Ca' d'Baron'? "Eh, I guess they must have been *baroni* at one time," says Philip Pasquesi.

Encouraged in my quest for the absolute, I further question my grandmother from La Rimessa. Campanile? It's named that because there's a bell tower? Right? Was there a church?

"No, there's no church," she says, "I don't know what was there before, but they call it Campanile."

I am not alone in trying to find reason behind the names of houses. Delia H. Pugh, writing more than thirty years ago in a scholarly publication called *Names*, also tried. "Every farm had its own name," she wrote. "And the people of the farm were known by the farm name rather than their own." No one could tell her, however, why a particular hamlet in North Wales was called "Rhoslefain," a name that means "the crying in the gorse." "It is a name—like yours is 'Delia,'" my grandmother might tell her.

I cannot give up, however. I take liberties and ascribe meaning where I have been assured there is none. What about Pellegrande? This means "big skin." Maybe, back in time, there was a big fat fellow who lived there. There's another house called Perdepolo, where Viterbo Ponsi grew up. He doesn't know why it received that name. *Perde* means "he loses," I reason. By supplying an extra *l*, you'd come up with *pollo*, which means "chicken." Could it be that the chickens of people long-forgotten were abducted by wolves? Or hawks? Or thieves? Maybe Perdepolo kept Pellegrande's stomach stocked.

Allow for grammatical errors, and I can tell you great stories of names bestowed by sardonic people who suspected an inside joke was the only luxury they'd ever have.

What of the little village Boccasuolo, built midway up a mountain on a shelf between a valley and a peak. *Bocca* means "mouth"; *suolo,* "soil." The town is an opening of earth on a sheer mountainside. Montecreto balances on another mountain. *Creto* is from the Latin, *cretum,* meaning "broken." So, then, the people tried to scratch out a living on a broken mountain. Which was kinder, a hole in the earth or a broken mountain?

I hear words I understand and continue my search for the concrete. The house named La Luna means "moon." Capiana? I can translate this. In true Italian, Casa di Piana; in dialect, Capiana, words familiarly merged. "The House of the Plain." Or perhaps it was the house of a stonecutter; a *piana* is also a squared stone. But for every one name I understand, there are ten whose origins remain a mystery. Doesn't Le Rive mean "shores"? "Is there a lake by this house?" I ask my grandmother from La Casella. "It means nothing. It's the name of the house," she says.

She recites a litany and offers no explanations. Legadé. Tambrullo. Capannone. Frateria. Canova. Moradina. Passonà. Roncombarlaio. Medale. La Cavedagna. She moves from one to another as if they were beads of the rosary. At the eleventh bead, the big bead, she pauses for mystery.

She tells of Cento Croci ("a hundred crosses"), a place with a wicked past where hideous crimes were committed, who knows when—maybe sometime between Christ and Columbus. Her mother told her this story a hundred times, she says.

"In old times," my grandmother starts, "the road they called La Via Vecchia, the Old Way, passed by there. At one time, they killed people. There used to be a restaurant, an inn. An old house. At this place, when people passed by, they killed—not everyone—but almost. And then, they cooked them and served the meat to the other people who passed through. Well, then, a priest passed through, and he found a finger in his plate, and he put it in his pocket. He went to the law and he showed them that they were eating people. They came and took them all away. The people who ate people. At Cento Croci."

What is the origin of this name?

The question hangs in the air like an ignorant joke. What, after all, is the significance of literal interpretation compared to a finger in a soup bowl?

CHAPTER

2

Chestnuts and Snowfall

THE SNOWFALL WAS so heavy in the mountains, say the immigrants from the Apennines, that no one could move from his house all winter. So deep that no one could work. Weather patterns have changed and now it doesn't snow as much as it once did, they say. Was there really more snow or less technology? Annual snowfall can be measured in inches and we could know for certain. But for their purposes can the unmeasured absoluteness of a snow cover be one way in which memory records with certainty the difficulties of a time when winter lingered?

The mountains are twisted, forged from calcified soil and clay. It is *terra che rende quasi nulla*—land that yields almost nothing—according to a song of the region, a theme common in songs of mountain people.

The land of the northern Apennines was a mixed blessing. On one hand, unlike their counterparts in other regions of Italy, Apennine *contadini* were far more likely to own their land. Those without land were in the minority. The holdings were small, however, and while the average family needed fifteen hectares to subsist, most had less than five.

Following the formation of the modern Italian nation-state in the 1860s, government policy and increases in taxes on land caused great stress for peasants who owned small parcels of land. Communally held land used primarily for grazing was transferred to private ownership, causing a decline in shepherding by decreasing the land available for grazing.

As cultivation of the land intensified, mountainsides were deforested to create new fields, leaving communities vulnerable to floods and mudslides, like the one which nearly destroyed the town of Sant'Annapelago in 1896.

These communities were isolated. In 1900, about one-fifth of all Apennine municipalities lacked any roads except foot paths and mule trails. Yet the communities were commercially tied to the vital affairs

14

of cities like Bologna, Lucca, Modena, Genoa, and Florence. Forced by an unreliable and meager agricultural output at home, the mountain people looked outside. They journeyed as merchants, shepherds, charcoal makers, woodcutters, stonemasons, and stonecutters. This diversity of skills led historian Roland Sarti to remark, "A peasant conditioned to appreciate occupational diversification was a peasant confident in his own ability to deal with new situations."

Inhabitants of the area began leaving their native villages in the 1890s, gambling that their lives would be improved by a journey outside, a "campaign" — *la mia campagna* — as the early immigrants called their expeditions, using the same word a soldier would. By the turn of the century, and again after World War I, emigration had intensified so much that those left behind spoke of depopulation. Beneath this transparency of bold movement, however, lies a canvas with a landscape that seems motionless.

Adele Dinelli pauses only to catch her breath. She talks quickly, sharply, with emphasis, using English, Italian, and her Bolognese dialect to get the story out. Getting it out, that's the main thing, the important thing. We can worry about the fine points later. She leans into you as she talks. She watches you. She doesn't want to be talking to someone who isn't listening. Watch the one-liners. They go by fast. Her voice is strong and intense. She bore the years on her back, and instead of breaking, it got stronger, an isometric trick of survival. When she sold her little house, located in a commerical strip, the buyers agreed she could stay there, rent free, until she died. That was more than ten years ago. She's ninety-five and this is 1987.

When I was nine years old, I was work for somebody else in Italy. I was do everything. From the time I was nine years old until seventeen, I went home just one time. My home was about three hours from where I lived. La Vergine is my place where I was born, in the *comune di* Lizzano, province of Bologna. I'm *bolognese*. One time, I went home, I was about fourteen, when I changed to work for somebody else. I came to my aunt's, it was August the twenty-fifth, it was a big holiday. And I went home because my boss, about eight days before it was that holiday, she hit me. That's why I went away from her. Because I don't do nothing to her. I say, she hit me because I don't have no mamma. I don't have no mother, you know, she died when I was a little girl. I was raised up with my sister. When I cry, I say to my boss, "There's a feast at my place and I'm going to the holiday over there." She was afraid I'd quit, so she let me go home. She give me four cents, you know, four penny. She give only four pennies, she never did before in her life.

And when I went home there was my aunt and she said at dinnertime, "Who wanna come to me to be my servant?" I said, "I do." I left my clothes where they were, and everything at my old boss's. I change jobs, I went to the province of Modena, in the *comune* of Fanano. Serrazzone was the town where my aunt was. And I stayed there until I got married, I was seventeen years old. She was give me like ten dollars a month. From nine years old until seventeen years old, I only draw ten dollars a month.

My daddy never gave me nothing. My daddy lived in the province of Bologna. But in an hour and a half he could have come and visit me if he wanted to—but he never did. He never would give me money, because my boss pay my father. They don't pay me. Where I was work, I didn't get no money at all.

When I asked to marry, my aunt, she make a dinner for us. I went in France the same day I got married. We went to Nice. In *Nizza* I was watching my sister-in-law's children. My husband, Mario Dinelli, opened up a store. He was from Fanano.

Where'd I meet him? I was watching the cows. He passed by the fields, and that's where I met him. Over there in the farm. I didn't go with him very long. I went with another boy about three year, but we broke up because he was rich and I was poor. He was from Serrazzone. But these people, they got a lot of land and I was a servant. The way I heard, his people, they think he was a rich boy and I was too poor. They don't want him to marry a poor girl like me.

When I was growing up I grew up by myself because I went to work for some people—and you don't get to go with your sister and brother. My brother, one was in this country, and the other one, I don't know. Both my sisters got married when they was young girls. When I was little, my sister was about eighteen years old and she raised me up. My mother was sick. She had me, but she never changed a diaper on me. She never nursed me neither. She was sick before she had me and then she passed away.

And then my sister raised me up until my father got remarried. And my sister, as soon as my father wanted to remarry, she got married because she don't want to be in the house when the stepmother come in.

And I worked all the time for the farmer people, worked in the fields. I never did nothing in the house. Never, never, until I got married. I never know how to cook. I never know how to do nothing, you know what I mean? Nothing! Today, the girls make me sick. They never work in the house, they don't cook for the husband—and they got the book and they know how to read. Me, they never send me a day for school.

I worked in the fields, you know what I mean, the land—cut the wheat, make the hay, put down the potatoes. There was just my uncle and me, that's all. I stay there until I got married. And I went in France. Then I come in this country to the coal mines.

Massima Vanoni, my grandmother, folds a bedsheet the way she closes a *tortellini,* with corners perfectly matched. She worked as a seamstress, and she is deliberate, methodical, and intense in every task. When she bastes a hem, the stiches are uniform and equidistant. She is neither careless nor carefree, like a child who has always been with adults. Yet, when she lays down the task, she can be whimsical, a child still.

I was born the fourth of May, 1906, in Sant'Andreapelago, *provincia di* Modena. Sant'Andrea is a little mountain town. It's a small village but very pretty.

When I was young, it had eight hundred people. But now, it's smaller.

My father was named Emilio Santi. My mother, Cherubina Morelli. My father was born in Sant'Andrea and my mother in Riolunato. My mother had a brother named Bartolomeo and a sister named Zelinda. My mother's father was named Silvio, and her mother, Caterina.

My grandfather Silvio transported food from Modena to Sant'Andrea with horses. There were no trucks in those days. And he sold things, wheat, corn, wine, all in bulk. He worked alone, then he worked with his son, who would have been my uncle. After my grandfather died, my uncle wasn't interested in the business. He sold timber to be cut for making charcoal and he had some men who worked for him.

My grandfather Silvio I remember vaguely. I remember very well that he wore a long beard, down to his chest. And my grandmother died during the *spagnola,* the influenza, in 1918. There were many, many people who died. In my husband's family two cousins died.

My grandfather Silvio had property. He had two *poderi,* they called them there. Farms. It was his land. He had *contadini.* He had land in Sant'Andrea and in Riolunato. I remember that the *contadini* brought milk, cheese, and butter. One was named Andrea Fini. And the one at the property in Riolunato was named Arcangelo Bernardi.

The earliest thing I remember is when my mother died and they showed me her corpse. That's the earliest thing I remember. I would have been four or five years old. She died during childbirth. I would have had a brother. But my mother had this baby in the winter, and at that time there was absolutely nothing—it was cold and you couldn't heat the houses. This baby was born and she got pneumonia. She died New Year's Day of 1910 or '11. And the baby died seventeen days after my mother. They named the baby Giuseppe, Joseph. He would have been named after my father's father.

When I was very little, around the time my mother died until the beginning of the First World War, I lived with my father and his mother. But during the time of the *spagnola*, my grandmother Caterina died, and I went to live with my aunt and uncle Morelli. This was during the war and they didn't need the food stamps to eat because they had food from their farms. So, the food stamps that would have been given to support me went to my father, and I went with my aunt and uncle. I always lived with them until I got married.

I started going to school when I was six years old. The first, second, and third grades were in Sant'Andrea, and then the fourth and fifth were in Pieve. I walked to Pieve. It took about a half hour. I always went in the winter. In the snow. I walked with friends who went to school with me.

After I finished elementary school—because you went there until the fifth grade—and then—I started to go to school in Pieve with the nuns to learn to sew.

In the morning, before starting work, there were prayers. Then, there was silence for a half hour. It was a little hard, but then you could talk while you were working but not really carry on conversations, just a few words. And then there was the reading. I read aloud many times. Other times someone else read. There was an hour of lecture, of catechism, of religious things. School started at nine in the morning and finished at 11:30. And then it was time to eat. Then, you could joke around, talk, and play together. Then you started again and worked until four in the afternoon and everybody went home. They came from Sant'Anna, Modino, from San Michele, from Riolunato, from all the surrounding towns.

(from Italian)

Domenick Linari pauses and thinks before he answers each question. He is as frugal with words as a merchant purchasing inventory. He is as careful with them as a miner with his lamp in the shaft. He searches for them and fits them precisely in place, like a master mason building a wall. He has been all three: a merchant, a miner, a mason. He considers himself uneducated, yet there are books all over his house. He has marked his place in *Brain*, which lies on the coffee table. There are books about history. There is some philosophy. On a bedroom shelf there is a volume of Friedrich Wilhelm Nietzsche. "Nietzsche—well, me and Nietzsche, we don't get along too well," he says. "It's really not his fault, though. I find him kind of hard to understand."

Have you been over there? You know where *la* Pieve is? Frassinoro, where I'm from, is across from there, that would be northeast. The only time I was at Pieve, I would walk there with my dad. And it took about a half a day to walk there, across the mountain. But I can't tell you just how far it is. Because if you go over the hills it's one way. If you go around the roads, it's twice as far. Montefiorino is another town that's close by. I saw it after it was destroyed by the Nazis. It was burned down and then it's been rebuilt.

My family had a few little pieces of land. It didn't amount to much. My mother made a living for us sewing. I went as far as the sixth grade. When I came to this country my school days were over.

We ate like kings. We had *polenta*—you don't know what *polenta* is anyway. *Polenta* is cornmeal mush, and we had a little soup and that was just about—you might as well say it was all we ate and be done with it. Bread, whenever they had flour enough to make it. Yeah, oh, we were well fed.

Teresa Saielli's house was always precise. The Italian ceramic tea set, nested like a chicken laying eggs, was perched on a dark wooden shelf above the desk. On the desk, which was covered by a piece of glass, was propped a black-and-white studio photograph of two toddlers, a smiling great niece and nephew, myself and my brother. Letters were kept in the top right drawer. The phone book and pens were in the middle. Bills were laid in the top left drawer, along with the checks that my father wrote out to the gas, electric, and telephone companies each month, and which she signed. There were many lovely things in her home, arranged just so, and never relocated from the time I was born in 1957 until the time of her death in 1984. She possessed elegant china and furniture, discarded and handed down by people for whom she ironed when blond wood came in and mahogany went out.

We lived in Groppo. We were *contadini*.

The land belonged to somebody else. We work in a farm, and somebody else owned it and the animals, too. They had cow and sheep, you know, you gotta go watch them in the farm, watch them all day long. I don't like the sheep. Cows, yeah, but the sheep, no. *Stupide.*

The people that owned our house were from Modena—they come just in the summer.

In Groppo there was a kitchen and one other room. In the other room, there was a big table. We got another place where you make the bread and the dough. Just like a kitchen, but smaller. There was a special oven in the wall where you cook bread. And then there were four bedrooms.

Then we went to Roncombarlaio because my brother Nello didn't want to hoe the fields. I didn't like Roncombarlaio. I was used to Groppo.

When my sister Nilde was a little girl, she had the tapeworm, you know, it comes from the stomach. Sometime they got it from the food. And when the worm come by the throat my mother would give her some whiskey. One time my mother no home. My sister go over there, you know, where the whiskey was, and drink all the whiskey. Then she was drunk. When my mother come home, she's scared to death. My sister was nine or ten. She had some worm in the stomach. Whiskey kills it. When it came up her throat she was afraid she'd choke. She took the whiskey, drank it all. She killed it. Oh, *Dio,* little devil.

I didn't go much to school in the old country. In the morning I gotta go watch the cow. I'm the oldest—I gotta stay home. The others went to school. Nilde go to school. Nello, too. Then when I was older my mother wanted to send me to school. I say, "No, I can't go to school no more!" But I learn for myself. Write and read and that's all. Not much, but it's okay.

My mother made the cheese. We had cows, and we make the cheese every morning. You gotta lot of work at that time. Now they do nothing. When they got the *castagne,* the chestnuts, they send me all the time over there to get them. I remember one morning when I was getting the *castagne,* I passed by where the priest lived. He come by the window, he say, "Teresa! Today is the feast of Santa Teresa, go home and pray!" So I said, "My father will fix me good if I go home."

I had to go cut the chestnuts over there in rain. I carried an umbrella. Over there by myself. Oh, the life. I'm scared to stay over there. Cut all these nuts. For what? Now, they don't do anything, the people. They live good now. Not in my time.

Some people make bread with the flour from the *castagne*. They make *polenta*, they make a lotta things. I don't like it. I like the *castagne* when you roast them—the *mondine*. *Polenta*, no.

Me, I went to first, second, third in school. My sister said, "You don't go to school because you don't like it." Yeah, you don't like it! You *testona*—hard head! Nilde even taught in the school for the kids. In Groppo. First, second, third. Three grades. Then some teacher from Modena—she got the certificate, she got all the exam—and Nilde, she gotta go out. If my daddy got money, send her maybe in Pavullo or Modena to school, she could teach all the time. When you don't got this (rubbing fingers of one hand together, a gesture indicating money) you don't do nothing.

I got the girl living here with me now. She say, "Did you go to college?" I start laughing. *Testona*! For college I work.

In the old country, for fun, we'd dance. That's all. Dance and when we were through at midnight have some bread and cheese, and eat. You know my Uncle Giovanni, the brother of my father, he had a place, most all the time we danced there. If you gotta room in the back of the house, most everybody would come there to dance.

You know what I remember? When Ada Pasquesi's mother got married. I remember. My mother was sitting down. At the time she was pregnant with my brother Nello. And me, I was just a little girl then. But I remember everything. I remember when they danced. Me, I'm just a little kids. I sit there by my mother. I remembered when they danced. And the father of Ada was more old than the mother. I remember it like it was today. I remember my mother and me sit down there on the chair and look at the people dance.

I had an uncle, my grandmother's brother, he was an attorney of law. When he died, my mother hit me with a broom because there was a feast at Riolunato and I was wearing a red dress. So I changed to a blue one. Then, on Sunday, I went out with the red dress and met a cousin who said to me, "Your uncle is dead and you're wearing a red dress?" And I said to her, "Give me the money and I'll go buy a black one."

Philip Pasquesi enjoys talking and telling stories. He says, "I got married the same year as your grandparents, the best year to get married. 1929. You know what a good year that was!" He tells a story that my mother says he tells every time he sees her. She was a little girl, seven years old and just arrived from Italy. He says, *"Maria Silvia, ti piace l'America?"* "Maria Silvia, do you like America?" "No!!!" The seven-year-old was adamant. Every time he has seen her for the last forty-five years he asks the same question. It still irritates her. Evidently, he knows.

I was born in 1901, December 20. The name of the little town is Cadagnolo, *provincia di* Modena. I come over here the eight of September, 1920.

Well, during the war, everybody was in the army. And I was very, very young and had to do almost everything. My sister—she's two years older—and I, we plowed the dirt. We had two cows. I done all kinds of things. I went after sheep down in Ferrara, down on the lowland. See, in the summertime they come up, and then when it starts to get cold they go way down to Ferrara and Padua. My uncle had about a 150 sheep and he had two sons who were going after the sheep, but they were called in the army. So he called me from Cadagnolo, I remember, the fourth of March, I had to go down to Ferrara and I had to take care of the sheep. It was not far from Ferrara, a little town by the name of San Martin'. And that's where I went after the sheep.

We had land out there and then I used to pick *castagne*, chestnuts, my mother, my sister, and I. Even if it rained we had to pick up the chestnuts. We had a sack over our head or an umbrella, and we worked out there even if it rained because those chestnuts they gotta be picked up, otherwise they can freeze, you know.

We used to dry them. And then they used to send them to the mill and make *farina*—the flour. And then they used to make all kinds of things. But now they don't do that no more. But that time, that was one of our main meals, that chestnut flour, because we didn't have too much, you know, we were very poor in Italy. We tell you, you don't believe it, but we were very, very poor. We used to eat a piece of bread, and a little, little bit of cheese—if we had it. If not, we had to eat the bread without it. The bread was made out of wheat and we had *segala*, rye, and we used to mix it and make bread out of it. The wheat flour was pretty high when you go and buy it.

The chestnuts were right around Cadagnolo. We had a *metato* right there for drying the chestnuts. It was like a garage, a room purposefully for that. We used to make a fire right in the middle. And the heat goes up and he dries the chestnuts. They're real hard, you know. Everybody had their own *metato*, everybody that had the chestnut trees.

We used to send it to a regular mill. We called it a *molin'.* The *molin'* was up by the Pont' di Sant'Anna, between Sant'Anna and Cadagnolo. You see, that's where the water is that comes down.

We buy *castagne* every fall now. You cook them with water and they're called *balucci.* Or else you can roast them in the oven, and you call them *mondine. Balucci,* that's what we called them in Italy. You can eat them either way. But before you put them in the oven, you gotta cut them with the knife, otherwise they do like a bomb. They explode.

My father's name was Angelo. Angelo Pasquesi. No, my father never came to the United States. He was working for the government. And he never come over here. But my father die very young. I was only eleven years old when my father died. He used to take care of the street. They call them *cantoniere.* And he used to get a check from the government all the time. In fact, when he died, my oldest brother—he was in America—we sent the telegram to him. He came home and took my father's job. Because they got that kind of a system. When you die, the oldest son gets the job.

He used to take care of the street. In fact, when I was a kid, he used to take me with him, you know, when he worked. He used to see that there were no rocks, because sometime they fell down in the street from the mountains. Then, sometimes, the street would get real bad and he used to fix it. Sometimes he used to hire people to do the work. And in the wintertime, we used to get a lot of snow over there. He was in charge of cleaning the snow on the street. So he had a horn. So he used to go and blow this horn. "A-oooh!" And they used to hear it, so they knew that they had to shovel the snow. They get a lot of snow up there in the wintertime.

My father had a good job, and beside that, he was shoemaker. He used to make shoes, most of the people over there, they had only one pair. I had a pair of Sunday shoes, too, because my father made them. But most only had one pair. Because they was so poor.

When it would rain, he couldn't go out and work on the street. He used to make shoes for the family. And we were a big family, you know. Boy, were we a big family! Oh Jesus. We were twenty-four, in one house, counting all my cousins. We used to sleep eight in one bed!

My grandfather Pasquesi was a big businessman, you know. He had four sons. And you know, he done so good, my grandfather. He had a lot of fields all around there. And we had eight cows. And he had four stables to put the cows in. He had 150 sheep, he had a horse, couple of dogs—he was pretty good you know. So when we divided, all those four brothers, you know what they got? They got two cows each, and they got one stable each, and then they got each a field. My grandfather, up there, he was pretty wealthy at that time. He was one of the wealthiest guys. And he was also a *consigliere* in the town, over here is alderman. My grandfather, he was pretty smart.

Fanny Cassidy's daughter prompts her to tell a funny story: "Mama, tell her about the undertaker who always came around to visit just in time to have Sunday dinner, and how the hearse would be parked outside." She tells me many stories, but when I hear the cane thumping the floor I know she's tired and it's time to go.

I was born in Italy in 1898, *provincia di* Lucca, in Toscana. My name is Fanny, *Fine.* And before I was married, Nardini. My family worked in the farm. The name of the farm was Gusci. The land was my father's land. We had one horse and two cows. We had vegetables. We have hay. We have oats, corn, beans, but not too much. Mainly for ourselves.

We grew silkworms. Oh, it's dirty work. I call it dirty work because it's too much work and dirty with all the bugs around to take care of. We gave green leaves, mulberry leaves, leaves *di gelso.* We were giving them these kind of leaves. The *gelso,* the tree, they was on the land. And after, when it was the time, around May, they used to blossom, the leaves, and we'd take these leaves and we feed these bugs.

We kept these bugs in the house. Yeah, in the house! You were supposed to give them the best room because they were very fragile, you know. Like, they could get sick during the night—the evening they was alright—but in the morning we'd get up and they was all dead sometime.

I didn't like it. We had to change it every morning when they were big and then we used to have to make little bundles, you know branches with all the leaves, and put it up the corner and when it was the time, they were ready to be picked up and put in a bundle. When they don't eat anymore we had to pick them up, one by one, and put them in the bundles and they used to make silk.

We start to have them in May, when the branches were coming up. We used to buy one big spot like that, and before, when it was the season, you know to feed them, that they were coming big, three or four months, in the end we have one bushel filled up with cocoons. Then, if you have some left in the spring they was come

out again and the butterfly leave the eggs there and before you
know it they leave and you have to pick up everything.

Well, for us at the time it was a little money to pay the taxes for
the house. That's what my father used to say. Pretty near everybody
have the silkworms. In the end, there were the big basket full and
we used to take it to the fair, to the market, and we sell. They made
the fair just for this kind of stuff. In one little place they used to
call Borgo Buggiano. Once a year. My father used to put it in the
basket—a big bushel—and take to the market. After we sell, I
don't know what they did. No, we never saw the silk. There was
just a little silk thread around the house.

Caterina Lattanzi was born in Nerito Crognaleto, province of Teramo,
in the Apennines of the Abruzzi. There is a framed color photograph
of the town hanging on her wall. "My town is beautiful, don't you
think?" she asks. She has waited her turn to talk, since I interviewed
her husband first. Now, he sits in a chair across from the couch where
we are sitting. Each is tempted to interrupt the other, but refrains,
except on a few occasions. Once during her interview, he says, "Can
I put my two cents in?" During his interview, she tells him to stick to
the subject. She is straightforward. She frequently jokes, teasing her
husband, who must be silent. "I'm the boss now, right?" she says,
looking at him.

There was Giovanni, Battista, Giulio, Cristofero, then another
brother Giulio, because the first one died, and then that Giulio died,
and there was another Giulio. Three brothers with the name "Giulio." Over there, if one child dies, then when you have another, you
give the second one the same name. The third one had typhoid. I
almost died, too. Then my grandfather died. My brother Cristofero
was really sick, he almost died, too. And the doctor came in, he say
he need some ice. We didn't have no ice in those days. This was
about 1914. And my father he took a sack, he went in the mountain, the *Gran Sasso d'Italia*, because it has snow in the summertime.
See, it happened in the summertime. And my father come back, he
brought some snow and put the bag on my brother's head. He have
a high, really high fever. Then the fever start to go down, down,
down. I think he saved him. Gran Sasso is pretty far. I think it takes
about three hours to go up there. I think he run pretty fast.

Anyway, when I wake up, you know, I don't remember nothing. I
ask for my grandfather. My mother say, "He died." And Giulio? You
know, my brother smaller than me. "And Giulio," she say, "he's die,

too." A lot of people died at that time, mostly old people. In our town, there were no more flowers left. They had fake flowers on the graves.

To me, my mother say lot of time, "You, I wish you were a little boy instead of a little girl." I feel funny when she said that. You know, I think she was thinking that girls are more hard for the mother than the boy, see. I don't know why she says those things. I feel like she liked more the boys than me. Anyway, I'm sure she missed me when I came to this country. She don't mean it. Because she got so much worry. She got a mother-in-law and my father was the only son and I think my grandmother was jealous, jealous because she, my mother, she might take over, you know what I mean? I think she had a hard time. And I never see my mother and my grandmother fight each other. Never. Maybe they fight when I wasn't around. And my mother took care of my grandmother to the end of her life, anyway.

My grandmother took care of me more than my mother. My mother worked in the fields, like myself when I grow up. We have a piece of land. You go up, you have to work for the beans, you have to work for the wheat, you have to work for everything, nothing come in. We didn't have no money. And then she have a lot of kids. And my grandmother took care of everything in the house. She showed me how to make bread, pasta. What I know, my grandmother, she showed me. My mother never had time. My mother, poor thing, I feel like she never bossed the house.

I married in 1921. It was bad in my family, but it was worse in his family. When I went over to his house, I worked more than in my house—more!

In the fall, the men have to go out from the town of Nerito. Almost all. The men, and women, too. The old people, the kids, stay in town.

His family had sheeps. About two hundred. We couldn't stay in the *mondagna*, in the mountains—too cold for the sheeps. We stayed in a *grotta*, big cave near Rome. There were people in there from all different places.

Everyone have a big bunch, like you have two hundred sheeps, and me, I have two hundred sheeps, and he have two hundred sheeps, and you put them all together with the people. It was damp. I was pregnant with my daughter. We have about eighteen people in there, have a little cabin to sleep in there. The *grotta* was so big. A thousand sheeps, some mules there inside. There was a

big fireplace. I sleep in a little bed my husband made out of straw
and cloth.

Me, my husband, his mother, his father, his brother, were all together. Five people. We cooked pasta and some soup with pasta, we
didn't have no potatoes, we have no beans, you can't make *polenta*.
And then we have ricotta from the sheeps.

Then, me, my husband, and his father stay another two months
in that *grotta*, and he and his father go to work in the morning, on
the railroad, putting in ties. I cooked in the morning. At noon I
have to cook for them and bring them the food. And me, all by
myself in the *grotta*. And I was expecting a baby. The first one. Anyway, I'm so scared when I'm think about it now.

Was it clean? Well, I'll tell you. All the time, all I know is, I never
took a bath. I went to wash at a little fountain. I washed the clothes
there. I don't remember if I washed my face in the morning.

Then I went back to Nerito and my daughter was born. I have to
go to work in the fields, while my mother took care of the kids. In
Nerito you have a little piece of dirt here, a little piece of dirt over
there. You have to go take care of the beans, the potatoes, the
wheat. You have to go wash clothes in the river.

Then, the next winter we went back to Rome with the sheep. We
had a little cabin. And I have my baby there, my son. He was born
in 1929, January, in a little cabin. I didn't have no mother, no
brother, no sister with me—nobody.

Anyway, that's okay. You know, I'll tell you in the old country,
almost all of our town, most of the single people, you see them
work, they do, it's the same story. One woman went over there, had
a baby, and another woman went with her husband and had a
baby. And in the towns it's all the same thing. You have to go *out*
to make living. Nobody had a good living. Now it bothers me more
to think about what I went through.

I never did go with the sheep before I married. I don't like it. A
lot of people have a lot of sheeps and making good money, then
you're okay. But our family had too many people and a small
amount of sheeps. You can't keep going. You can't have wealth with
that. Me and my sister-in-law, together with the men, walking,
bringing the sheeps to Rome from Nerito. We stay about three
months and then my mother-in-law and the kids come to Rome.
And my son, he didn't recognize me. He forgot about me.

You're behind the sheeps all day, all day. You have to be where
the sheeps eat, you know, you can't let them go across the street,

they have to stay there. The owner, he have all this property. You rent it for three months and then you have to go another place where they have another contract.

For the men, well, it's hard too, but for the women it's harder because they do the same job as the men. There's work, you have to wash clothes, you have to cook. The men don't cook. And you're behind the sheeps all day. In the winter. It's cold. You're no dressed proper. Over there, they didn't wear pants in those days.

Could I do it again? No. Oh God, no. For me, I'll tell you, now I'm making a good living. I never did it before, what I'm do now. I'm enjoying my life now.

I enjoy my family, and my kids is good and my husband is pretty good, anyway, I'm a little bossy.

Menghina Mocogni pours coffee gracefully. She tilts the coffee pot with her right hand. The tip of her left index finger is pressed delicately on top of the pot's glass dome. She stands a respectful distance away from the cup as she pours. She asks each guest if she has served enough. She offers cream and sugar. She sits down. She offers sweets to the guest on her left and the guest on her right. She gently insists they take one of each. She takes her own, and places it on the saucer, balancing it against the cup. When her guests have taken their first bite and first sip, she herself begins.

I was born in Piandelagotti in 1896, July 25. My mother had eleven children. *Dio!* Too many. Not too much because of the number, because they were people that were fairly well off—they had animals, they had a nice farm—but the work!

I was the youngest of all, and then my mother died when she was forty. I was seven years old when she died. And she left nine children—because two were already dead. One was born and then died, and the other with a hemorrhage at six. Oh, there were troubles, there were troubles.

My oldest sisters took care of the house. And my oldest sister already had a husband, and my poor mother had even nursed her first son. Like, I nursed Mario and Nello Ori's sister. We lived near their family in Piandelagotti, across the street, and I had my Louie who was little and Nello and Mario's mother died after the baby was just born. So one time I nursed my Louie and the next time her. Eh! *Come si faceva?* What else could you do?

This would have been '23, in Italy. She was so happy, Mario and Nello's mother. She was so happy that she had a baby that was the same age as my Louie. She said, "Menghina, I have a little girl now, too." Because she had three boys. And then, four months later she had a hemorrhage and she died. She was so happy, and then she died with this sickness. *Oh Dio, quanto dispiacere*—what grief.

I went to school until the third grade and then I had to go to work, *eh Dio*. Instead, after Mussolini came in, it was required to go to school until fifth grade. That's good because only until the third grade is very little. I had to go watch the cows. *Dio, Dio, Dio*.

I got married in Piandelagotti in 1920. I was twenty-four. My husband's name was Giosue Mocogni. He was from Sant'Anna. Me, from Piandelagotti. How did we meet each other? At the *festa*. Because on Sunday, you'd always go to some event in town. I met him *in paese*, right up town, in Piandelagotti. *Che mondo*. And then they all said, *"Eh, ma sposi uno di Sant'Anna?"*—"You're marrying someone from Sant'Anna!" They acted like I was going far away— never mind coming to America!

After I got married, I lived in Sant'Anna in my husband's house, with my sister-in-law and *nonno* and *nonna*—my mother-in-law and father-in-law.

In '20 I got married and in '22 Giosue came here to America. He left me there. He left me in Sant'Anna for ten years. Finally, I said, *"Basta ora*—enough! Either come back to Italy or I'm going back to Piandelagotti!" Oh *Dio*.

To tell you the truth, my *nonna*, I loved. With me losing my own mother so young, I became very attached to her right away. I had a lot of respect for her—she was so nice, I was very attached to her. But there was a sister-in-law. She was jealous. You know how awful it is when people are jealous?

I stayed there ten years. Giosue stayed in this country three years, Giosue, then, in '25, he came back to Sant'Anna for one year because there were things to take care of after my father-in-law died, and he came to settle things with his sisters, you know divide up the property. Giosue had applied for his citizenship papers, and when he came back to Italy he said, "I'm going back to America and when I get my citizenship papers, I'll come to get you." And in '26 my Joe was born. He was forty days old when Giosue left. Forty days! And then I came here in '30, and my Mary was born in '31.

We had gotten married in Piandelagotti. At that time, you had to get married in the bride's town. We got married in the church, then we had some refreshments at my house, and then we went for the meal at Giosue's house. My poor feet! It took an hour to walk to Sant'Anna. We were married in July—at least the weather was nice!

Well, the shoemaker Carlon' Pasquesi fit me. The bride had to have new shoes—he was a good shoemaker, but the shoes were so tight. *Eh Dio! Mamma mia!* I'll never forget it. And then I danced all night. Smashing my toes. I had told him, "They're too tight." But he said no. I was no good for walking, let alone dancing! The musicians were from Sant'Anna. They played well. The accordion, the clarinet. Oh, they were so good! We danced all night, and then in the morning we got up and went to Mass. And the house was a mess, all the plates had to be washed. I was so tired I was crazy, and I had to work.

(from Italian)

Four Stories about Sewing

Domenick Linari, who doesn't get along too well with Nietzsche:

My mother wanted me to be a tailor in the worst way but I just didn't want it at all. I couldn't sit down. I couldn't see myself. I mean every now and then mama would make me sit down and do a little work, I'd almost die. I imagine it's interesting, I suppose, like if you do a coat for a man. She used to do like wedding garments, they used to come to her because they didn't trust the other ones, they didn't do it good enough. I remember her cussing about them wedding gowns. They were so hard to work on. But I imagine there is a satisfaction in seeing that you have done something that looks good on a person.

My mother made a living for us sewing in the house. It was mostly men's clothes. See, she didn't want to do women's clothes because they were too fussy. She made suits, pants, shirts. I used to make all the underclothes.

She learned to sew by herself. She was never one day in school and she says my uncle encouraged her—my father's brother, he was a jack of all trades and a master of none. And after she got married, and she came to Pratelnuovo where we lived. He encouraged her all the time, and she said the first time she cut out a pair of pants she cut the pieces, she says she was sweating because she knew she was going to ruin the material. She was sure of it. But she said my uncle was there and said, "You're doing okay, you're doing fine." "I made a pair of pants," she says, "they wore 'em, and I guess they were not too bad."

She had quite a reputation as a seamstress.

Teresa Saielli, who defied the priest on the feast of Santa Teresa:

I went to Pieve. There was a tailor. I went to ask him if he would help teach me to sew. I didn't want to come to this country anymore. I was having trouble with my papers. It wasn't going well. First there was one problem, then another problem. It was right after the war was over.

I went to ask because, see, I wanted to learn how to sew men's clothing. The tailor told me, "I'll take you," but then I started to think, "People, will start talking." You know the people. Then, I decided to marry Roberto.

Gina DeBartolo's mother is her hero. She says her mother killed snakes and hawks. Her mother was a seamstress who taught herself her craft, boldly telling customers she could sew what she had never before attempted. "My mother was, you know, a good, strong woman," Gina Leonardi DeBartolo says in the living room of her sister's house, where she has moved with her ill husband in a last-ditch effort to prevent him from being moved to a nursing home. She, too, would club snakes to protect her nest.

My mother was no farmer, she was a seamstress. Her home was called La Torre, "the tower," and she went from one family to another. Well, they'd hire by the day and she'd carry her little portable machine and she'd go and sew probably a week in one house. If somebody was getting married, she'd sew sheets and the bride's dress.

One time she said she even made a groom's suit and she said, "I was young and I was courageous and they asked me if I could make a man's suit and I said, 'Yes.' " I can imagine what kind of suit she made! She said, "I went over there to sew and she brought out this material and I started cutting the suit, and well, I got down to the pants, and I only had enough for one leg." And she said, "It was a Saturday, and when I went home that night I couldn't sleep. I got up early the next morning." Luckily the material had been bought at the local store, and she found another piece of material and bought it. And when she came out of church, she had the material, and the lady told her, "Maria, I looked over that suit that you're making but I only could find one leg for the pants." And my mother said, "Oh, no, no, no, you made a mistake," she says, "there's two legs." She said, "Right away, I cut the other pants leg

and I wrapped it up. And when she came down she went straight
for the material. When she opened it up, there were two legs. She
said, 'I could have sworn there was only one leg.' " So she learned
as she went along.

But she was a good seamstress because she sewed here in Highwood, too.

Massima Vanoni, who was always old for her age and remains youthful:

There was was a room called *La Scuola del Lavoro,* the School of
Work, and there was a nun who taught. Sister Albina. I liked
school. I went there almost until the time I got married. The nuns
took in sewing, and then we would do it and they paid us a little.

They taught us needlework, *il ricamo*—embroidery. We learned all
the different stitches: *il punto filet, il giliuccio, il punt'erba, il punto a
croce.* You started with a simple stich, then little by little, you learn
the ones that are more difficult.

There was a little poem I knew called "Fila, Bida!"—"Sew, Bida!"
It went:

> Fila, Bida!
> Mi sudano le dita.
> Se può venire
> quest'inverno
> Voglio tanto filare
> che mi voglio stancare.

> E quando veniva l'inverno:

> Fila, Bida!
> Mi gelano le dita.
> Se può venire
> quest'estate
> Voglio tanto filare
> che mi voglio stancare.

> "Sew, Bida! Sew!"
> "But my fingers sweat so!
> If only winter would come
> I could succeed.
> I'd work so fast
> I'd drop with fatigue."

And when the winter comes:

"Sew, Bida! Sew!"
"My work would be nice
but my fingers are ice!
If it were summer
I could succeed.
I'd work so fast
I'd drop with fatigue."

CHAPTER

3

"Like the Grace of God"

"L'ITALIANI SONO dappertutto—come la grazia di Dio."
"The Italians are everywhere—like the grace of God," Menghina Mocogni said.

The mountaineers took work with limited life spans. Seasonal labor. Short-term projects. Abandoned projects. The scope and pace of work in North Africa was determined by the foreign policies of governments in Rome. Work on railroads through the mountains was cut short by the Great War, the project never resumed in peacetime. Work on the Panama Canal was curtailed by malaria.

During the growing season they worked the land; in the winter they were stonecutters, stonemasons, charcoal makers, and woodsmen. This seasonal exodus from the mountain towns of Modena, Bologna, and Tuscany included women, particularly single women, who took jobs as maids—serve—or as wet nurses in cities like Milan, Livorno, and in France. The work they found in Italy was serving the signori, just as they would later find on Chicago's North Shore.

From an area covering fifty square miles of corrugated earth, an area that includes corners of four provinces—Modena, Bologna, Toscana, and Reggio Emilia, their boundaries determined by dukes whose authority was cloven by mountain ridges—people journeyed to Australia and Argentina, and everywhere in between.

From the Frignano, merely one impoverished area of this region, people spilled out seasonally all over the globe. They went to cities like Livorno, Pisa, Florence, and Rome. They descended the mountains onto the plains to work construction jobs. They labored throughout the Mediterranean—in Corsica, Sardinia, Libya, Tunisia, and Algeria. As miners and agricultural workers, they worked in southern France. They worked as miners and factory workers in Germany, Luxembourg, Switzerland, and Belgium. In Great Britain they were ice cream vendors. They came to the Americas—North, Central and South.

Rosa Fiocchi, born in Lizzano in Belvedere, in Bologna, spoke of her husband:

In Lizzano, up in those mountains, there's nothing much to do in winter except they have a big snow, they can work for the town, shovel snow, something. So every winter the workers would either go to Sardinia to make charcoal or go to Germany and there they could go in the ore mines or work in the foundry. He worked in Germany. Then the last year that my husband was in Italy, he went down to Paola in Calabria. The contractor they worked for had a lot of work in Rome. And he wanted them to work in Rome, so they all moved there. But not Caesar. Caesar came over to the United States.

For many years before the mass exodus of Italians between 1900 and World War I, *i montanari*—the mountaineers— left their homes to find work, just as the Appalachian left home to work in Detroit or Dallas because the mountains could not provide enough succor. This recourse to temporary emigration became infectious.

In 1921, more than 10,000 people of the inhabitants in the communities surrounding Pavullo, nearly 12 percent, were temporarily absent from their homes. In communities of higher elevation, where agricultural opportunities were more limited, the numbers were higher. In Frassinoro, for example, 1,086 of its 6,182 inhabitants decided to emigrate; and in Pievepelago, 1,187 of its 4,825 inhabitants—almost 25 percent—went outside to find work that year.

One example of the profound impact of emigration on these communities can be seen in the attention given it by one institution, the church. In a meeting in 1919, with the Cardinal of Bologna present, the archbishop of Lizzano gave a critical analysis of the immigrant communities he had visited, including Dalzell, Illinois. In the study, entitled "Emigration and its Dangers as Measured by the Clergy," Don Alfonso Montanari argued that emigrants departed from the church's teachings and returned with destructive ideas and habits. Young men, he wrote, were particularly susceptible to corruption. They returned to their home villages alcoholic and obscene, opposed to the church and civility. They returned from the urban centers of corruption, he wrote, with the spirit of evil and bolshevism, as "apostles of Satan." Whatever the value and accuracy of the archbishop's observations, they attest to the velocity and intensity with which change was occurring in these communities.

By the 1890s emigration was laced into the yearly rhythm of these mountain communities. By the 1920s, it remained as promising, as predictable, and as unavoidable as birth, the growing season, and death.

Sante Pasquesi, born in 1888 in Cadagnolo, was a respected man in the community who assisted many immigrants with correspondence and legal matters. He was said to have had beautiful calligraphy. This reminiscence is taken from his memoir, *La mia vita*, which was written in 1933.

. . . The evenings, from after supper to bedtime, especially during the month of November, were spent around a fire that burned slowly in the *metato* to dry chestnuts. In spite of the dense smoke, we spent our nights here, listening attentively to the older people's conversations, which consisted more or less of the accounting of their harsh experiences in Maremma, Corsica or Sardinia or they talked of some relative or friend, who, at least according to the letters, was doing very well in a land very far from Genoa, called either South America or North America; it didn't really make much difference to them which one of the two it actually was. If a skilled story-teller happened to be present, he would have had the floor for the entire evening, to my great delight, because these tales interested me more than anything, particularly those about wizards, fairies and enchanted palaces. At the end of a story everybody would say it had been a good one, but it left me with such a fear that I hesitated to go to bed by myself for fear that the meanest wizards would try to take me to their enchanted palaces and that I wouldn't be able to find my way back. . . .

An uncle that had gone to North America sent me, once in a while, Italian newspapers published in the United States, and as I read them I became interested in this new land to the point that I wished I could go there myself to find work. Slowly, with diplomacy, I tried to find out what my father's feelings were on the matter and, actually, I found them not too hostile, but I had to promise to return to Italy for my military service. We set the date of my departure for the following spring and in April, instead of May, I returned to Cadagnolo to get ready to leave.

From talking to people who had been in America I found out that to go to an American metropolis it was necessary to have a trousseau similar to that of a future bride: At least one new suit (of an American cut, of course) and the same for the shoes, so that you had better come to an understanding with the local tailor and shoemaker to see that no mistake would be made in the matter.

Adelmo Bertucci was ninety-seven years old and living in a nursing home when I interviewed him. When he died in 1984, the *Chicago Tribune's* obituary called him "the dean of Chicago area golf course superintendents." He had worked for forty-six years as superintendent of the golf course at the Old Elm Club in Highland Park. "Active in retirement," the obituary said, "Mr. Bertucci had his driver's license renewed at the age of 95." It did not, however, mention that he was an accomplished accordionist or that he wore a cardigan with the insignia of the club. There's only so much room in an obituary.

My grandfather was shoemaker. He immigrated to Sardinia in the wintertime and they come back in the spring. And they make a campaign there. Sometimes they make some money and sometimes they don't. They been robbed from the contractor a lot of time. My father been in Sardinia, too, three or four time. General work. Under the contractor. And then they came back in the spring through the city of Livorno.

My father used to have a horse and wagon for passengers and merchandise. He would go to the city of Lucca and load it up. And they had the passengers come from Sardinia, Corsica, then he load them up. He took me with him to Lucca sometimes when I was a small boy. To see the country. He used to put me on the basket on the back of the wagon.

Like I say, I came in Highwood and Highland Park in nineteen hundred and seven. Highland Park first because an old Bertucci live there, and from there, after, I moved to Highwood. We had four that were companions. One was John Servi, Alberto Ozzi, another one was Tommaso Bertucci, my second cousin. All from Pieve. I had a brother here. Joe Bertucci.

Then me and my brother went back to Pievepelago. We went back and in the summer, I went to Africa. In 1910. Algeria. A city called Constantine. My trade was a blacksmith. I had some friends over there and I got the job. One was a Morelli. The boss. I was there one year. I like it, yeah. It was pretty hot. Work around the fire, was pretty hot. All the time. We learned to speak French. I used to live with a French family and two guys from Spain. And then I went back to Pievepelago and made my mind to come in America again.

Viterbo Ponsi is looking through a book of photographs of homes in Highland Park. He's not finding any that he worked on as a bricklayer. He says the trade is in the blood.

I spent my fifteenth birthday on the island of Sardinia. In the winter, everybody from our parts went away to work.

My father was a farmer but on the farm was woods. We had two or three animals. My father had chestnut trees. And walnuts. There was enough to eat, but for money, no. The land wasn't like *la giù*, down below, on the plains in Modena or in other areas. The land was ours. It was there in Sant'Andrea. It was a place called Perdepolo. It was where all the Ponsis lived.

My father spent twenty-five winters in Sardinia. In the winter he went there, left my mother and his kids with the animals. In my family, there were four brothers and two sisters. We were never together. Never! Because one would be gone, one at home. Even my sisters. I was the youngest, and at fifteen I was gone from the house. At sixteen, I was gone to Sardinia—and nobody was supporting me anymore. I worked as a laborer with stonemasons. I had a cousin there. They were all *paesani* there. The contractor, the boss, was from Modino. He would come to Sant'Andrea and Pieve every autumn and ask who wanted to go to Sardinia to work. My father spent twenty-five winters there. In the spring he had to come home to farm a little, to plant some grains.

There were a few people who stayed there in Sardinia all year but most didn't because they would catch the fever. After April you had to leave because there was the fever that started out in Spain. You've heard of *la spagnola?* Where we were in Sardinia, it was a place that was all slough, all marshes, near the sea. I only made two emigrations there. Then, the next fall, I went to Libya, in '11 and '12. When there was the war between Italy and Turkey. Italo-Turkey. Italy wanted Libya. I went in '11 and '12 to Libya. I went to Derna and Benghazi. There I was building walls. I was a stonemason. After that, there was no more work. I got that work originally because there were two old people who called me: "Viterbo, go ahead there, you'll find all your *paesani* that you know there." And I stayed there seven or eight months. In the summer I came back home for a month, then I went back to Tripoli. I had a cousin who had opened up a restaurant in Tripoli. Afterwards, a couple of Italians came to live there, too, but when I went the first time there wasn't anyone else. We ate military food. I stayed almost two years in all.

The government gave work to the contractor. They hired for the jobs. There was a contractor from Bologna and one from Milano.

I was in Tripoli, Benghazi. At first I was in Derna. In the middle of the city there was a mountain of sand. There was a strong coastal wind that carried the sand. But when the wind blew, the sand would go in your eyes. It would go in your nose, in your mouth and ears. It was awful. It was a wind of sand. You had to stay inside. My cousin had a wooden house, a barrack there. It was near Eritrea, and they fought, the Arabs against each other. They were with Italy. They were odd. Thieves. But brave in things of war.

They paid well there. And then after there was no work, after the Turks left, I left, but the Arabs continued on with the war. They always fought. So the Italians stayed there. I'm not sure for how many years. At the time of the Second World War, they lost it.

To live in the barracks was free. The government built them for the workers who were doing the jobs. We ate like soldiers. Beans. Pasta. Rice. We ate bad.

And then after that work was done they sent me to construct walls in a place called Azzizzia. There was a little train that went along the coast. It was all sand. All sand! And sometimes to make a trip which normally took two hours, it took four hours because the wind covered the tracks with sand.

So, along the tracks there were these little houses, little forts. In these forts, there were Italian soldiers stationed there to send the Arabs away. We only stayed there for three days. We ate with the soldiers and they gave us a place to sleep. Then, one night, the Arabs attacked the fort. Boom. Boom. Boom. All night long. We stayed there three days. We were waiting for some building materials to arrive so that we could build more of these forts. But the stuff never arrived. So, we went back to Tripoli.

And then after a little while, I went back to Italy. There was no more work. This would have been around '14.

After I got home, I found someone who knew an assistant supervisor at a job in Piacenza. He was a Bartolotti from Pieve. The contractor was a Minghelli from Pavullo. He was building a road behind a little town. Then, in '16, I went into the army.

I had a cousin, Paolo Dori, who went to Scotland. I was supposed to go there too, but then I found another job and I didn't go. I went to Sardinia instead. I don't know how this Dori ended up in Scotland. He had an ice cream parlor.

After the war, I went to work in Genoa. I got a job from the guy who was my sergeant in the army. When I got my discharge, he asked me what I was going to do when I got back home. I said that I was going to try to find work as a mason—I had done that kind of work in Libya. I liked that trade.

You know, it's in the blood. My father was a stonemason. And

my grandfather too did that kind of work. When I was a little boy,
my father had a bunch of sheep. In the winter they would go down
on the plains, near the sea, where it didn't freeze, to graze the
sheep, in the province of Ferrara. And there would be these little
stone huts where the shepherds slept. So, when I was a young boy,
I used to find stones and make little houses that looked like the
ones on the plains. It's in the blood. My father was a stonemason.
And my grandfather was assistant at the church in Sant'Andrea and
he made the facade of the church.

In my family, it was impossible to be together. Like I said before,
we were four brothers, but we were never together. Eh, sure! One
took work in Africa. Another in Rome. Another in Switzerland.

                                                        (from Italian)

Adeodato Fontana's trade was stonecutting. In the United States he
left the trades and opened a business, a grocery store. A quiet man
with an air of dignity, he seems to have been able to swim easily
between the world of his *paesani* of Sant'Andrea, workmen all, and
the world of the *americani*. His friends were men of Highwood and
Highland Park, but his fishing partner was a doctor. He is a mountain
boy who took to America like a fish to the sea.

I was born in Sant'Andrea. My sisters Rafaela and Veronica were
born in Sardinia. Most of the time my father went to work in Sardinia, in Maddalena. He was a *scarplino*—a stonecutter. They used
to have a lot of caves, you know, quarries, where you work on the
stone, chop it up. He made a lot of monuments. He had a nice
cave, his own cave. There was just me with him, and my brothers
sometimes. My mother came from Sardinia to Sant'Andrea after she
married my father and she never moved. All my father's life he
worked in Sardinia. His father, too. My father went to Sardinia by
himself. My father was a smart man. He had a cave by himself. He
was working for himself. If you were a bricklayer or stonemason in
the mountains, there wasn't too much work. At that time when I
left for Sardinia, there was no work. Nobody was working. Everybody worked away, in Africa, in Australia, wherever they can get
jobs.

I was eleven years old when I went to work in Sardinia. My
brothers didn't stay there too long. I'm the one. I stayed there more
than my brothers. I spend a lot of years there.

My father was a good mechanic, you know, in the stone. He cut
the stones for a lot of monuments. Not everybody can do it. He

made one for Garibaldi, a monument in Caprera, they called it. Caprera on Maddalena. My father used to cut the stone pieces. He made a monument to Garibaldi, my father. He cut the stone for the tomb in Anita to Garibaldi.

I saw Garibaldi. Right down there in Maddalena. Not far from where he lived and he died. I still remember.

I used to live just a few blocks from the sea. You know, I used to jump in the water all the time. Oh, like a fish. My father would get mad sometime. I wouldn't get out of the water. Boy, I loved it. I was a kid, you know, like a fish.

Teodoro Sassorossi sits on a folding chair in the shade at the edge of his garage. His cane is propped on the arm of the chair. We talk. A neighbor walking on the sidewalk passes the driveway. "Where are you going?" Sassorossi bellows out toward the street. "Vado in paese," uptown, the other man says without stopping. We continue the interview. Two children who live nearby come by to talk to him. One circles us on a bike. He examines the tape recorder and asks what we're doing. Sassorossi tells him he must be quiet. I continue the interview. A friend waves to him from the sidewalk and heads toward us. She sits down on the chair next to mine. They talk. She has recently had her picture in a local newspaper article featuring her needlework. The neighbor returns from uptown with a grocery bag. He ambles down the driveway and sits with us. Sassorossi gives him a hard time about the purchase, which is beer. The moral of the story: Never conduct an interview in a garage.

My full name, Italian name? Teodoro Sassorossi. Sassorossi. You have five s's there? I was born August 28, 1898. Tomorrow is my birthday. Thank you. I was born in Pievepelago.

I started working when I was thirteen years old. A water boy. It was road construction, see? I carried the tools. I had to arrange the tools for the scarplino, and to carry water to the stonemasons and whoever else I was working for. They were constructing the road that goes from Riolunato to Sestola and Fanano, along the Scoltenna River. See, there was no street then. They were just building it. Before, there was just a little road you could walk on. They didn't have cars then. They went with horses. Asses, mules, in that method there. See? And I worked under Bartolotti, a construction cooperative in Fanano. Other people contracted with them, and you would go wherever they had other people working.

I stayed there until the fall, and then I went down to the plains

with the sheep. See, I went with the sheep down to the province of
Ferrara and the province of Rovigo. From there you crossed the Po
River, Italy's biggest river, and go either south or north from there.

Then I went to Sardinia. I went to Sardinia three times, starting in
1913 with my father and my brother. My father was a foreman who
had a gang of men who were building a section of railroad in Sardinia. I stayed there until the spring. In the summer you worked
around home, but there wasn't much to do. Then in the fall, you'd
go back to Sardinia.

We didn't make charcoal ourselves. We cut the wood and another
company actually made the charcoal. They were almost all *toscani*
who did that work. They would pile the wood like a pyramid and
then cover it with dirt and leaves. Then they would put a fire inside
and it would burn slowly, slowly, until the wood was carbonized.
And what came out was charcoal, *carbone*.

There were people from Pieve in Sardinia. There were some from
Sant'Andrea too. There were some from Sant'Anna. The ones who
directed the work would get workers from Sardinia, too, like these
landscapers around here do with the Mexicans. But in the summer
we came back home because there was malaria, and in fact, the last
year I got the fever from malaria.

My father was born in Pievepelago, but not right in town. Me,
too. I was born at Fontanini, it's a little hamlet that's called Fontanini, outside Pievepelago near Cadagnolo. There were eight or ten
families but now there's just one. My father was the *contadino* for
Galassini. It would have been a house with six rooms plus the *can-
tina* below. That's where you keep the cheese cool, where you keep
food that needs be kept cool. Then my father went away because at
home there was only *la miseria*, misery.

My father worked in coal mines in Texas. Thurber, Texas. Then he
worked in Chicago. He stayed in Chicago with a family named Pa-
nerali, and he bought out their part of Fontanini. After Chicago, he
went back to Thurber, Texas. Then he got rheumatism, so he
couldn't work in the mines anymore. He came back to Italy, then he
came back here and went to work at Lake Forest College as a jani-
tor. He worked there the whole time he was in America the last
time.

In 1913, he came back to Italy, and that year there we went to
work together in Riolunato on the road, like I told you before. He
never went back to America. Then he went to Sardinia, home, Sardinia, home, and then at the end, he was head of the forestry de-

partment, working with plants in an area between La Rocca and Sant'Andrea.

My father went to Sardinia instead of back to the United States because he thought he could earn a living closer to his family. He tried going to America, but in those days, all of the old-timers came to America for three or four years, and then they went back to their homes. They didn't think of leaving and taking their families, to make their homes here, to live here. Ninety percent were like that. That's what they figured, they had ideas like that. But then he went back home and stayed there a while, he saw that it wouldn't work. So he left every fall and returned in the spring.

My mother never left Pieve. Once, she went to San Pellegrino, a sanctuary nearby, but she never worked away. Just to visit the sanctuary, that's the only trip she ever took.

(from Italian)

In his youth, Zeffero Pacini says, he was a *giron*, someone who liked to move around. At ninety-eight, he is more limited in his movement, but his concentration and his intensity suggest a mind that has no problem moving around. His wife and daughter sit nearby, ready to interject and interpret if he doesn't hear or understand. Despite this cadre of women who are stronger than he, he talks like a man used to being in charge, with a list of tasks set before him. He talks about what he wants to talk about, and moves from that subject when he is through. I have seen him taking a stroll from his house down the sidewalk. Even assisted by a walker and a grandson, he is still a *giron*.

I was born in 1888, the fourth of September, in Gramolazzo, in the province of Lucca. We were *contadini*. We had sheep. The land belonged to my family, even our little house.

C'era la miseria. There was misery. In those times, it was hard to get even a piece of bread. There was nothing there. After I came in America, then there was something, when I came in America. We were three brothers and we only had my mother. When I was fourteen years old, my father died.

As a boy, I started to go to do different things, but you couldn't do anything because there was nothing. The kids of the *contadini* kept the sheep, there was nothing else to do.

When I became a young man, *un giovanotto,* I went out of the country. I went to Germany. I was seventeen years old when I went to work in an iron foundry, working with iron. In Differdange, in

Luxembourg, near the border of France. They used coal to make the iron. The working conditions were very nice because it was a huge factory. There were four thousand workers. You put pieces of coal in the furnace and the iron came out of that. It was dangerous because the iron was all boiling. I stayed there twenty months. It was good money. They paid by the hour in Germany.

There were a lot working outside the country. There were many Italians.

After the First World War, I went back to my little town where there was marble work and I started to work there at Carrara, in the province of Massa Carrara. When I left the marble work, I came to America. I came to Highland Park where I had a cousin, Alfredo Bernardi. It was him who gave me money for the trip over. With his address, I came to America.

(from Italian)

I never met Joseph Muzzarelli. My only acquaintance with him comes through reading someone else's interview with him. Born in Fanano, he went to Switzerland in 1899 in Canton Fribourg to work as a construction laborer at a chocolate factory that was being built. He worked in Switzerland for several years before emigrating to the United States in 1906. As a miner, Muzzarelli suffered a disabling back injury in an accident. He points to a picture of John L. Lewis on the wall and calls him a great leader. He worked as a gardener in Lake Forest for General Wood, a powerful man in the Chicago business community who headed up Sears and Roebuck.

I was born in Italy, July 27, 1884. I came in the United States from Switzerland, April the seventeenth, 1906. I emigrate at fifteen. I was work in France for several months, you know. And then I went in Switzerland.

I was in Canton Fribourg, Department Le Guyère, between France and Switzerland. They was building a big chocolate factory. And I work over there. And then I came and see my daddy. And back over there in the same labor. Oh yeah, I learned French. I remember I still have some book. Now it be a long time because no people around here, you know to speak with them.

I was only three years in Italy in the school. The first, the second, the third class. And then, I emigrate. My idea was emigrate all the time. Change the situation. And then after I was married I was deciding I want to emigrate to see better condition for my family in the future.

Menghina Mocogni, who pours coffee as she was taught in Firenze:

There was no work. There was no work. Then, everything would get better after the winter when you went to work as a maid. We would go to work in Firenze in hotels. I went for seven years.

You went away to Firenze and you went to the offices where they sent you and asked if they had work because there were many places that were looking for maids. Sure, I wanted to go because you made good money, it paid for expenses, and you know, when you have parents, things are different.

We waited tables. There were a lot of American people, you know, in the hotels they came there to study, to study Italian, and so we served these people and cleaned the rooms, that's all, near the station in Firenze. It was a beautiful hotel.

The free day was Thursday, every eight days. And then we would go and find some other friends who were working. We walked around there on the avenues, in the gardens.

We went away to work once a year. For example, in October we went back to Firenze, always to the same boss. Then, the hotel where I was working had little work, and the *signora* said, "Oh, I'm sorry, I would keep you if I could." So they found me another place. They found me two *signori*. They were Germans but they were very nice, so I was a maid for them. I cleaned, I helped cook, everything. And then they said, "*Dio*, go to bed," because they were sure that I had worked too hard. With them, I had only three rooms to do, and in the hotel, you could never keep a room clean! And then at the hotel you had to stay up until midnight, until the last train came in. Because then people would come from the station to the hotel and you had to serve them coffee or maybe make up beds. And then I got up at six in the morning. It was a long day working like that.

And after I had been there for two months, these Germans said, "Come away and stay with us." They said to me, "If you stay with us, we would treat you like a daughter." *Ma ero giovane!*—I was so young! I went away when I was fifteen the first time. I was nineteen when I was working for these Germans, but I didn't want to go to Germany. They asked me to go with them for many years, but to go away and then I would regret it—I had my sisters and brothers, *macché, macché!* Never mind.

What a life! I liked Firenze. There were a lot from Piandelagotti, from Sant'Anna, and places nearby. If not, there was Milano for maids, but it was too far. There were people that went to Pisa. But in Pisa, they didn't pay much, so to go away to work for so little, they wouldn't go. *Insomma*. This is life. Now, we'll have coffee.

(from Italian)

Teresa Saielli, who defied the priest on the feast of Santa Teresa:

When I go with my sister in Milano, I'm fifteen and my sister, thirteen. To work. Work for the rich people in the house. They make me do everything. Clean house, cook, everything. I got no kids to take care of that time. My sister Nilde, thirteen, she worked in a house and she got some kids to take care of. Whenever she see me, she start crying like I was a mother. Poor Nilde. Me, I'm fifteen, Nilde, thirteen. Isn't it terrible?

It was far away from me where she lived. We go out just one time a week. You know. Like on Sundays, just a couple of hours, then we got to go back in home. We go around, find the other girls, because a lot go in Milano. And then, when I take her home, she start cry.

A lotta girls go work. And then they stay all winter, then they go back in the summer, they go in the old country to work in the farm. Work, work all the time. Go over there and watch the sheep.

The rich people I worked for didn't do nothing. They make me do everything.

To find work, you go over to the convent—they find the work for you. If you need somebody to work for you, you go over there and ask, and the nun finds you somebody. In Milano, when I go there, somebody take me over there. A lot of rich people they go there and ask for somebody.

And when you go over there and work for rich people, they take care of you! You go outside, they say you can stay away one hour or two, then you gotta come back. They take care! Especially when you're young. When you're young it's worse. When I go to bed in the night, I say, "Tomorrow I'll be home with my mother." Oh boy, so young like that.

At first you think you go, I don't know where. It's no fun. We make nothing. Today, they make good money. Today it's different.

Everybody go. We wanted to go, too. That's the trouble. My mother, I think, she *non* sleep good, too, have these kids far away.

Eritrea Pasquesi tells her life's history as if it were an operetta. There is a beginning, middle, and end. There is pathos and humor, crescendo and diminuendo. She plays to her audience. As a child in Texas, she sang with a Salvation Army sister. She sang for her family and a house full of boarders. She says she was always *la canterina della famiglia*, the little singer of the family. She was born in 1907 in a Texas coal mining town, but her widowed father returned to Italy with four young daughters. Shortly after, her father died of pneumonia, leaving *le quattro orfanelle*, four little orphan girls. She and her sisters left the mountains each winter for cities to work as maids. When she came back to the United States, she worked as a seamstress and laundress. In Highwood, she continued to sing in variety shows and at the church. She has in her possession a pocket King James Bible given to her on Christmas Eve 1914 for never missing a service at the little red schoolhouse where Miss Mitchell taught miners' children to sing "Jesus loves me, this I know."

When I was eleven, there was four of us left, my sister Vanda went to Pisa to work for some rich people and she took me along. My sister Ribella went to Florence, Italy, alone, to work for rich people. Svezia was too little, so she had to stay in Pievepelago with her godmother. But I was in Pisa with my sister Vanda. And in the summertime, we would all come home, but in the winter we had to go away to make a living.

I lived in Pisa, would you believe it or not, I lived with an old woman and an old man, and they were Jewish. And they kept me and they fed me, and they made my little dresses and she would send me—she was Jewish—but she would send me to church, she knew, she'd say, "Tomorrow is Sunday, child, go to church." She'd make me go to church. I stayed with them for quite a few years. He was a leather merchant.

She used to get such a kick out of me. When they would eat, she'd make me sit in the corner over there and I would tell her jokes, and she'd laugh.

I learned a little about Jewish life, too, cooking, you know that. No pork, naturally, you know. And he used to go all the way to Leghorn from Pisa to pick up the matzohs. She made her own sausage out of beef. I remember helping her. She'd make me go shopping or do little odds and ends. Like cleaning vegetable and she would make me clean the vegetable and she was so fussy. So fussy. "Wash! Wash! Wash!" And I got so tired of washing in that cold water.

But I'm glad because I learned quite a few from those people. How to be clean, how to wash your hands every time— "*Lavate le mani!*" Wash your hands! That's all I ever heard. And it stayed. Even now, I wash my hands a hundred times a day.

At that time, I didn't even know there were Jewish people. I didn't know what Jewish meant. You know, and they never taught us. In Italy, they taught us Catholicism and that's all.

The only time there was something different, she would sit in the dining room and read a book. And me, I was curious you know, she was turning the pages the opposite of what we turn them. And I said to her, "*Signora*, I learned in school and you don't turn the pages like that. You have to turn the pages the other way." "Go away, child. This is how it is done by my people." Then I asked, "Is that music?" You know the Jewish language looks like music. "No! It's not music. You can sing later. But this is not music! Go! Go!" And she would chase me away.

She used to sew my clothes. I remember one time she bought me a cute little hat with cherries on each side, so when I went up to Pieve, I was the only one that had a hat on, and you can imagine, and it was a beautiful hat.

I used to just sing for them. She would make me sing while they were eating, oh what was that song about the bird? "*Cardinalino, che viene stasera portando l'amore*"— little cardinal who comes to-night bringing love.

I went there until I was fourteen, and fifteen years old, I went to Livorno to work by myself. They put a tag here and they shipped me. "Eritrea Galassini must take the train to Bagni di Lucca. From Bagni di Lucca to Livorno." I found the job through somebody in Pievepelago.

In Europe, you know, honey, when they can say, "*tengo la serva*," you know, "I have a maid," it's a big thing. This one in Livorno was a merchant. The one in Pisa was in leather. And the one in Livorno, he was not Jewish, he was like us, and he had all kind of candy and *saponette*—little cakes of soap. He was a salesman. I guess he sold all sorts of things.

You had to say, "*signora*" qui, "*signora*" la,—"ma'am" this and "ma'am" that. Yeah, even if they haven't got much, they always make sure you know. This one even had a nurse for her son, and the nurse was from Piandelagotti. They had a beautiful living room with a piano. They never opened it.

One of my sisters was in Florence, one of them was in Pisa. And one was in Livorno. And then we'd meet in the summertime and we'd be up in Pievepelago in just this poor little house. We bummed around, especially me. I really did bum around. I used to love to dance, and I'd watch for all the dances, go to a *festa* in Pievepelago, another one in Sant'Andrea, one in Riolunato.

I worked in Livorno just one year. Because then I had to come to America. In fact, I had to go home. I was going to stay there. And then August, it was the fifteenth of August, I got a letter, or telegram, I forgot, that I had to go back because we were leaving for America in September. My older sister decided. Because, see, she had a boyfriend here in Highland Park. Tony Crovetti from Pievepelago. I didn't want to leave. I had all my friends there, my boyfriends. They gave us a party and there was a picture taken. It was my birthday, the second of September. And I have a picture of all my friends in front of the theater there. They gave us this going away party. We had a glass of wine and a piece of cake like they usually do.

CHAPTER

4

"All My Young Life":
Recollections of World War I

IN THE LAST YEAR of my grandfather Vanoni's life, he said goodbye to my brother who was going to Florence to study art history. My grandfather, who was ill and confused, believed my brother was going to war. It was as if my grandfather mistook his grandson for his younger brother, Gaetano, who had died in a Milan military hospital nearly sixty years ago.

World War I, it has been argued, was a turning point in modern history. It changed the course of warfare, transportation, and communication. It blew open a world with different rules. If you are looking at military strategies, perhaps the view of the war can be confined from 1914 to 1918, from the date of the declaration of war to the date when peace was announced. For those whose youth passed during this time, the time span is not so crisply delineated.

The episodes and experiences of those days were not extracted and deported when the armistice was signed.

In my conversations with men who fought in the war, I heard a difference in the stories of those who served in the Italian army and those who served in the American army. Those who served in the American army told anecdotes; they told tales which were optimistic and verging on buoyant. For these men, serving in the war for the United States was their first act of patriotism. The war experience, though painful and grueling, was tied to the optimism of a young nation.

The men who served in Italy spoke with resignation, regret, and bitterness. For them, the war was tied not to a promising America, but to a desperate country devoid of hope.

It is as if, in the telling of the tale, the narrator never let go of his emotions of 1918. If you were a doughboy, wrapped in optimism and

banners the color of the American flag, the story you carry with you
is different from one that ended with church bells tolling grimly in
mountain villages.

Adeodato Fontana, who took to America like a fish to the sea:

I came here to Highland Park in 1910. I went back to Italy 1913.
Then, they hooked me in the service. I spend six years there.

I was mostly in Austria, in Trentino. I was on the front line. My
brother saw me on the front line and came over. I didn't even recognize him.

What I went through. You know, they used to call it Monte Santo,
they had a lot of fighting there. Every time there was bombing, I
laid down, you know. Nowhere to hide, just lay down. I stayed
there. I was kind of numb. I couldn't get up. The lieutenant says,
"Hey, Fontana, look out, you gotta bomb in there. Be careful!" Right
behind me. It didn't explode. Then I wake up! I looked. "Oh *Dio!*"
Lucky, that's all. Oh, I'll never forget that. Soon as I went home, I
says, "I'm gonna get out of here, out of Italy." See, when I was in
this country the first time, if you don't go back in the old country
and serve, you can't go back there for thirty years. And me, I have
my father and mother in Italy. So after that, my sister Rafaella—she
was here—says, "You better go." So that's why I went back there,
just for my folks. I'm glad I did because I was free, I was free to do
whatever I please after. And I'm glad. I paid.

Walking, walking all the time. You gotta move. Then they kill you
when you reach the place. You didn't know if you were you or
somebody else. No transportation. Oh *Dio.* That ain't life. But like I
say, if I don't go there, I'd never have seen my folks. That's the
trouble. I'm glad I did it. This ring, my mother gave me. For good
luck, and I still got it.

During the war, I remembered America how many times! But
when they say that you won't see your folks no more, what choice
you gotta take? One or the other. One of the two.

There was one guy from Italy, he went back for a vacation and
the government got him for the service. He went to town for a
hunting license, like an idiot. "I was free," he thought, he had a
card, but it was no good and so they kept him there. I see him with
the *carabinieri* go down to Pieve. I says, "What's that matter?" "I
don't know." He didn't know it himself, either. Called for the service. They got him in the service, too. Just to get a hunting license.

Yeah, there were a few in this country who decided not to serve in Italy. But very few. Maybe a couple. Everybody liked to see their family, you know what I mean. Even so, you like to go back, you know, to see the country, see what you used to know.

When I got back from the war I stayed in Sant'Andrea very little. I was broke like a bum. I knew more people over here in this country than over there because I left Sant'Andrea when I was eleven years old, you know. I was in Sardinia and that's all.

When I think about war, boy, it ruined my life. Six years is a lot of years, you know, for a young fellow. Ah, they ruin you. I mean, if you start some kind of trade, mechanic, or something, you gotta leave it. When you come home, what's the use to start something? Six years in the service. Six years. All my young life.

Louie Bernardi was born in 1891 in Maserno in the Modenese Apennines. He is thin and his pants are big for him. A car mechanic by trade, he walks fast, too fast, through his yard, pointing out tools, tires, parts and materials he has saved over the years. "This ladder here," he says, "used to belong to my brother Donald before he died." Propped by a cane, which he uses only occasionally because it moves slower than he does, he forges ahead to his garage, a brick building built with the help of friends, with salvaged, second-hand bricks. Inside, there is a heater made out of a metal drum. Laying sideways, the rusted barrel is supported by iron legs. A hinged piece of metal sawed out of its belly serves as its door. Unmatched pipes are soldered together to make a chimney. The pipe zig-zags to a hole in the roof. "It works pretty good," he says.

When I was up working in Lake Forest at McCormick estate, I was talking to the superintendent and I let him know that I got this order that I was in the draft. Then I asked the superintendent, I says, "Superintendent, well, I see here we got to a point, we either gotta go serve the time here or in Italy. What d'you think?" He said, "You better stay here."

Well, I could either go back to Italy or go here, but I volunteered here. In Rockford, at Camp Grant, I took the aviation. And I served two years with the aviation. Sixteen months in France, Germany, and Italy, and seven months in this country. When I enlisted, the end of six months we were in France.

See, when I was working at McCormick's, they sent me to a mechanic school in Chicago run by two Italian race car drivers. When I enlisted in the army in Rockford, they asked me if I had a diploma in the mechanical field and I told them, I said, "Well, by God, I dunno if I got it with me, but I got it in Chicago." So I went through like nobody's business with the aviation.

So after we make the application in Rockford, this other sergeant took me and my partner, Fonso Bellei, the butcher's brother, over into the shop. He had motors all apart and start to ask me, "What is that?" "Well," I say, "that's a valve." "What's this?" "A piston." "What is that?" "Piston ring." That was enough. And so me and Fonso, we passed the test like nobody's business.

Well, I enlisted late in the fall of 1917. I went to Texas and we start to work around the planes. I was one of the first fellas that knew how to put the motor together. The pilots were working, flying, practicing, and when they got through with one plane that didn't fly anymore, they put it on the side and start out on a new one. And we got there and started to work that motor.

So we went along about six months there in Texas and then before we knew, we were in New York. We knew we were going to cross. So, we went across, we traveled in the first group. It was a German boat—the first American boat captured in New Jersey. And then they overhauled it. We were on that boat. *Von Steuben.* And when we start out, there was three ships loaded with all kind of troops— aviation, navigation. *George Washington* and *American* and *Von Steuben.* The three ships. We traveled together from New York to Brest, France.

The next we knew we were in Alsace-Lorraine, and we land in a little town closer to the front, but it was still about forty miles away. Then the last time we landed in a little town, it was up much closer to the front line, in line to Verdun, a little town called Toul.

My job in the field was to receive those planes coming in to see if they're okay and then they could go out again. We didn't do much overhaul because we used to send them to Paris motor division. And there they had machine shops where they rebuild them brand new and send back the motor. All we did was put the motor in the plane.

When I got my furlough I was in the first assignment, but to go to Paris. When I saw my name on the bulletin, I says, "Oh no, I'm going to Italy." I was the only Italian in the squadron and we had one Polish. So I went to the commander, and the sergeant said, "Well, why do you want to see the commander for?" "Well," I says, "He's got my name in that bulletin and it's going to come off. I'm going to Italy." And, by gosh, the colonel had made a note of this in New York before we left because they had asked us what nation we were from and if we had a family over there. So I got twenty-six

days in Italy. So I had a nice furlough, heh? See all my family. Oh
that was great. We were done and we did our best. Everything that
we had coming, it was given us.

Well anyhow, we got back to New York the fourth of July, 1919 —
they wanted us to reenlist. So they offered me. "Nothing doing. I
put two years of service and I think I did my service and I'm going
home." And the sergeant knew that I was from Italy. He says,
"You're not going home to Italy?" "Well, I'm going where I'm gonna
make a home." So we went to Rockford and I got the discharge
right there.

Henry Piacenza is one of the only "old-timers" at his granddaughter's
wedding. Henry, in a tuxedo, holds court at his table as people come
up and say hello. He can't carry on a conversation because the Elvis
impersonator and back-up fifties band is compromising his hearing aid.
When I interview him a few months later, his daughter and son-in-
law warn me, "Pa can't hear, you know, you'll have to talk really loud,
otherwise he can't hear you." We sit at the dining room table. The tape
recorder is between us. There are no audio reception problems when
we're discussing something that interests him and there's no rock and
roll.

Nineteen-fifteen, I got called in the army. I went for training with
three guys I knew, our picture is on the wall there. Up to Rockford,
Illinois, Camp Grant. It was a military camp, see, they train the people before they send them across. So I was there about three
months in Rockford, Illinois, and then from there they ship me out
to North Carolina to do some training yet. And then from there
they shipped me across to France.

We fought in France against the Germans. And then I went to
battles, before I got hurt. I went through one — Chateau Thierry,
first battle I was in fighting against the Germans. And then from
there I went to St.-Mihiel, and then, what the heck do you call it?
Châlons.

See, the Germans was trying to get land to put an end to the war,
see, and we were trying to push ahead all we can, see? And geez, I
see the dead all along, just like that, in the ground. You couldn't
walk unless you stepped on somebody.

From there I went to Argonne Forest. That's where I got hit.
That's where I was wounded. I got shot. October 12, 1918. Shot in
the shoulder and hip. The day I got wounded, I was on detail and

went back to the second line to bring the food up to the company. On my way back, that's when I got it.

And from there I was in the hosptial in France, for not very long, and they shipped me to the United States, down in Newport News, Virginia. I had three or four operations there before I came to Fort Sheridan.

What a life. You want to see all my medals? I'll tell you what they are for. This is the Purple Heart. Everybody that gets wounded they give one of those. Purple Heart. "Enrico Piacenza." See, these are the different fronts I went to. Can you read it? The Marne. St.-Mihiel. Meuse. Argonne. Ainse. And this is the Victory Medal.

These guys in the picture? That's Isaia Santi. That, of course, that's me. This is Bertucci. This is John Pasquesi. All the ones that went in the army with me, they're all dead now, except me. I'm the one that got shot, and I'm still here now. Figure that out, will you. Isn't that funny? The only one I saw in the war was this guy here, Pasquesi, up on the front, the only one I ever saw. I saw him in the first battle we had. I met him up there. He was in transportation. Those days they had no trucks, you know. They had the horses, the mules. And he used to drive four old mules and take the supplies up to the front lines and back. So one day, I met him. I was so surprised. Because you know, it's a pretty large country. Jesus Christ. So it was funny to meet that guy, geez, I was surprised because we were bachelors together—we bached together in Highland Park.

Tony Casorio was born in Accera, near Naples, in 1894. He came to the United States at age fifteen. He has worked as a gardener all his life. He is a tiny man who walks in quick duck-like steps, bending, stooping, digging with stamina at age ninety-three. His yard is meticulously trimmed. Tiny boxwoods line the walk. Flowers bloom from spring to fall in a well-orchestrated landscape. In his house, in the room that gets the most sunlight, are minute stems, roses, he says, planted from seed. They have taken years to emerge from the soil to the height of two inches. He gives the impression of a man without a grudge. He punctuates his conversation with "wonderful, wonderful, wonderful."

Nineteen-seventeen, the registration come out, when I was working for Harold McCormick in Lake Forest. Registration come out for the army, you know. So I went over and registered in Libertyville.

September 14, we had an examination. We went through so many doctors, you know, one measures, another see if you got anything wrong. I see everything was alright. Except when I went to measurement, you know, they maked a mark on my back. And when we went out, John Pasquesi say, "Tony, they say they don't want you." I says, "Why? Nothing wrong with me. I want to go."

So I went to the office, I ask one of those officers, I says, "Sir, is there anything wrong with me?" He says, "No, we wish we could find all like you, you know, healthy like you are. One thing wrong with you is that you're not even five feet." That's true, you know. And I says, "Well, what difference does that make, five feet or six or four?" I says, "If the man he wanna go," I says, "they should take him."

Then after they took me, they asked me if anyone want to go in school, automatic school—machine gun—I says, "Yes."

And then we started school, you know a couple hours a day. I was good. Very good. And when we went to rifle range, the major and captain was right behind me. But I was only about 115 or 110 pounds. So when I was shooting, you know, that machine gun, it just shake me up, you know, tight to hold, you know, but it shake me up. And I couldn't see where the bullets was going. And now the captain and major and colonel was right behind me, they just want to see me, you know, there they was teasing me all the time. You know, they liked me. I know that, so I turned around and the captain says, "What's a matter, Casorio?" And I says, "Captain, I can't see where the bullets are going." And he says, "Never mind that." And then the colonel says, "Never mind, Casorio, we've been looking at you for half an hour," he says. "You're doing wonderful. Keep a go."

One time, they give a party, you know, and they want to put me on the table, want me to say something. I was interested to talk about that we should go and catch the Kaiser and this and that. And they had even in the camp newspaper that I was talking. Talking about that I would like to go over there and catch the Kaiser and bring the hat back, you know. And then they put it in the newspaper.

First I was at Camp Grant in Rockford. Then transferred to Texas. They sent me to Thirty-third Division. Thirty-third Division was in Texas, in Houston. And then from Texas they sent us in different division. So we went from Texas to New York. Then to France. And then from there keep every day a going, marching. For ten days. There was no truck. Even the big guns, they have to pull it with mules. That wasn't like today, you know, they got a truck, a tank. They got everything.

Every day we was walking, walking, walking all the time with guns and with everything. We battle in what do you call, Argonne. Cansavoy and St.-Mihiel.

When we was in the war, you know, I tell you, it was just a mess, the holes all over, big holes that you could build up houses right on without digging a basement. Fifty feet across. From the bombs. Trees are down, blown up. Oh, night just like daytime. And gas. Cyanic gas. One time, you know, there were so many bombs, I was out of post. Every night I was out of post. It must be two hundred or three hundred yards. We find out how far German lines could be, you know, we didn't want to get too close. Me and two more, you know. The boys up here, you know, and I was up there, you know, in case the Germans would advance, you know, and then I could notify behind so that they could get ready, you know.

And one time, I got lost, oh. This is funny. This is one of the worst things I've been through. See. You know the Germans, they had the bathrooms outside, the holes with two-by-fours. And there was so much gas, so much gas, and so many guns shooting. I tried looking for a shell hole so I could get in. I was on the ground, looking, with the hands because it was night and I couldn't see where I was going. Until I find the hole. I fell in the hole, you know. I couldn't smell it. It was a German toilet. So I went right in and the dirty stuff just here, you know. I got out of there. I took the gas mask off. Oh boy. Oof. I couldn't stand it, the smell, I put the gas mask on again. I went out. I didn't care if the Germans coming or no coming or what they would do to me. And two months before I got another uniform, you know, and the boys always keep away from me! That was one of the worst things that I've been through.

Leo DePalma wintered at Sutton Terrace, the same apartment complex in Fort Lauderdale as my grandparents, for many years. There were three, two-story buildings. The buildings were full of people from Highwood. In the morning, the men played *bocce* at a court off Commercial Boulevard. In the afternoon, they played cards, *scopa*, at poolside. We are sitting at his kitchen table in Highwood. Toward the end of the interview, he unwraps a piece of hard candy. He offers me a piece. I take it. Butterscotch. Transcribing the interview, I hear the crinkling of the cellophane. The tape recorder has captured forever the sound of candy rebounding against teeth as he discusses Mussolini: "I'm glad I was here because I no like that party anyway because he doing the dirty work all the time. You had to join."

I was the youngest in the family. I was born in 1894 in Corato, in the province of Bari. Work on the farm. We didn't own it. We had olive trees, almonds, grapes, all kinds of fruit. I stayed home all the time until I was twenty-one, then I went in the Italian army.

I was in the Italian army and my wife was my girlfriend, see, for many years. So every time I go on furlough, my wife wanna get married, see. And I figured, "I'm on the front line." I say, "So I get killed, won't do any good to you."

I spent most of my time on the front line in Austria.

So finally, the war was nearly over. And I had no more danger to my life. I went furlough to get married to my wife. Only had ten days. To get married, to the church, you have to take three days, to announce it. I only had five days. So in this five days, I was in furlough myself, the town was declared infection town. The government ordered all the GI on furlough to stay in the town in quarantine! So in the morning, I had to present myself. Then I could go away, see? Soon as they call my name, I say, "Here," and then go away home. We stayed together for four days. That was the best four days in my life.

Enea Cortesi is one of the Sant'Andreol', one of those born in Sant'Andrea. Born in 1895, he is a bachelor. "Never found a girl," he says. He talks about domains exclusively male: *bocce* and *ruzzolone*, blind pigs, union halls, steel-mill foremen, card games, and construction crews, without sounding rough and macho. He is a tall gentleman, who must end our discussion so that he can eat lunch at McDonald's and join the men uptown at the *bocce* courts, where his age commands attention and his picture-perfect follow-through ensures he is still asked to play.

I got called in the Italian army in 1915. When I went to the army, my brother was in the same regiment that I was. The king's guard. They called them the *granatieri*. Then in a few months after they declared war to Austria, and I went to war. I was in the Austrian territory, my company, the day that Italy declared war to Austria. I remember when I come in they say, "Today Italy declared war to Austria." You know, alongside France, England, the United States. I was there when I got wounded. In two places. Plus the grenade exploded a piece of iron and I got a sciatic nerve, it's almost broke. Then I went to the hosptial, it was near the end of 1918.

First I went to Gorizia, a little city on the bottom of the mountains. Then we went to Trentino by Trento, but we didn't reach

Trento. Not me. We occupied Alto Adige. Then we come back from
there and we went up to the other front at the bottom of the mountains. Because in the mountains were the *alpini*, they called them.
We was nine thousand *granatieri*. We come back two or three
thousand. That's all. From the battle.
The Austrian army was coming in, we used to shoot: poom,
poom, poom. They like to kill with hands. It was either kill or get
killed. That's how the war is. Because *a noi altri*, for us, those people didn't never done anything wrong to us, to me personally, and I
never done anything wrong to them. But you know the government.
They send you there and you gotta kill. If you don't, you get killed.
That's what war is.

Zeffero Pacini, who despite using a walker, may still be a *giron'*:

I was a prisoner of war in Serbia. It was a pretty place, but, you
know, they treated us like animals, because we were prisoners. We
worked on the railroad. Those times you don't forget. I was near
Gorizia when they captured me, but they took me to Serbia. They
gave us hardly anything to eat because there was nothing at that
time. The Germans lost the war, and all the prisoners went home.
And after the war, I went to my little village, and I found work
with marble, I was a stonecutter, in the province of Carrara.

(from Italian)

Domenick Linari, who doesn't get along with Nietzsche:

Maybe I was a rebel or something. I didn't want to go to the service. I didn't go. I got out of it somehow. I didn't go here. I didn't
go in the First World War. I was supposed to be too young, of
course. And Second World War, I was too old. So, no war for me,
and I didn't complain.

Viterbo Ponsi, who says the trade is in the blood:

Minus a month, I spent four years in the war. In the Italian army.
I went in January of 1915 and I was discharged at the end of December of 1919.
In the war, I breathed mustard gas, that would make a good
novel, you know, to tell about breathing mustard gas during the
war. They had masks but mine didn't fit right. It took me a long
time, and a lot of money too, to be cured. I couldn't hold the food

down, there was pain. When I ate lunch, throw up. See, if you can't keep the food there, you get weak and weak. Some doctor put me on a diet of toasted bread, like baby, light food. You know, if you're working, you can imagine, you can't eat only that. Then one doctor, he put me in good shape. Take a year, pretty near.

Domenico Lattanzi came to the United States in 1913 at the age of seventeen. He later went back to Italy and married, returning to the Highwood area in 1928 with his wife and children. He talks very fast, wanting to get the story out. His stories have a big outline that is filled in with many details and detours. In the end it winds its way to the punchline. His wife brings glasses of Seven-Up into the living room. I accept, he declines. She insists. He tells her, "No, you drink, I gotta talk."

Before I leave Rockford, I call my father to say, "I gotta go in Texas tomorrow." Nobody had a telephone in those days. There was a telephone just at Frank Benvenuti's house in Glencoe. I call down there and ask him to tell my father to come to Rockford for awhile.

Then, in the middle of the night, I heard, "Lattanzi, Lattanzi, Lattanzi, Lattanzi!" I said, "What?" "Your father is right outside here."

When my father came he says, "Benvenuti called me at Lake Shore Country Club." He was working there.

He came to Rockford from Glencoe with a cab. He says, "We gotta say something." You know, I don't have much to say, but I told him, I says, "I gotta go tomorrow." The cab waited. I says, "I got a little locker at home. I'll give you the key so you can open it."

He says, "Alright."

He stayed just an hour. We had a nice talk. An hour. It was plenty.

I was in the service seven months. I got a fever. They discharged me. Then when I come back to Glencoe, it was all old people left. I was young. I was ashamed. I said to my partner in Glencoe, "Let's go to Waukegan and buy a uniform." I went up there and bought a military uniform better than the one I had. And every so often I put it on and people thought I was on furlough.

Caterina Lattanzi's addendum:

Can I tell you something? My husband served in the United States army. Okay. Six months. After six months, it come the peace, we didn't have no more war, okay. He's in the American Legion.

He went back in Italy, okay? Went back in Italy right after the war. Then after six years, the United States had a law, all of the men who served in the war could have one year to come back to live in the United States. He was one that could come back.

Well, okay, he went to Rome to tell them, you know, he wanted to come to United States. The Italian government told him, "You served only six months in the United States. Over here you're supposed to serve one year." So, they took him in the Italian army for six months!

And then, the deadline was coming to go to the United States. I wrote to him. I said, "Listen, if you go in the United States, I come too, I don't stay here." He told me, "Listen, if you want to go, you can go. Go in the post office, I have ten thousand *lire* in the post office. Take it out. Make passport." That's what happened. Good thing. To the United States, I'll say, thank you, I come in this country. Otherwise I didn't have no chance.

From *La mia vita*, reminiscences of Sante Pasquesi:

We were working at the Moraine Hotel in Highland Park when the United States entered the European war of 1917 and the older of my two brothers had to quit his job to serve in the American Navy.

He who leaves for war always goes toward danger and it's natural for those who have relatives in the war to live in constant worry. This held true for us. I wasn't called into the army because married men with children were only called if there was a shortage of men.

The men and women who worked in the hotel were, for the most part, young; consequently, in a short time, many of the young men were drafted. It was necessary to replace them, but the administration wasn't glad of it because older people had less energy to work.

Peace, implored for so long by the entire world, came for some countries in November 1918; for us on the eleventh of this month. Everybody was happy. Every corner of the world, including ours, was celebrating. Gradually the soldiers came home and our family, like many others, was reunited. At that time you came to make money to then invest in your native country. It became, for our advantage, and in the future, for the advantage of our children, an adopted land where we felt to be the same as the native citizens as far as duties and rights were concerned.

Massima Vanoni, who was always old for her age and remains youthful:

I remember that I saw posters on the walls in the village where they called up each year, each *classa*. And then they came to the *classe* of 1878, '79, '80. I was about eight years old. And I remember that I didn't understand what these notices were about. Later, I understood what they were. Almost all the young men left. People cried. And the discharged returned, those who could. Many lost their lives. They didn't come back.

Did they want to go to war? I remember that generally many were disgusted.

My father was in the war. He was wounded. And so they made him a baker and he didn't have to go to combat anymore.

When someone from town died, usually they sent a notice to the city hall, the *comune*, and they would tell the priest. The priest would go to the family's house to tell them that a son or father of the family was dead. When your *zio* Gaetano, your grandfather's brother, died, it was the priest who brought the news to the family.

After the war, very slowly things fell back into place. But very slowly. During the war, like I said, they issued food stamps, and with those you could get food. There was a ration.

Almost all the men went, except the very ancient. All the young men from our town left. In your *nonno's* house, three sons went, your grandfather, Angelino, and Gaetano. Gaetano died in a hospital in Milano. After the war they brought his bones back to Sant'Andrea.

I remember that when the war was over, the people who remained and those who returned home, there was *allegria*, celebrations. There was enthusiasm. When the war was over, I remember that the bells rang and there were celebrations in the towns when they heard about the armistice. That everyone was happy. Those who were dead, their people cried. But those who remained were overjoyed and celebrated.

(from Italian)

CHAPTER

5

Stopovers

IMMIGRATION IS FREQUENTLY depicted as a linear process: a person begins at point A and ends at point B. In the lives of Highwood's Italians, there were frequently points in the middle, stopping places on the journey, stopovers only in hindsight. For many, at the beginning of the journey, Highwood wasn't even an option.

At the turn of the century, Rosa Fiocchi's father, for example, was in Sunnyside, Arkansas, a plantation in the Mississippi River delta where Italian peasants had been recruited to work as sharecroppers. An uncle settled in Vineland, New Jersey, an important settlement of Italian immigrants on the East Coast.

Families from the Frignano, including members of the Ugolini, Pichietti, Santi, and Biondi families, settled in Memphis where they went into the grocery business.

Other Highwood residents spoke of relatives in Detroit or Fresno, California. Louie Bernardi tells of a cousin, Joe Bernardi, who left a coal mine in Ladd, Illinois, to try his hand at farming in Minnesota: "He bought a farm someplace in Minnesota. He stayed about two years and went back again in Spring Valley. Well, I guess he didn't find the farm was good enough."

Despite a perfectly rational explanation to the question, "And why didn't you stay there?" I suspect there are other answers that were equally as important. If, for example, one winter, Mike Lorusso had met a girl he wanted to marry in St. Paul, would he have stayed there? If Gina DeBartolo's mother had despised her brothers, would life on an Indiana farm have been more attractive? If Pia and Ciro Gibertini hadn't seen a mouse in the drawer, would the family have stayed in Chicago?

The options of people are shaped and limited by economic and social circumstances, but these stories suggest the power of chance and the inevitability of quirk in historical process.

63

I interviewed Mike Lorusso at his daughter's home. On reviewing the tape, I find it betrays the problems of the uninitiated interviewer. We're talking in the kitchen. His daughter is washing dishes, and when he can't hear, she helps. I listen to my voice on the tape: "No, don't worry, you're doing great. You're doing beautiful." Grandchildren and children stop in all morning. A young great-granddaughter breezes in. He says to her, "Michelle, so aren't you going to say hello?" She says, casually, "Hello," and goes about her business. He says, to no one in particular, "Yeah! Hello." It is as if I am hearing my grandfather rebuke me for rudeness.

My name? Michele, in Italian. "Mike" here. I was born in Valenzano, Bari, April the fourth, 1895. We were six in the family, two girls, four boys. I'm the second in the family. My father had a team, he had a pair of mules and carried stone and commercial stuff.

When I left? In the first part of February 1919. I was fourteen years old. My father was in Chicago with my brother and an uncle. I think my father came here in 1905. They were working at Fort Sheridan. Teaming. Drove a team of mules. In Italy, it was for himself but over here it was for Uncle Sam.

I lived in Chicago until the summertime, then we come out and work on the railroad, going out to Montana, work on the railroads. The road was built already but we had to fix it up. We kept it up. I did this for five years. Well, I worked all over. I was in North Dakota, even the state of Washington.

There was a county office. You go over there and ask for a job and they'll give you a job and they'll send you out. But you had to pay some money. Yeah! You had to pay money to get the job! Six dollars, eight, ten. All depends.

First year it was me, and my brother and my dad, too. That's when we was in the Montana. Then, my dad, a year later he went in the old country. Me and my brother stayed here. I had four uncles, *zio* Anton', Roc', Joe, and Pepin'. They all worked on the railroad. They all went back to Italy.

We slept in a bunkhouse. The company, the railroad, they furnished that. You didn't have to pay nothing when you work on the railroads. They give you everything free. There was no stove, nothing. We had to build a fire like an Indian. Cook outside with wood. We ate anything, potatoes, pasta, meat. We'd get a chicken once in a while from the farm, because there was nothing but farms out there. Sometime we were right in town, sometime far away from the town. And you'd go to the store, the general store.

It's a pretty good state Montana, but too cold in the wintertime. One day it was fifty-four, fifty-eight below zero. It's right underlying Canada. The place where we were was Cut Bank, Montana.

They paid fifteen cents an hour at the most. A dollar and a half a day. Work ten hour every day.

I worked on the Great Northern. A year later, it was the Northern Pacific. No union. Union? Huh! Them day nobody knows anything about the union. Especially the Italian and Greek. Nobody talking English anyway. How can you put the union when you don't know the law?

I was crazy for work in them day, but no more! Yeah, yeah. In the wintertime, I come back in the city. It was warm there. Do nothing for three or four months. I stayed in St. Paul, Minnesota. Then one winter, I stayed way out in Washington. Worked for the Milwaukee-St. Paul. I work nothing in the winter. I lived on the money saved during the summer. I save a little bit. Them day, for a dollar, you go a long way. So I was a couple of winters in Chicago. One in Washington. Then Minnesota.

Traveling, traveling. Them day I liked to travel. In the wintertime in Washington we were in Spokane. It was a nice town. Then, I worked near St. Maries, Idaho. We were staying in Plummer, Idaho.

Them day, the trouble was, we wasn't with the family. We always like, just like a hobo. Today here. Tomorrow over there and go. And you go and find friends and they gotta go over there and I gotta go over here. Crazy.

Gina DeBartolo, whose mother killed a snake to protect her nest:

My father didn't stay in Chicago. He bought a farm then in Indiana. When he bought his eighty acres, he thought he had an estate. And my mother was no farmer, she was a seamstress. Well, my mother hated the farm.

At first, we lived a year in Chicago with my uncle so my father could save enough money to buy equipment. My uncle Joe Leonardi was in the grocery business. At the time they had such a beautiful old house. The first floor was almost like an English basement with one step down. And on the second floor, they had a kitchen with a big dining room, and then the living room, and there was a beautiful wooden stairway. Upstairs, they had a big master bedroom with an alcove with a nursery. And they had a fireplace in the dining room, a fireplace in the living room, and a fireplace in two of the bedrooms. My aunt had some boarders living there. There was John

Santi from Santi Brothers' Dairy, and Amedeo Picchietti and Aldo
Piacenza.

My Uncle Joe had a horse and a wagon and they would go down
to the market and fill the wagon up with fruit or vegetables, and
then they had their little customers along the ways, mostly store-
keepers.

So we came over in 1908, and then we went up in the farm in
North Judson, Indiana. This was a Polish-Bohemian community.
There were developers in Indiana where we were, and there happened to be cross section of railroads. There were four railroads, because that was the time when transportation was by railroad. There
was the Pennsylvania, the Erie, the Baltimore and Ohio, and New
York Central, all happened to intersect right in that particular section. It was about seventy-five miles southeast of Chicago. And so
there were these developers then, like there are now, and they
would advertise or men would run excursions to sell this land. So
my father bought eighty acres.

We stayed there on the farm my father bought, until my little
brother got blood poison; there was a lot of medical attention and
he died. Well, my father went to pay the doctor bill, and he asked
the doctor if they couldn't make an arrangement with part of his
farm, and this particular farm had a nice house. I think it was one
of the nicest houses my father ever lived in. 'Course there was no
plumbing, you know, and there was no heating. We had a big old
stove and had to go out in the woods and find the wood and the
stumps to put in it in order to heat up the house. And then we had
a coal stove, and then we had a pump that was inside and you had
to prime it to start it, and when we'd get up in the morning, if your
hands were wet, they'd stick to the handle. And so, it was pretty
primitive. But nobody else had anything.

Well, anyhow, the doctor took the forty acres where the house
was, and my father bought another forty, that was much better
land, because that first eighty was terrible. It was all sand.

And at that time he raised onions and pickles and potatoes. That
was your cash crop. So we planted an acre of onions and an acre of
pickles and an acre of potatoes. We wore overalls because we'd have
to kneel in this black muck and weed the onions because there
would be so many weeds and you'd have to be careful so the little
onions would be there. You could get two hundred dollars out of an
acre of onions and at that time that was a lot of money. And the
pickles, you had to pick them every morning. I'm sure you know,

the smaller they were, the more expensive they were, and if they got beyond a certain size they wouldn't buy them.

Heinz had a platform along the railroad and all the farmers would get together, maybe one time one would go with a wagon and horse and pick up everybody's pickles. Then the Heinz man would weigh them and grade them and pay them.

Well, my father went to work on the railroad but that didn't last long because he wasn't the kind of man who worked on the railroad. So he started doing the same thing he was doing in Chicago. He was really a jobber. He knew all these merchants, the vegetable and fruit merchants on South Water Street, and he would usually get a train from one town to the other, and he started taking orders for fruit. And then he'd come home with his orders. And, I was twelve years old, he'd say, "Alright Gina, sit down and write so-and-so's name, Indiana, one case of oranges, half a case of lemons, a bunch of bananas." Then we'd mail those orders in and they would send them out on the train by express and the next week he'd call on them. He'd collect for what they received and take any new orders. And besides that, he had the Spanish peanuts. So he made a living on that. Well, it wasn't such a good living.

You know, the farm left such an impression on me. I think that it was such a way of life, and yet we only lived there five years, which isn't very much. But my mother always wanted to come to Highwood where her family was, so my father sold the farm and he came up here to Highland Park, looking for a farm.

I remember this so distinctly, you know, one day I go out and I see something in the front of the house and I went over there and I told my mother, "There's a big *bago* out there in front of the house." And my mother comes out and it was a snake. Oh, my mother gets so frightened. But my mother was, you know, a good strong woman. She goes and gets a hoe and puts the hoe on the snake's head and she finally chopped the head. And when my uncles came on Sunday my father was showing them how brave my mother had been. She'd killed the snake. And another thing. I guess we had some little baby chicks, and a chicken hawk would come down and steal one of the baby chicks and the whole chicken yard was getting all in a flutter. The rooster was hollering, and the chickens were hollering, but the old chicken hawk would come down and pick up and away he'd go. So my mother goes out there and the mother hen and the hawk were fighting, so she takes the hoe again and hits the hawk and kills the hawk.

Well, anyways, so my mother finally got to Highwood in 1918.

This account is a translation of the memoirs of Aldo Piacenza, local poet, painter, and merchant. Born in Sant'Annapelago, in 1888, at La Torre, he came to this country in 1903.

On a major street of Chicago called Fulton Street, there lived five Italian families from our towns of Sant'Anna and Pieve, who had arrived before me.

One of these families consisted of the two brothers Leonardi of Pieve. They had come to America several years before and then returning to Italy, had taken wives, and with their wives, natives of Sant'Anna, came to the United States. One of the wives was named Gaspera Ugolini, who was married to Domenico Leonardi, and the other Caterina Rossi, who was married to Giuseppe Leonardi. The other families included, one of Sant'Anna, a certain Fernando Bertucci with his wife and children, and the other families, Pichietti and Giuseppe Ori, with his wife and children. Lastly, there was a certain Ferrarini of Pieve. They were in the fruit business and evidently things, they were doing well.

I lived with the two Leonardi brothers. I can say that I was extremely fortunate to find myself with this family because there I found all the Christian virtues, and they saw me, so young, and did not refrain from giving me all the guidance possible to keep me far from the danger that someone so young could have encountered in this big city.

Next to the Leonardi house on Fulton, there was the family of Ferdinando Bertucci, in whose house there lived a man from Sant'Anna named Alfonso Santi, who came to America years earlier and to his credit had become a foreman of a division of workers in a factory called the National Biscuit Company. Through this Alfonso, after four or five days that I was introduced to him, I was employed in the bread department, putting stamps on top of the loaves at a salary of five dollars a week.

I started to familiarize myself with the city, visiting the public gardens, the art museum, the public library, the zoological gardens and all those grand and beautiful places. This is how I spent Saturday, my day off. But this didn't last long because a law was enacted that forbade children under the age of seventeen from working in factories. In order to do this you had to produce a birth certificate, which I could not show them, so, as a result, I was out of work.

What could I do then? After several days I went to this Giuseppe

Leonardi for help, and it was he who suggested to me to go on my own, selling fruit. What should I sell? Start with strawberries, he suggested. And this is how I started, with a box on my shoulder on several streets he had suggested. To attract attention, I had to shout like the fruit vendors do. But with no language and little experience I couldn't do much, so I proceeded with this work for several months, waiting for something better to present itself.

And again, through this Alfonso Santi, I found myself another little job in a little pastry shop, working at night, and even though I could not work legally, I could enter unobserved. The distance to go to work at this shop was considerable. It's true there was the streetcar but I got another idea. At this time before the automobile, the streets of Chicago were swarming with bicycles and I was dying to have one, not only to take me to work, but especially for riding around for pleasure during my hours of leisure. And so I found one at a low price and acquired it, and there I was, happily seated on my bicycle.

But one afternoon, coming back from work, crossing an intersection, I was hit by an electric train that threw me to the ground, and left me unconscious with my left leg completely broken.

The fracture left me unable to work for more than four months. During this time I was bedridden, I received a letter from my parents, asking to send them two hundred *lire* right away, because they were in dire need and a bill was coming due. Thus, they did not know about my sad situation, and during this time I didn't have even one dollar. While reading this letter I started to cry bitter tears, the kind when one feels utterly alone in the world. Hearing me cry, Domenico Leonardi came in and asked me why I was crying. So, I showed him the letter, and as soon as he read the letter, with a smile, said to me, "If this is what is making you cry, don't worry about it." And in fact, he sent the two hundred *lire* to my parents. So you see another proof of what good people they were, that even though my father already owed him seven hundred *lire*, he still sent another two hundred.

After four months, I returned to work in the small shop, and stayed there for several months. But I didn't like working at night, so I left this job to go work in a hotel.

The pay at this time was very low and I was able to save very little. Without language, with little education and with no training in a trade, I made very little progress at this time. And then, I couldn't give my parents what they wanted and what they expected. I spent several years before I could contribute substantially to their well-

being. After five years I was once again at the same factory where I
had been let go earlier because I wasn't old enough. I was a young
man with a nice salary and I was happy enough, even with my
work, and would have happily remained there, but because of an
unpleasant difference of opinion that occurred—in which I felt I
had been wronged—I left again from this last job.

I remained out of work and indecisive for a little while and finally, after having thought hard about it, I decided to leave the city
of Chicago and go to a town out in the country called Highwood,
about thirty miles outside the city.

From *La mia vita*, reminiscences of Sante Pasquesi:

The train stopped under an enormous glass roof of the old-fashioned platform filled with smoke, the conductors ordered us to get
off, and we knew that finally we were in Chicago. Now, I was finally with the uncle whose newspapers had tempted me to under-
take this American adventure, and together we went to visit another
relative. Then, we went from Chicago to Highland Park, where my
uncle had been living for some time and where I was to make my
home if I could find a job. I was hired to work in a brick factory
with a low and also undependable salary, because in case of mechanical trouble we would have to suspend work, without getting
paid, while the machines were being repaired; this happened often
since the mechanic was a Scot who was always drunk.

Finally I decided that this job was not for me and I went looking
for another one, but with very discouraging results. Even though
jobs weren't lacking, employers wanted strong, experienced laborers
that could speak at least a little English. Lacking the proper qualifi-
cations, and with my uncle's permission, I decided to move to Chicago. In this enormous city with other people I knew who were also
unemployed, I went every morning to look for work, with little success for fifteen days. Finally, with the help of a cousin, I found
work in a bakery called Gonnella where I was happy to go, knowing that some friends of mine and schoolmates worked in these surroundings.

Any idea I had that these friends would help me with the new
job or with the English language soon proved to be an illusion.
With indignant surprise I ascertained that a good number of them
had forgotten there was a past between us, close friendships, and
that it would not be to their advantage to be caught using their already forgotten, first language, and, finally that in observing my

shoes, with their row of nails, they didn't want to keep company with me, so as not to run the danger of being labeled an immigrant.

But since I knew so well the capabilities of these already seasoned "Americans," I decided not to bother them so that their high social position wouldn't be jeopardized on my account. Under these circumstances, there was only one solution, to work diligently and learn the English language as soon as possible. As a result, in the place of these renegade friends, I put a nice book of English-Italian grammar with which I spent my leisure hours.

After a few months, I threw aside the shoes with the nails, even though they weren't completely worn out, a bit disdainful with that shoemaker who had thought of putting the nails there, and I started to speak in broken English, having a little knowledge of its grammatical rules.

Two years later, I was joined by a brother, two years younger than I, who got a job at the same bakery where I worked; we kept each other company. Both our salaries were paltry, but being regular, they permitted us some small savings. Every once in a while we sent some money home, not because there was a need for it, but to assure our parents that even though we were far away, it was our desire to be generous toward them to show our gratitude. So, indirectly, they remained convinced that it was our intention to be industrious and to stay on the path of honor and virtue.

It would have been better if my job had been during the day because in the winter I would have attended night school which was then available without charge in various parts of the city so that foreigners would have the privilege of learning the English language more rapidly. But my job was from eight p.m. to eight a.m. Upon investigation, I learned that at the Dore School on Harrison Street near Halsted Street, adult foreigners were permitted to attend classes during the day also. Even though it was a torment and I studied, sleepy and exhausted, I didn't miss this opportunity. From nine a.m. until noon, I regularly attended the class to which I was assigned.

My father started to remind me in his letters that I was to be drafted in October 1908, and, before I left Italy, I had promised him that I would return for my military service.

At this point, I had only one year left of life in America and on one hand, I was sorry that the time to go back to my country was approaching because now that I was more experienced in my job, my salary was higher and I could have saved more money. On the other hand, it was worthwhile to return to Italy and prove to my parents that I kept my promise. I also imagined that I had grown in

the estimation of my family and the community, now that I had
seen a foreign land where they spoke a different language which I
understood a bit, and now that I wore more elegant suits and shoes
without nails.

Fanny Cassidy, whose tapping cane signaled it was time to leave:

My father said that women have a better life in America than in
Italy. And he wanted to send us to America. Before we came, my
father had been here, too, for a short time. He worked in the Crack-
erjack factory. And he saw how the women did. So, he said, "Le
donne fanno la vita meglio in America che in Italia. Dovete andare in
America." And he sent me to my aunt. And she knew that a friend
worked in a pants factory on Monroe. I didn't know anything. I
didn't even know how to speak. It was pretty hard, you know.
When I was doing some work in the factory, it was my first job and
nobody teach you how. You had to do it by your own mind. And
the first time, the boss came, saw my work, and he said, "No, no,
that's no good. You can go home." And I had just arrived. I don't
even know the way to go home. I knew only that I lived at 1014
Randolph.

We worked by hand. There were some who used the machines,
but I hadn't ever seen a machine. I worked on the hems of pants,
on the pleats. I worked there from 1913 to 1915.

There were days when I made ten cents a day because they paid
by the work done. There was a ticket in the pants, you take the
ticket, and they pay you for however many tickets you have. And
then, when I began to learn, I made a dollar a week. Era tough. It
was very tough. There were a lot of Italians, a lot from southern
Italy. I found some good women who taught me. I liked the work,
but I would have liked to know more. A lot of times the Italians
would teach me once, and then they would go work.

I worked five days a week. From the morning at 8:00 until 4:30.
They were starting a union when I was there, but it began after I
left. Then, after, I knew the work pretty good, I made a little more
and I got up to five dollars a week. It was alright.

My husband came from Highwood to Chicago to visit my family.
He was from Modena. My sister's husband, Bernardi was his name,
was coming from the same town that my husband come from. It
was there that we fall in love. He was a nice, good man.

When we got married, we had a dollar and thirty-five each. We
got married in Chicago on Grand Avenue in a church. My wedding

dress, I paid nine dollars. It was silk. And my husband, he paid nine dollars, too, nice big suit.

(from Italian)

Pia Gibertini serves the meal at noon. She and her husband, Ciro, operated a boardinghouse that catered to Italian immigrants, as well as private dining rooms patronized by the wealthy and performers from the nearby Ravinia theater. It is easy to picture her passing from table to table, serving the Italians seated in one room, and the opera stars and well-to-do patrons in the other dining room. She is small and intense. Her eyes are deep-set and her cheek bones expansive. She says to me, "Excuse me, are you finished, may I take your plate?" She concentrates as she lifts up the bowl of artichokes, elbows bent and hand extended away from her body. She is methodical and unhurried. Even in her home as she clears the table, she is a professional.

The reason we came up to Highwood is because my husband, Ciro, said that in Chicago the baby had to stay inside all the time because it was dangerous outside and it would be better to find a place in the country, he said, that way there would be good air.

I was happy to leave because the work that he was doing was very dangerous. He worked at Lakeside Fish Market in Chicago, and the first year he worked there, two men died, because, you know, they worked outside, and then would go into the ice house, and many of them caught pneumonia. And those days there wasn't penicillin. These two men were the same age as Ciro. Still young, they died. And so he said that it was too dangerous and that it would be better for us to go up there and do something else.

We moved a lot. It was hard to find places to live. We lived on St. James Place in Lincoln Park. We had to go to eat at a restuarant because we had no kitchen. We went to a Greek restaurant. Then we lived at 2855 Belmont Avenue. It was a place where there were a lot of Germans. And we lived on Belden Avenue. Before, we had lived in an apartment on LaSalle Street. It was a place where the people were desperate. It wasn't a nice neighborhood; it was an ugly neighborhood. But we couldn't find another apartment. The apartment was big enough. More or less. Right away we found mice. We opened a drawer and a mouse jumped out. Ciro slammed the door in the landlady's face.

Eritrea Pasquesi, the *canterina* of the family:

I was seamstress in the garment center. It was on Maxwell Street. And I worked there until I got married in 1929. Nat Rebeck and Company. We came in '23 and I lived here in Highwood with my sister Ribella. I got to Chicago with the Northwestern train, then walked it to the shop.

There was nothing here in Highwood for work in those days. Especially sewing. And I didn't want to do nothing else. I wanted to sew. Some woman, they used to call her *La Ferraresa*, because she came from Ferrara, was working there and she took my sister Vanda and I. They put me in the finishing department. Putting on buttons and hemming dresses.

I was the greenhorn, you know. In that department they were all Italians. One of them was Mary Carani's mother, from Highland Park, and Inez Turelli, she was there, and they would help me along. But they put me right away on a machine. From a hem-stitching machine, they put me on a pleating machine. Then they put me on a buttonhole machine. And anyway, I was a busy little girl.

On Tuesday we got paid. I got twenty-one dollars a week. First I started with eighteen. The girls did the sewing. But the designer, the cutter, the fitter, they were all men.

I'll tell you what I did. We worked on Saturday until noon. And this friend of mine, Frances, we'd hurry up, we'd pick up a sandwich at the ten-cents store, baked ham sandwich for ten cents, and then we'd go to the Chicago Theater, the famous Chicago Theater, that they're trying to keep now, you know, they're trying to make it a landmark, to go see a movie with Clara Bow. Then I would take a train home. I didn't go every week. Whenever there was something, like Rudolph Valentino, Clara Bow, something that we liked. We walked it. It was fifty cents up until one and after one, it was seventy-five cents. So we'd have to break our necks to get down there to see the movie. There was one, it was called *The It Girl,* Clara Bow, and Rudolph Valentino, *The Four Horsemen of the Apocalypse.* And Wilma Bank in *The Sheik of Arabee.* At that time there was John Gilbert and Norma Talmadge.

To learn English, it took me, to really get it nice, a couple of years. And I studied on the way from Chicago. I used to write my words down. Classes? I had to work, like most girls. They should have sent me to sew, to learn how to become a designer because that was my line—that's what I would have always liked to do. But it took $150. Where did I have $150? Not only the $150—but no work, no money coming in. I had nobody to sponsor me. But I got along.

Enea Cortesi, whose follow-through in *bocce* is picture-perfect:

When I first came over, I stopped in Chicago. On Western Avenue and Lake Street, but I was only there for a few months. I had my brother there. He was working in a tavern and for a marble company.

Nineteen twenty I was in Chicago. I worked on what they called South Water Market where all the fruit came from California by train. And we used to go on the track and load it on the wagon, horse and wagon for the people that owned the horse and wagon. We loaded up the wagon and then we go to the store and unload before noon. Then we used to sell it to those stores, even from Highland Park and Highwood. We used to weigh the stuff that was the owner's and take it home with the horse and buggy. There were the two Pichietti brothers, they used to have a store uptown on Central Avenue. South Water Market, that was all retail stores.

Then, I went to Gary because there was no more work in the market. I had a chance to get a job at Gary, Indiana, in the steel mills, and I took off. In Gary, we used to keep on building, improving the building, new building, construction. For the steel mills. The foreman, boy, he used to like me. Many times, he asked some of the friends after I left, "Tell him if he's running out of work, tell him to come back and work here." I was in the steel mill in '21. Then I found the job here. Otherwise I would have stayed there. I used to live with a friend of mine. Domenico Galassini. He used to own a bakery in there, in Gary. He's from Sant'Andrea.

When I came over there was no taverns. They used to sell even in Chicago. But not with the license. My brother, he used to work in one in his spare time, in a tavern, the owner was a *genovese*, on Western Avenue and Lake Street. And from my bedroom I used to see the elevated train at night, *r-r-r-r!* That noise! And I would say, *"Bella mia Sant'Andrea"*—"My beautiful Sant'Andrea!" With all that noise. My brother was used to it. He was sleeping.

After I moved up here, I went down to Chicago every once in awhile, but I don't like to live there. No, I never did like to live in the city. You're more free up there in the country. You get friends around here. Down there, there is all kinds of people that you never know. Around here, if you live here a few years, you get to know everybody in the neighborhood. Even if they are a different nationality. But not in the city. In the city sometimes you don't even know your next-door neighbor.

Mariuccia Piacentini

Adele Dinelli

Domenick Linari

Fanny Cassidy

Domenico and Caterina Lattanzi

Domenica Mocogni

Adelmo Bertucci

Rosa Fiocchi

Viterbo Ponsi

Adeodato Fontana

Gioa and Zeffero Pacini

Louis Bernardi

Leonardo DePalma

Tony Casorio

Enea Cortesi

Pia Gibertini

Julio Brugioni

Giosue Brugioni

John and Yole Bagatti

Delma Muzzarelli

Mary Baldi

Louis Baruffi

Everett Bellei

Ester and Guy Viti

Giulia Mordini

CHAPTER

6

"Down in a Hole, There"

INTERSTATE 80 CUTS ACROSS northern Illinois cornfields. They are mostly flat and entirely Midwestern, and in October they are plowed under. What does the Interstate traveler think when he catches sight of a red angular mountain, an enormous elbow jutting from the side of the fertile Midwest? It is crude and harsh and bald. Further on Interstate 80 he sees to the south another cubist heap, then another. These slag piles are signs that this farmland was once coal country—in towns named Spring Valley, Cherry, Ladd, and Dalzell. These are ancient Midwestern pyramids built by enterprising pharaohs and laboring immigrants.

In those places, there are few traces that a coal industry ever existed. In Texas, in Iowa, in areas swallowed up by Birmingham, Alabama, and on northern Illinois farmland, there were once huge immigrant communities of coal miners. The mines and mining communities are buried, like geological strata of sandstone and shale, under new layers of American generations.

By 1920, the towns of the northern Illinois coal fields had reached their peak in population: Spring Valley, 6,493; Cherry 1,265; Dalzell, 903; and Ladd, 2,040. Thurber, Texas, located halfway between Abilene and Fort Worth, was an immigrant town of coal miners with a population of 10,000. Bevier, Missouri, had a population of 1,868. In 1925 more than 11,000 miners were employed in Iowa.

The mining industry in these areas began to unravel in the 1920s and the residents began to leave. Competition from coal fields with higher-grade, anthracite coal, lower labor costs at nonunionized mines in Appalachia, and a shift to oil and natural gas all contributed to the breakdown of the industry in these regions. It was from these areas, as well as from mines in Indiana and southern and central Illinois, that many of Highwood's immigrant families came.

Immigrants from the Modenese and Bolognese Apennines were first recruited to work in U.S. coal mines during the late 1890s. The earliest immigrants went to the mines of Colorado, New Mexico, Alabama, and Illinois.

In 1908, the Italian Chamber of Commerce in Chicago estimated in its *Bulletin* the number of Italians in Midwest communities: In Spring Valley, there were 2,300; in Oglesby, there were 1,000; and in Ladd, there were 1,300. Nearly 700 of South Wilmington's 1,500 inhabitants were Italian. In the same bulletin, a certain Fabiano of Fanano is credited with initiating the emigration from the mountains of Modena and Bologna. After Fabiano "made money here and visited Italy a wealthy man," it says, "many Italians from the provinces of Bologna and Modena, numbering more than 2,000, joined him on his return and settled in Spring Valley, Seatonville, Ladd, Dalzell and many other places. . . . " Was "Fabiano of Fanano" the first? As my grandmother said about the houses with names, *chi sa, chi sa,* who knows? I can't say Fabiano was indeed the first, but, at any rate, it is certain that from the mountains in Modena and Bologna and these coal towns in Illinois many of Highwood's families came.

The Italian immigrants entering American coal mines in large numbers in the late 1890s were preceded by skilled miners from Germany and the British Isles. At the turn of the century, with technological advancements, the industry needed unskilled laborers. After 1900, Italy and eastern Europe fed these unskilled workers to the American mining industry. This infusion of Italian and other southern and eastern Europeans into the coal mines reflects the staggering growth of these groups in the United States. By 1910, 71.9 percent of European immigrants were from southern and eastern Europe.

Nationwide, there was hostility to the newest immigrants. In certain regions, such as Pennsylvania, the first arriving Italians to work in coal mines included men who were brought in as strikebreakers, a development that further polarized ethnic groups. It was a reputation difficult to erase despite the integration of the Italian miners into the labor movement. Miners of northern European origin considered the new arrivals unskilled workers who were taking away jobs from Americans and bringing down the standard of living because they were willing to work for less.

In 1911, Congress's Immigration Commission echoed this perception: "On account of their lack of industrial training and experience before reaching this country, their low standards of living as compared with native Amerian wage-earners, their necessitous condition on finding employment in this country, and their tractability, the south and eastern Europeans, as already noted, have been willing to accept the rates of compensation and the working conditions as they have found them in the United States." In this way, Italian miners were treated no differently from any newly arriving immigrant group—they were greeted with suspicion and hostility.

By the time most of the Italians arrived to work in the mines, the United Mine Workers had made substantial gains throughout the country, particularly in the Midwest coal fields. In mines organized by the United Mine Workers, the eight-hour work day had been firmly in place before the turn of the century. One victory it could not clinch, however, was the guarantee of steady employment. If the voyage to America had changed many things for the immigrants, it did not change the unpredictability and the seasonal nature of their work.

Just as the unkind terrain and winters pushed the Italians of the Apennines to other parts of the continent to find seasonal work, so did the coal mines of the United States. The habit of going everywhere, *dappertutto*, to find work did not begin or end overnight. A seasonal migration, already set into the clockwork of Italian families and communities, helps explain the fluidity of Italian emigration. Rarely did an immigrant come with the notion of making a permanant home, particularly during the early stages of immigration. Usually, he came with the intention of working for several years, saving money, and returning to Italy.

This bond with the homeland is reflected in a message sent to Italy in a poster in 1899 by Bolognese and Modenese miners working in Carbon Hill, Illinois. It expressed both fervent religious and proletarian sentiments, and was displayed in their hometowns on the feast day of the Madonna of the *Querciola* (Our Lady of the Young Oak).

> From Carbon Hill (Illinois, United States of America), to fellow workers of the mother country, the Bolognese and Modenese emigrant workers greet you. . . . The harsh necessity that compels us to such a dangerous and disconsolate distance, that has buried us alive in these mines with all the elements threatening our unending existence of labor, are not enough to destroy our tender feelings for religion, for the country, for the family that form a single inflamed affection in the heart of the exiles. . . . The fields of Illinois are vast, but still we sit here crying, thinking of Italy.

Although the immigrant miners found themselves in "this American republic, however Protestant," they did not forget the church and did not cease to pray to God and to the Virgin Mary, wife of the carpenter from Nazareth, "mother of the Divine Worker of the Universe who gave up his blood for the true salvation of all workers, all the poor and all the oppressed," as the poster declared.

Carbon Hill was one of the coal mining towns of northern Illinois, part of a corridor running east to west that includes Coal City, South Wilmington, Spring Valley, and Cherry. The miners' hometowns—Fanano, Serrazzone, Sestola, Maserno, and Grecchia—were towns of Highwood families. The names on the Carbon Hill poster were the names of Highwood families.

The seasonal migration pattern of the Italian workers continued in America as it had in Italy. Now, instead of going to work in Switzerland or Algeria for six months during the winter, the immigrant miners moved from mine to mine. It was during shutdowns and strikes that many of the Bolognese and Modenese first went from coal mines to Chicago's North Shore. They latched onto new opportunities when current ones failed, a reaction to the unpredictable puffs and breath-holdings of the American economy.

Louie Bernardi, the mechanic with his brother's ladder:

Well, I'll tell you to go back and really refer back to what we went through—we did go through something then. Anybody, like our family, another family, that left the country, they didn't find it so sweet in any other place where they went neither.

My brother, Donald, "Domenico" in Italy, he came direct to Spring Valley in 1906 and started right in there, right away, then about a year and a half later, he sent a letter home for Angelo. But Angelo, he got sick and he didn't come, so I took his place. I was a little young. I was seventeen years old.

Well, from this town, Montese, it begin to be quite a few were leaving. Leaving the country. Some went to Brazil, some went to South America. And we came to North America.

The majority that left at that time, those days, was either going to work in the railroad or in the mine or in the factory because it wasn't many from this part of the country in Italy that went to the farm. We didn't have anybody to lead us to that. The only recommendation that we got was to come over here and go to the coal mine.

The majority of the countrymen that left the old country had the idea of coming here and make a little money, I guess. See, that was the point. Because they was so poor in the old country that, I guess, they started to spread to the coal mines.

From Maserno, well, from Montese, the big town, we might say, there was about nine of us in that group. When we got to New

York, some went to St. Louis, some went to Canada. It was only
two from the expedition that went to Spring Valley.

Well, we came here, we went to the mine, and the mine didn't
pay very much. They paid so much a weight.

You was down there, you had your own space to work in, they
called it a "place." Well, it would have been about fifteen or eighteen feet frontage. You had to dig that coal, the coal was four feet
high and it was all pick-and-shovel. My place was here—like this
dining room—the next place was like the living room.

To get that coal out, they had a driver with a horse down in the
mine, and they pulled the car from the place to the main gate so
they could get that coal up. The mine was about six hundred feet
deep.

I wasn't scared the first time I went down because in this cage,
they used to put eight or nine or ten at a time, see, and naturally,
you see the other fella, and you just follow the other fella. The elevator, they used to call it a cage, was closed then for safety. The
mine had the steps too, but, hey, that was for emergency. Hardly
nobody ever used them. One time I had to use the steps. I missed
the cage one time. Well, I would have had to stay down there all
night and so I started on the steps and I made it. You could make it
up the steps, because we were young people, in about five or six
hours. But you got up there.

When you finally get up to the top and you see the sunlight you
had enough. Pick and shovel. Pick and shovel. We were hauling
about a ton, a ton and a half. When that cart came to the cage and
came up on top, it went through a scale and you get so much a
weight. But you don't get much more than a dollar for one cart.
Had to be pretty well full, took awhile to get one dollar. Eh, boy.

Lotta times you go down and it wasn't much coal, well, maybe
you get one cart, that'd be one dollar. Some day, we stay down
there a long time and the drivers don't come. So in that day, you
don't leave with nothing. Oh boy, I'm telling you.

There were some mines that had better contract and they used to
work full time. Like nine hours. Every day. It depended on the contract in the mine. At the time, most of the market for the coal was
the railroad and the factory because there was no gas power, no
electric power.

They organized this union but then the mine disappeared. But in
the big mines that kept open, the union went ahead and did it.
There were a lot, like me. I signed up with the union when I was in
Spring Valley but then I wasn't working there and I went to Rock-

ford and worked in the factory. No union. You had to work ten hours for $1.72.

Well, when you go out from where you were raised and look for something else, and you got to pay the consequence, and you got to pay the consequence.

Adelmo Bertucci, "dean of Chicago-area golf course superintendents" and an accomplished accordionist:

I worked in Colorado at a place called Aguilar, a slave camp, they owned all the house, all the land. If they tell you get out, you go. Normally in the mine, I work about three or four days. Then there was a saloon keeper, we called him Nicolo. He put me there to be the blacksmith. I used to play the *fisarmonica*, the accordion, and I gave him a lot of business when I used to play, when they have the dances in the saloon.

It was all kinds of people, Japanese, Greek—all different nations there. If you don't work, alright, the sheriff, boom, he kill you. No monkeying around. Throw 'em on top of the wagon, take 'em down to Trinidad and goodbye. It was pretty rough.

Myself, I never had any trouble. When they went in strike in 1904, they have the support from the Illinois union. They used to send the money. The miners went down in a camp. They put them down, all together there, and when they tried to come out at night to get the water or something, you was liable to get shot. The guard, boom, from the company. No union. They don't want to put the union. They don't want no union.

I worked in Illinois, Taylorville, for six months but that 'twas the union. The union put up the props, the timber for protection. In Colorado, you got to put them up yourself.

There were people in Colorado from Pieve, Roccapelago, from the neighborhood. Some, they work hard and then they go back. 'Twas some Japanese, too. They was very well organized. The Japanese had to go inside and dig the coal. The manager take care of the rest for them. When they go home, they find everything ready to eat. 'Twas a good organization, the Japanese. The Italians, they think about themselves, the Italians.

Oh, I saw a lotta accidents. Yeah. When I worked on the black-smith shop, the whistle blow most of the time. Taking out people wounded or broken leg or dead. Blow the whistle.

My brother Joe was one month before myself in Colorado. Then I go and join him. Then we come back in Highwood and work on the road construction. We was tired with all those company rules. It was dangerous, and to work there you have to shut up. Then you get along alright.

It was mostly Republican. All Republicans. The company, they force the people to do this and this and this, the company. In Ludlow, they still got a monument down there, all the martyr that been shot down. They put up a monument for the victims that been fighting there. There was a strike. And then the trouble from the camp, down in a hole, there.

Domenick Linari, who has trouble with Nietzsche:

My parents couldn't get it out of my head to leave Italy, so they had to let me go. I was going to go someplace. I was going to try to better the living for us. I had decided my dad wasn't going to let me go because they were sinking ships during the war. And my mother finally said, and after all, you know, my mother was like any other woman, she was the boss of the house when it came right down to it. She decided, "Well, if he's going to go, you might as well let him go and be done with it."

I came in 1915 during the First World War. Sixteen years old. I come with a brother of my dad that had been here before, and there was two other brothers that lived in Iowa already. So I went to Iowa, of course. Worked the coal mines. In Madrid.

I borrowed the money. I didn't have any money to come over with. It cost a hundred dollars and I borrowed it from an acquaintance, a guy that I had just done a big barn for. He was an old crab but he kind of took a liking to me for some reason. I guess I was a kid. Everybody likes children. So I decided to ask him if he'd loan me the money to come to this country and he said, "Sure I'll loan it to you. Absolutely." And he loaned it to me.

When I was a kid, I worked with a cooperative outfit, builders, that was right there in Frassinoro. That's where I started to learn the stonemason trade. Work over there, especially in them hills there in Italy, it's seasonal because—I guess they don't any more, for some reason, whatever it is, the weather cycle is changing—we used to get terrific amounts of snow. Used to get falls of snow, you'd be marooned in there for days and days. And so nobody could work, nobody could move. So in the fall of the year, they used to close down and then open up about the first of April, try to work again. In the wintertime there was nothing going.

I remember—especially some people coming from this country—
there was a belief, maybe that's still followed now, that when you
change from one part of the world to another the air is so much
different that if you're not careful it'll kill you and so on. And so
when they came back to Italy from the United States, they had to
lay around for so long and not do any work because it was too
strenuous on account of the thin air. To me that was a silly thing—
laying around for a couple of weeks or so, not doing anything because it was a different air.

And I used to see them people dressed, they'd bring some clothes
from here and they'd be dressed good, I thought. So I decided that I
was going to go over to the United States, fill up a couple, three
bags full of money—because I figured it must be laying around all
over—and I'd come back home. I'm still looking for the money.

I never regretted leaving Italy. Then, of course, the war dragged
on, and I tried to get money together to get my mother and the
children and my dad over, because the life was so much better in
this country. Although we lived in a coal camp, we lived in shacks,
you might say, but things were different, completely, than what they
were over there in Italy. We could eat. Food was not such an important thing as it was over there. Over there you'd work to try to get
a little food. Maybe it was enough and maybe it wasn't; maybe you
went hungry at that time. Now, it's different over there in Italy, of
course. I was there last summer. Things have changed, altered completely.

At the time, I wanted to get my father's family all over here. I
couldn't convince my old man. Oh, no, he wasn't going to go. He
wasn't going to pull up stakes. He believed in staying home and
working that little piece of land by hand. My mother was willing.
But he refused to.

Well, around Des Moines, Iowa, there in the coal mines, was full
of our country people from around there. Them and the Croatians
populated the mines. My wife was Yugoslavian. Markun was her
name. Mary was her first name. She was a nurse. I met her at a
dance. She was a good dancer, so she got my eye because she was a
good dancer. She was born in Olyphant, Pennsylvania. Her grandfather and grandmother worked at the coal mines in Iowa. My
wife's father came from the ore mines of Minnesota. Then he
moved to Pennsylvania. He got pneumonia about six months before
my wife was born, and died. My wife's mother was left with four
children. Her father and mother in Iowa sent for her. That's how
my wife got to Iowa.

There didn't used to be too much of people from one nationality marrying someone of another nationality. The old-fashioned people, they told me to my face that I was a ruined man when I married from another country. It wouldn't have been so bad if I'd married an Italian, even from a different village, but not to marry somebody from way out, some other country—that was awful. But I guess it didn't make any difference. I was stubborn enough.

We had a great big wedding! We went to the priest, got married, her mother had a little dinner for us. Then we went to work. Our big wedding consisted of that.

When I came, the miners were already union in Iowa. It made a great big difference in the working conditions of the immediate work. It was quite a while later that the wages and so on began to improve.

Before that the life of a miner wasn't considered anything, just, especially the immigrants, there was plenty of 'em coming all the time anyhow, so it didn't make any difference. If you killed one, you got another one, that's all, so what's the difference?

I was driving a mule, oh, I had been here about two and a half years or so. I was driving a mule and the mule, of course, was stubborn. I was stubborn and the mule was stubborn, so I was beating him up. And the foreman caught me at it. He started yelling. And I said, well, I was mad, I said, "He's gonna do what I say or I'm gonna have to kill him." He said, "Oh, no you're not! We can always get a driver, but a mule costs money."

Most of the foremen in the coal mines in Iowa that I worked, in fact, all but two of them that I know of, were Welsh. From England. In their Welsh country there is a lot of coal mining—seems like half of the country is coal mining. So the foremen, the superintendent, and so on were Welsh. I knew one Croatian that got to be a foreman, and an Irish. And I was in line to be the next foreman hired when I left over there. So I was going to be the first Italian foreman. But I got mad and left. I came to face the Depression in Highwood. If I would have stayed there I would have been much better off, but I didn't have brains enough, so what are you gonna do?

What I did, I studied continuously when I was there. I was always like that. I always enjoyed studying. It got to be I was an expert in ventilation in the coal mine, an expert detecting carbon monoxide, carbon dioxide, and different things like that. We used to have different names. We called it "black damp" and "white damp" and so on. The miners used to call it a simple name.

And so I could make use of some of that. I had studied with a chief engineer of the coal mines of a company that had seven or eight mines there. And I knew a lot of things. For instance, there

toward the end, not very long before I quit, I was foreman for the
city of Des Moines digging tunnels because I was supposed to be an
expert in ventilation. Whether I was or not, I was getting paid for
that anyway. So, my knowledge might have helped in some other
way. But as far as mining was concerned, mining went to pieces,
anyway, over there, in the immediate region.

I drove a mule for a while, but I got run over by a car. Got out of
it alive, a carload—about a ton and a half—only about this much
room under the axles. They dug me out from under there and all I
had was a scratch in the back. So I decided that was enough of
mule driving.

I dug coal very little. With the coal that I dug everybody would
have froze to death, I believe. I started out doing something else.
For some reason, I guess the foreman maybe liked a kid that wanted
to try, so he give him a chance, and I was an expert timberman,
they call it, I was an expert track layer and things like that.

A timberman sets up the shores to hold up the top. A lot of hard
labor. But I was supposed to know what I was doing. We used to
put the legs upright and the cross pieces so far apart. For some reason, sometimes when you look at the timbers across the top it looks
like the top is coming down. Instead it's the bottom coming up.
When the air hits the bottom, it begins to swell. It looks like it's
starting to break up the timbering, the shores, it looks like it's the
top coming down. Well, I discovered it a couple of times and that's
why I became an expert, naturally.

An educated person, I suppose, has not too much trouble learning
the language. The uneducated has a lot of trouble because he
doesn't go about it grammatically. When I came here, when I started
to work and I couldn't understand the language, I wanted to learn
so bad, I worked trying to get a night school started because I knew
you couldn't do it in the daytime because we had to work.

So I got a bunch of us together and my uncle helped because he
could speak fairly good. He went to the teachers that were teaching
us two nights a week and it costs us twenty-five cents for two
nights' school. But there was a bunch of them so they were making
fairly good money for the time they were there. The wages in the
mine were only two dollars and ninety-nine cents a day anyway
and it was good wages, supposedly, at the time.

But everybody used to tell me when I'd try to get them together,
they tell me, "You don't have to learn, you don't have to know the
language to dig coal. You gotta have good muscles and be willing to
work." So finally I got a bunch of them together but it lasted only

twelve nights and each night three or four of them were falling out. First thing you know, we ended up with only about a dozen of us that paid to have the school.

But I learned more in that time. I learned kind of the way to go about it. I got a couple of dictionaries and books. We didn't have a newspaper delivery or anything at the time. If you wanted it you had to get it by mail, subscribe, so I subscribed and got the American newspaper.

They used to make fun of me about that newspaper. But I learned a lot from it. Because in an article I'd recognize ten words, but the ten words brought another word or two along with it. The pronunciation wasn't any good, I had to learn that, but you could pick it up fairly good out of the dictionary.

These guys that didn't want to go to school used to say, "Hey, tell the boss about this, I got some trouble with this or the other." So I was cocky, a young kid, "Why should I, you don't want to go to school, why don't you tell him?!" And I was supposed to be the interpreter. I had to because they needed it.

The Croatians, they were just as bad as the Italians. They were just as bad. They practiced their own language and they seemed to have no ambition to learn the language. And it was a lot of Croatians where we were. Like I said, the Croatians and the Italians made up the mine. The blacks lived in segregated camps. There was quite a few. From the South, they come up from the South most of them, Alabama, Tennessee.

The Swedes were the best. As soon as they got here they wanted to learn the language. They tried. After I learned a little bit—not that I could pronounce the English language good, because it's hard for the Italians to learn that—I would talk to Swedes. The ones that had been here maybe a year would speak nothing but English. You couldn't understand what the heck he was saying but he was trying to speak English, anyhow. Where the Italians, the Croatians, they spoke their own language, that's what they wanted to speak.

You must remember that the miners, like almost any labor group—they work with their hands mostly, and the hard work and the worst job possible, you might say that nobody else wants to do it—are not educated, so consequently are not too proud, they're not so active trying to learn something. So, and they have a habit of depending on the mouth, mouth to mouth for information. Maybe one out of a hundred could, maybe could read us a little English in the newspapers, so what did they want the newspaper for, you might say.

We didn't go to school up in the hills where I come from up
there. My mother and father, as poor as they were, they made me
go to school for a while and I went as far as the sixth grade, which
is not quite comparable to sixth grade here. But I liked to study and
I enjoyed it, so then I kept on. I got a certificate from the College of
Ames in ventilation, which you had to study in order to get it. And
study also brought about a better knowledge of the language.

I was the tradesman of one local there for a while in Zookspur, a
coal camp. About a year and a half later, I gave up the job and
went to Carney.

I never heard of anything like a socialist party in Carney. There
was some talk about Spring Valley and there was, I remember
somebody talking about it, somebody that came from Illinois. I don't
remember. They were trying to start a socialist movement but I
don't think it got anywhere.

If the company had a market for coal, you worked, you even
worked day and night to try to fill the order. If they didn't have an
order, we just stayed home, that's all. And there was nothing else to
work at where we were. We were out in the country, out in the
middle of nowhere, no means of transportation, no cars. Cars didn't
come along until after 1922, 1923. So you worked in a coal mine
when it worked, and when it didn't work, you used up what you
saved up—a few dollars—and try to make a living, or went in
debt. Mining wasn't easy, I can tell you that.

The poor coal miner. Outside of the mine they were kind of
talked about, the miners being rich because they were getting so
much money, they were getting so much an hour. But if you get ten
dollars an hour and you only work one hour a day, it's only ten
dollars. But they figured you worked eight hours. And they figured
that you worked 365 days a year, too, which never happened.

Oh yeah, yeah. There were a lot of serious accidents. I helped to
dig one man out in 1918, yeah, or was it 1919, I forgot exactly
what it was. I moved from one mine to another when I went from
Zookspur to Enterprise. And then I went to Melcher. The week that
I started there, there were three men killed. A ton fell on them and
killed them. Two brothers got killed one day, a couple days after the
funeral, another one got killed.

So, the way it is, you're in there, you're used to it, you know it's
not going to happen to you because that's what you feel. If you
didn't feel that way, you'd be scared. And so, everybody went to
work like if nothing had happened. Maybe they watched a little bit
more for a few days.

It's hard to say whose fault it was. The company said it was their fault. The union said it was probably the fault of the company, that they didn't do a certain thing right. So you decide. In any kind of a doing, the workers try to blame the boss and the boss tries to blame the workers. Every place I've worked it's always been the same way.

When I decided to leave the mine, I was running them tunnels, like I said, for the city of Des Moines, and had a gang working for me. We had to change shifts because we worked three shifts, eight-hour shifts in twenty-four hours. So every two weeks we had to change and I had to fall into the night work and my wife was scared to stay home by herself. She was always scared of the dark. And so after I worked there for so long, I went to the superintendent to talk about it. He got kind of snotty, so I quit.

And I said, "Before I go back to the coal mine"—the wife had two brothers in Chicago working—"I'm going to see how things are on the outside, see if we can get a job."

I took the car and decided to come to Chicago. I didn't know where I was going. I had their address that's all. And I got to Geneva, I stopped for gas, and while he was gassing it up, I went into the station to buy cigarettes, I remember, because I used to smoke, and there was a map hanging on the window and I looked at it and I happened to spy Highwood.

And I had heard of some of the people from over there, that come over and work in the summer, then go back to the mine in the winter. And so I looked at it and said, "Well, maybe I'll go up and see what Highwood is like."

I got my directions on the map and come up here. When I got to the corner of Highwood Avenue and Greenbay Road, right there—Giannetto had the place there where the Chinese restaurant is now—when I got there, there was a lot of people standing all over and I knew over half of 'em. And I said, "This must be Highwood."

So I went to work here, I got a job as a laborer because I'd done mason work in the coal mine a little bit, and, like I said before, when I was a kid I served my apprenticeship over in Italy.

So I saw there was a lot of stonework going on so I wanted to get to that, but first I wanted to get the layout, see the terms that they use and different things so I wouldn't look completely green. So I worked as a laborer for three weeks.

I said, well, I'll go back to the mines for this winter and then come back next spring. I told the wife what it was like and she thought it would be better if we moved over here, also.

And when I went back in the coal mine, maybe I didn't like it because I'd had a taste of the outside—I don't know what it was. But it seemed like every day I got hurt a little bit. Not enough to do too much damage but something happened every day.

One day I was laying a track and something hit me on the head. I looked around, I thought somebody had hit me with a club, and finally I found a piece of rock that had fallen from quite high up and it hit me on the head and knocked me down, almost knocked me out. So I looked at it and I thought about it for a little bit and I said, "That's enough. I'm not going to work in the mine anymore." So I went home, called the foreman, told him I wasn't going back. We came over here, I been here ever since.

Julio Brugioni shows me a photograph in an old Des Moines newspaper. A man in his late thirties wears a mining cap. His face is black from coal. He holds a little girl. Before the photo of him and his daughter was taken, he said, she cried because she was so frightened by his blackened face. Usually when she saw her father he had already washed. But the photo assignment called for a miner just emerging from the mine.

My birthdate was the twenty-second of February, 1900. I am eighty-seven years old. I was born in Fiumalbo. At Calunga. Casa Lunga. "Long house," it means. It was a big, long house, see. There used to be seventy or eighty people living in that little bunch of houses. We had the earthquake years ago and it shook all them old houses. One's still standing. The rest of them, they're all rocks.

My daddy came to this country here way before 1900. And then when he was fourteen years old my brother came with my dad. Stayed here four or five years and then he come back. And they left again. I came over here when I was twelve years old and six months.

My father came the first time to Bevier, Missouri. Up in the coal mines. Oh, there was a gang that came from Fiumalbo. And there were some from Pieve, too. They all went to Number Seven Mine.

There were some of these people, recruiters, that come to this country to see if there's work, they scout around. And then they let the lawyers know where the work is at. And then, they send for people in Italy. Those suckers, they get money by making your passport and all of that. Then they ship you. They ship you just like a bunch of cows. They don't give a damn if you make it. If you make

it, you make it—if you don't make it, it's just your luck. That's the
way it used to be.

Before my dad was married, before he came to America, he was
in Africa. Making railroads. He was a young punk. The contractor
was an Amedei. Agosto Amedei. He used to take them to Africa.
Then this Amedei quit Africa and he came to America and then he
went to Colorado. Then he opened up a mine and he called the
people to come over. To work for him in Colorado. They were from
Fiumalbo.

Used to be in Fiumalbo, Pieve, all them places, they used to go to
France, to Portugal, all over. Because there's nothing up in Modena.
What the hell. Ain't no factory to work in. You had to get out of
there. Down on the plain at those places where you've got good
ground you can farm, you can produce and you make enough for
your family. But up there where we're at, you ain't got no chance to
make a living. If you have one or two in your family, maybe, but if
you have three or four, you can't make it, you might as well get
out.

Over there, you do a lot of work. For what? For nothing. Heck,
going after wood, it was going like from here way down to Highland Park, maybe three miles. Walk down there and cut them, make
a load, put it on your back, then take it home. Three or four trips a
day. For what? You have to have wood to warm yourself in the winter and to cook because wood was all they had up there. They
never had no gas. At that time no electricity.

Fiumalbo has got men all over the creation. He's got some in
South America that I know of. Some couldn't come over here, you
know, so they tried to go to South America and maybe in time they
come over here to this country, they could have a chance to come in
here, to sneak in. They go down there, Argentina, Brazil, all them
places. Work in agriculture, the farms, for these big concerns, cotton
fields, banana fields. They don't make much, but it's just as good as
to be in Fiumalbo or *la* Pieve, because what the hell they got up
there? It's all right if you go up there with money. I know two of
them that came from South America. There was a lot that used to
sneak into this country. In a boat. They was lucky to get in. And
they'd go from one place to another. They'd stay maybe a month
here and they knew the police were after them. They go down
south, they come back here, then down south. Then a few years go
by and the police would forget about them. Then if they happened
to get married, they'd say, "I got married. I fixed it."

In Missouri, there were lots of families from Fiumalbo. A lot of
Amedeis. Eh, how many Amedeis! We had a lot of Amedeis here in
Highwood, too. Fraulinis. Amedeis. Coppis. Amedeis, *quanti*? How
many? Christ sake! Amedeis, there's hundreds of them. Eh. Lotta
Amedeis. Christ Almighty. In Highwood, there were a lot of Italians
but mostly they came from the mines in Illinois. Pepperneck. Bush.

Some of them from Italy went to Texas. They got low coal down
there in Texas. They got three-foot-high coal. Meanwhile in Missouri
you got all the way from four to six or seven foot and Illinois you
got six, seven, eight, ten foot high. And Iowa the same. Iowa is
better—all the way from four to six foot high. You can work there
pretty good with four foot, five or six, but if you have two and a
half or three, that's pretty damned low. You have to scoot down like
a cat all day.

I came here in 1913. There were some from Fiumalbo killed in
the Cherry mine disaster in 1909. Well, they were talking, when I
came, about this mine. They had mules down in the mines. They
had tons and tons of hay. The superintendent set this hay to fire.
And instead of calling the men out, he burned mules, men. Cherry
Mine. Yeah. Disaster. Everyone killed. I heard about it when I got
here.

When my father first went to Missouri, they weren't union. Before, they never had a union and the company used to give you
what they wanted. They rob you on weight. They rob you on
everything. After, they had checkweighmen—like you belong to the
company and I belong to the union, and then I watch the scale and
you watch the scale to see if you're cheating me. Before, they didn't
have nobody. Just dump the coal and they had the company man,
that's all. Write down what he wanted.

There were shaft mines in Missouri. One thing about Missouri,
and even in Iowa, they ain't got no gas in the mines. These here, in
Illinois, they got a lot of gas. No, Missouri was good coal. Soft. Was
the best coal to make steam. For the railroads, to make iron, it takes
a lot of heat. And that Missouri coal burns with a lot of heat. More
than other coal. Because you got a lot of wood in there. It's made
out of wood and leaves and grass, you know, all that bullshit, and
the weight of the earth pressed it millions of years, to form coal. In
the mines we used to find ferns, plants, clover. I used to find pieces
of snakes. God knows how big they were when they were alive.
Long from here to over there.

It's hard, the work. At first when I started it was all by hand. You
had to dig it, with the pick, and you have to drill by hand and you

have to load it by shovel. And then, when I was in Iowa you didn't have to do all of that, you just drilled it by electricity, cut it with the machines, loaded it with a machine—the shovel was just as wide as this room—and it would take whole chunks of coal bigger than this kitchen table.

The first lamp was oil. It had a wick, a wick like a candle but only it was bigger. *Stuppini* they used to call it. When you used to go the store you used to say, "I want a *stuppini*." They had them in a package. You put oil and a *stuppini* in the lamp, and then you light it, like a candle, only this little lamp had a hook. It used to make smoke, *ssshh*. And then they changed to carbide. Then, the last I had, an electric battery. You had seven pounds of battery on your belt—you had a belt four inches thick—and seven-pound weight all day long. And it had a cord that come up here to the cap and you had a lamp that used to throw the light. And every night you used to charge the battery.

They made a lot of new mines in Missouri. They made Number Nine. Number Eight. Sixty-eight. We used to own a mine. We worked ten years in there. We had it all in good shape, then overnight she got flooded full of water.

I drove a mule, off and on. Whenever your room, your place, is finished, you wait for a room. Then you work for the company, you don't work for yourself. Sometimes you wait a week or two and then you drive the mules if you enjoy driving. Or do other work. If they need you to put down tracks. Or sometimes they need you to put up timbers, so you go and set up timbers.

I was a shot-firer, too. At Number Nine. In fact for a long time. I done it eight or nine months. Three or four men went down, one on each side. One goes north, and one south, east, and west. Four of them for shot-firing the mine. And you go and set fire and you run like hell. Ping. Poom. Ping. Poom. Yah, I liked it. It's short hours. When you're young, a runner, what the heck. In an hour and a half you're done. You've got your day's work in. But you run like hell.

I was good in the mine. One of the best.

The mines used to strike all together. But you strike once and a while for what? They make you stay out six or seven months, and then maybe they give you ten cents raise on a ton. What the hell is that? Ten cents. You stay out six months without doing a damn thing and them days when you go in the mine you was lucky to make five dollars. And you bring five dollars home, you got three or four kids. You pay rent, this and that. What the hell you got left?

You stay out six months. When you go back you haven't got a damned penny left. That's how it used to be in the mining camps. It was like those towns where everybody gets the hell out of there, you know, ghost towns. Poor people. They didn't give a damn, the company. For ten cents they used to fight. They take your ten cents, they make money. But you don't make money. How the hell can you make money at ten cents an hour?

Once I had a jack hit me on the head. There was a guy helping me. I told him to not move the shovel and I went up there to the place to move the machine. The machine was over there; I was supposed to bring it over here. And he made the shovel go. And there was a jack that was holding a timber, but they had three or four jacks under this timber, the shovel was in the back by the jacks. That sucker hit that jack, it threw that jack, and it hit me in the head. The jack, made out of iron. Good thing I had on a cap. It busted the iron cap.

In 1935 I went to Iowa. Waukee, Iowa. It's not a town, it's a mining camp. Close to Des Moines. I worked there until 1944 for Northwestern and Central Coal Company. Then I got sick and tired because it was killing too many men in that mine. Three or four at once. From what?! From the ceiling coming down. Because you used to cut an opening, we'll say from here to that house over there, without any retaining wall—if the whole damn thing comes down, how the hell can you get out? Finally my wife said to get the hell out of there.

When the mines close? It's like anything else. Suppose this mine shuts down, that's five hundred men out of a job. Okay, then there's another mine that's working, they try to go get in there to get work. They might, a few get work. But the rest of them, they can't because it's filled up. They have another mine. Where are all these miners going to go? They can't go all in that one. There might be four or five hundred men working there already. They can't let them in. The rest of them, they'll have to find different work. Same if you're in a factory. Your factory, it closes up and you go try to find work in another factory, you might have a chance. But not all of them. Some of them will have to find themselves something else.

And it's bad. The poor people suffer. I mean they should have something that you get out of a job, you should have another. Plenty of work on this earth. Can't you see they leave everything go to the dickens? Bridges, that they are gone, roads, that they are gone, buildings, even in Chicago, that are gone. Why don't you restore them and make new ones? Sidewalks all gone to the dickens.

They let everything go. These rivers, straighten them out, instead of having all this water when it rains, flooding everything. Straighten 'em out! Put 'em to work. You got machinery. You could do a lot of things. Why?! Because they don't want you so you'll have too much money and say, "To heck with you." They want you to stay around, they want to keep you under, see? You stay under here, under this table here. Don't get on top of me, the rich man says. You stay right there. They give you that much, just like you got an animal. You know what I mean? The rich man don't care for you. He don't care. He cares because he have to use you. If he don't, he have to work himself.

A queen, she said once, "Why don't we do away with the poor?" And the king, he said, "Who's going to do your work? You going to have all the kids do your work?" "Oh no," she said, "we need a cook to bring the food for us and work for us so we don't have to work." See? If they cut us off, if it was left only the rich, if all the poor dies and there be nothing but the rich, who's gonna work for them? They'll have to do their own work. But this way, you do the work and I set back—I'm the rich, you do the work. It's very easy. It's the same in the coal mines. You take the rich, they got a mine, he don't care if you get killed. Not a one. It's like when I was a mule driver, I loved a nice mule that they had, he looked like a horse. And they wanted him pull more coals, more coals, more coals, and I says, "You put any more coals on him, you'll kill him." And then he says, "Don't worry, once he's dead," he said, "the harness is still around." See how much he cared for the mule? I cared for him because he was so nice and gentle. But the owner, he wanted more money off him. So, instead of putting two or three tons, he put four or five. That's how much he cares. But you, me, I'm a human, I can leave when I've had enough, but the mule, he want to kill him, you know, pull and pull, he can only pull so much, but he's not a railroad engine.

Giosue Brugioni is much younger than the others I have interviewed. At seventy-eight, he likes to be the bad boy, mocking priests, stonemasons, and people who are not from Fiumalbo. The priests, they like money. Stonemasons are uptight. In Pievepelago, they eat pigskins, and that's why they are nasal and whine when they talk, because the pigskins get stuck in their throats. He squeals, imitating them. His wife, Ann, American-born and of Italian descent, says, "Isn't he the dickens!" He tells of one time when a stonemason made him so mad that he took a sledgehammer and knocked the scaffolding out from underneath the tradesman, who jumped to the roof for safety. "They called me the wild kid," he said.

My name is Giosue Brugioni. I was born in Bevier, Missouri, in 1909. I went back to Italy 1913. That was before the First World War, you know, and they used to say if you didn't go back and serve in the army, then you couldn't go back to Italy—that's why my dad took the family back to Italy. When he was over in Italy, then he changed his mind, and he left the family over there, and he came back to the United States.

I went to school in Italy, in Fiumalbo. And then 1927, I came to the United States. Mussolini was in power. Eighteen years old, you was supposed to go in the army. So I left before that. I didn't want to go in the army. Them days, you had to be American-born, or American citizen, otherwise you couldn't come here. So that's why I had a chance to come back.

My dad, the first time he came was 1898. And last time he went back to Italy was 1919, after the First World War. First, he went to Walsenburg, Colorado. Well, at that time, they were trying to put the union in the coal mines, and you know they allowed the people from the South that were working without the unions, and they had a lot of trouble. You know a lot of people got killed. I think when they had the strike was in 1904. In Walsenburg. And then when my dad went to Italy in 1905, then 1906, he got married. And then he left my mother and one of my sisters and he came back over here. And then 1908, he sent for the family. He was in Bevier, Missouri, then. So my mother came, my mother and my sister, and we was there until 1913.

Well, when he came to Colorado from Italy, there was no union. He was working in the coal mine, ten hours for fifty cents. Them days, there was no insurance, there was nothing. The company, they give you work, but then if you got hurt or killed you didn't get nothing. Then after the union, if you got hurt, you were supposed to get so much.

My father never worked in coal mines before coming here. There was no coal mines in Italy. He was a farmer, and then he went to work with some company that was making charcoal. Down by Rome. Down by Grossetto—Grossetto, Italy. He was cutting the wood. And then when he came here, he worked in the coal mine. There weren't too many Italians at that time. He said he was the fifth one, he said, the fifth Italian that was in Walsenburg.

I didn't live with my dad much because when he brought us over to Italy from Bevier, he came back over to the United States right away. And then he was in the United States from 1913 till 1919. Six and a half years. And then in 1919, I went away a couple of years. I went to Corsica to work. I used to load cars, you know the big wagons that used to transport wood and railroad ties and all kinds of stuff. I worked in the little town, Pietro Corbara. It's about thirty-three miles from Bastia, Corsica.

When my father came in 1898, there was some guys from Fiumalbo that was over there, that's what he told me. I had an uncle got killed over there in the coal mines. Giosue Nizzi. An explosion. They were digging coals. You have to drill into the coal to shoot the coal and sometimes you find a pocket of gas and a spark, anything when you drill can set the fire. And it exploded. See, they had a lot of explosion in those mines. Like in south Illinois they got gas. He was about thirty-one or thirty-two years old. He got killed before I was born. I was named after him.

From Colorado, my father went to Iowa. And then from Iowa he went to Missouri. He left Colorado because, see there was gas in those mines, and a lot of people used to get killed. It was dangerous. And they didn't have no safety lamps or nothing in them days. It was Rockefeller's mine.

I know a lot of these Lenzini in Highwood, they come from Colorado, from Walsenburg. One was named Gino Lenzini. And Desi Saielli from Highwood, she's a sister to them.

It was dangerous then, besides that, the unions, and the strike and all of that. That's why Rockefeller sent for the army. My father had just left. He left before that. He went back for a visit but not to work in the coal mine.

My father always told me, "If you go to go Colorado, it's just like Fiumalbo." He said, "They got the same mountains and same air and the same rivers," and he said, "it's a beautiful country, you know, and people like to fish or hunt and stuff like that." He liked it. Like he said, if there wasn't all that kind of trouble, he would have never left. He would have stayed up there.

The Rockefellers were the owners. Nobody, most of these big rich people, they don't like the unions. They don't want there to be controls.

I know my dad was telling me there was one guy organizing for the union from Fanano out there. There was some other people, you know, from different parts, where there was the union, they went up there to try to organize the miners. The miners wanted the

union, because once you got the unions, they got to establish the
contract and they pay so much, whatever the union and the contractor get together. But before, they said, "Well that's so much a
day, so much an hour, that's it."

After Colorado, my father went to Valley Junction, near Des
Moines. Where he was working, there was a smaller mine. See,
well, the coal in Iowa—someplace, see, like the mine that I worked
before I came here in 1935-36—see, they had two veins, the top
vein was four feet, then it went down sixty feet deeper, and they
find another vein of coal, it was twelve feet high. In Colorado, the
coal, it's all high coal. The mine in Iowa that I worked when I went
over there in 1927, it was only two feet and a half. You had to
crawl underneath.

In Illinois, they got high coal too, most of those mines. See, most
of the people that worked in Illinois, they were making much more
money than people working in Iowa and Missouri because they
were bigger mines and they had a bigger contract, see? They were
making money, but they were dangerous because most all the mines
in Illinois, they had gas. See, like when it was when they had the
big explosion in Centralia in 1947, about 111 people got killed. Instead, in Iowa and Missouri, they never had those kinds of troubles
because there's no gas.

My dad was in Iowa for about three years, then from there he
went to Missouri, and he stayed there when he had the family and
he stayed there until 1919 when he went back to Italy. In Missouri
the mines were unionized. There was a lot of mines, there was
about fifteen or twenty mines when my dad was there. There was a
lot of people from Fiumalbo, Pieve, from Sant'Anna—mostly they
were Fiumalbo, though.

My father was digging coal and then he was a timberman. They
used to put up timber, beams, you know, where there's a danger of
caving in. Over there in the coal mines, every morning they got
these company men, test the rock, you know, they hit them with
something, and if it's loose, they send this timberman. They put up
timber to hold the rock up. My dad, he was very good, because
that's all he did from '98. I think he was there twenty-one or
twenty-two years. That's all he did when he was here in this country. Of course over there in Fiumalbo, he had his farm called Lago.
That means "lake." There used to be a lake, now they got a sports
field there.

You be careful in the mines. You look, you be careful, but sometimes it don't even pay, you know. A piece of rock, you know, the

rock is pretty heavy, and if you're down working like this, bending over, and it hits, most of the people that got killed, it broke their spines. The spines, mostly the spines when they're bending over. And then sometimes even in the wintertime it's hot down there, you know we used to work, we used to take everything off, just wear the pants. Sometimes not even the shirt, we used to take it right off. See, because in Iowa, they're all shaft mines, in Missouri, too, and when you go down about three hundred feet down, and then you go ten miles underneath, see, and the push airs, you know they got the fans that push air over there, but by the time it gets over there, that air is hot. And you sweat. And when we come out at night, sometimes, you're sweating. All your clothes are wet. You're dripping. The minute you get off the cage, there's a wash-house there, and they got it real hot, winter and summer, and you take all your clothes off and you take a shower. There's maybe seventy-five showers, you go underneath there, you take your shower. Then you dry yourself and you stay there because they got a furnace there, it blows steam day and night because even at night, you see, they need a lot of heat to dry the clothes for the next day.

No, I was never afraid in the mine. The trouble is, once you get used to the coal mine, you never want to leave. Eh, because, you're independent, no boss, no nothing. If you work, you make money. If you want to take it easy, you make less. Once you get used to it, you don't think about it. More, when after you're out, when it's many years you don't work there, then sometime you say, "I wonder why, you know, I went through there, those dangers, there." But I worked there just the same and never got hurt except I got my finger smashed between the timber and the car that was loaded with coal. A carload is about two tons, two tons and a half. It depends how much you want to put in. In some mines, like in Madrid, it was a big mine, they had big cars, it would hold about four, four and a half tons. The mine that I used to work, it was two tons, two and a half. I lived close to the mine there in Granger. And I lived in Madrid.

One company was Norwood White Coal Company from Des Moines. And the other one in there was Dallas Coal Company, the last one that I worked. In Bevier was Midway Coal Company.

It was 1927, the winter of 1927, when I first worked in a mine. It was altogether different from when my dad worked there. Of course, my dad, when he left this country in 1919, it was just like now. They had good unions. John L. Lewis, he was one of the best union men in this country. And they had good unions. Now they use oil, gas, and stuff like that. But them days, even up to the Second World War, they used mostly coal in factories, power plants, houses, and big buildings, and all of them, they were burning nothing but coal. But then they were starting using oil.

I worked 1927 until 1931 in the winter in the coal mines. In the summer I came here to work. Eh, I knew a lot of people in Highwood. My uncle 'Mingo Nizzi, he was in Iowa, then he came to Highwood, and he stayed here two, three years, then he went back to Iowa. In the summertime in the coal mines, it was only one day, two days a week. A day and a half, and so I said, "What the hell, I don't make nothing here," I said, "I'll go back over there, I'll work four or five or six months." Because in the summertime, they don't need too much coal. There was no demand.

I worked as a tracklayer, laid the track. But you know, when you lay tracks and you put timber, you got the boss, you know. He tell you, well, you got to do this, you got to do that. Instead when you dig coal you're your own boss. If you don't want to work, you take it easy. Nobody could tell you nothing.

We used to take care of our places. We used to put up our props and try to make it safe the best we could. Mostly when you work, you kneel down on your knees. They had those kind of pants with the cushions underneath. You get used to it. When you're young, you don't care too much. But I used to love it. I used to love that work in the coal mine.

You know when the coal comes up, way on top of what you call the tipple, about fifty feet high. They dump it there, and, automatic, the cars open up and dump through a chute, and it goes into the railroad flats. And there's two men that look at the scales. One belongs to the company and one belongs to the union. They're checkweighmans. That's what they call them. They check the weight. Because if there's only one from the company, they would steal you alive. In some place they got the black damp. It's dead air. It's not good air. That gets you in your lung, then you get sick. You get asthma. That's why sometime you don't sleep for two, three nights in a row when catch that. That's what they call it. Someplace where there's no more coal, where it stays there empty, the company's supposed to close it off. See, like, where we used to work, you know, it was just like you go through a door and then you wind around, to dig the coal. See, if I work here, it's called *la piazza*, the place, and then between my place and this other place, they used to leave about six feet of coal, like a pillar there, to hold the rocks up. And they're supposed to seal it off with cement after the coal is all lol

gone. Cement blocks. But when they didn't do the seal good, then this black damp accumulates. And once you work close to there, you get it, it gets in your system. I watched out because I didn't want to get sick. Because once you get that, it's hard. It affects your system.

If it's a big company, then they can afford to keep the mine in good shape. They keep it good. But some company, maybe it hasn't got too much money, they say, "What the hell, if the miners get sick, it's too bad for them." But, see, there's supposed to be a mine inspector once a month that goes down and check the old place and the new places and everything. Because sometimes, you know, the companies, they pay the mine inspectors off with money. Old Man Menoni, Joe Menoni, used to say, "Money, it isn't everything, but just about."

Your grandfathers didn't work in the coal mine too much. Piacentini worked in Carney. And your grandfather Tony was in Centralia. See, the mine exploded there but he was already here and he never went back to the coal mine.

Then, there was a place where your Nonno Piacentini went, they named the little town there, Carney. Carney, Iowa. You ever heard of the Carneys up in Lake Forest? They used to have the mines in Madrid, near Des Moines. Because they were a big company, they had a lot of money. And once you got a lot of money, you keep the mines in good shape, too. And they used to run big mines. Like in Madrid there were about five or six hundred miners working there in the Number Four mines there, Madrid. And Number Six. Then they had mines all over, down close to Des Moines, down in through there.

Did I go to church? No. Not even now. I'm against the priests. Sometimes the church helped you. If you paid. I figure, myself, my idea, to me it's like a business, all over the world. I say that's nice for young people, kids or something like that, but when they get a certain age, don't force them. Let them do whatever they think is best. If they think it's okay to go, like a lot of them, that's okay. But to me, I couldn't see it.

John Bagatti kneels, applying a sealant to the base of the house where it abuts the driveway. The white stucco house is so neat and clean it's hard to believe it needs work. He wears coveralls. On his knees are worn, rectangular protection pads. He is a cement finisher by trade. He was born in 1902 at Modino, near Pievepelago. He came in 1919

with a group of young men that included my grandfather, Nello Piacentini. There was a standard greeting between them, the story goes.
"*Eh, Nello, ci siamo in cinque*"— "We're down to five." With each wake,
the number decreased until the private joke, like an elbow nudging
the ribs, was, "*Eh, Bagatti, ci siamo in due*" — "down to two."

I come over in this country, seventeen years old. I told lotta guy I
was going, but they don't believe it. They say, "In the coal mine!
Me, I don't want to go in the coal mine like that!"

My mother, even my brother didn't want me to come in this
country. He say, "Oh, you spend a lot of money to go over there,
who gonna pay?" "Don't you worry, I'm young, I pay for it." I borrowed money. My sister, she gave me the money. Take me quite a
while to pay it back. But I pay.

Everyone that come over with me was from Riolunato. Everyone
that come over with me in this country after the war, every one, he
die. I guess I don't go. I was ready to go a few years ago, but now
I'm pretty good.

When I come over, my brother was down in Texas. I had one sister and one brother-in-law in Texas. Thurber. I had a lot of *paisani*
over there.

In Texas, my sister have a boardinghouse. She have fourteen or
fifteen who were there. She cooked. She had plenty to cook. Soup,
that's all. One rabbit, maybe. Not too much meat. Now, every time
you eat, you gotta have meat. Her husband got hurt in the eye. The
dust. And then he don't work no more in the mine, he helped her
in the boardinghouse, see.

When they stopped the mine in 1921, my sister and brother-in-
law, they give up the boardinghouse and went back to Italy. Everybody disappeared from there, you know. Some went to Colorado.
Or Iowa. Lot went to Italy. There's nothing else to do.

I was in Texas, I don't think I worked more than two months.
Well, me, I was glad when they stopped the mine. Because I didn't
like the coal mine in Texas. You had to dig under, take the dirt out.
From Texas I went to Iowa. I went to Zookspur. Between Des
Moines and Madrid, Iowa. My brother went to Colorado. I was
ready to go over there, too. But in Colorado, there was a big storm,
the storm take the railroad away, no chance to go in Colorado that
time. I change the ticket and went to Iowa.

In Iowa I got sick. I stay in the hospital over a month. I had
pneumonia. Catch cold. In the mine it was warm, come out with
the pants wet. Eh, no, no, no. Iowa is a poor place, too. At that

time I was there, have to go over to the boardinghouse, wash yourself. Over here in Illinois, it was better, better yet. We had a big washhouse.

Even in the hospital, I didn't think of going back to Italy because we had a poor life over there, too, you know. I never was home in the wintertime. I was working the railroad way down from Marinello to Pavullo. Digging. Make the tunnel. There is a lot of tunnel from Marinello to come up in Pavullo. They quit building the railroad during the war. Then from there, we went to Bagni di Lucca. We didn't have no chance to make money over there at Pieve. And the family was gone, you know.

In Iowa, I don't make enough money to pay the board neither. I come over in Highwood. Was in the summer of 1922. In the spring. From Iowa, a lot of people come over here in the summer. There was a lot of people work in the golf, work in the building, work in the road. I don't like too much even Highwood because when we was working we had a boss. Three men, one boss.

And I worked a little bit with your grandfather Nello Piacentini over there in Exmoor golf course. But, me, I told him, "I gotta go make money." In the construction they were making more money, but at that time there wasn't much construction. In the golf, in the wintertime, they laid you off, you know. They don't keep you to play golf.

I don't like too much, for sure, because you got a boss all the time. In the mine you're your own boss.

Then, after I was in Highwood three or four months, I go back in the coal mine, way down in south Illinois. I was in Bush, Illinois, it's near Herrin, a small town down there. Close to Carbondale. I went with a bunch of guys to southern Illinois. I go with the friends. They told me they need some men over there. That's why I went over there in Bush. There was a lot of guys in Highwood from Bush. Ugolini, Medio, you know him? Two brothers Cirotti. John Morandi. Tiriolli.

The mine in Illinois was all different from Iowa. In Illinois, it's like you work over here in this room, you take all the coal by and by. You dig 'em down, you load 'em and send 'em out. It's as big as this living room, see. Now, in Iowa, the coal was different. I had to work on the knees. In the Texas, even more low, like the table. You have to dig up under the coal, and even on top, and take 'em out. I worked on the back. I was young. Well, that mine I was working in Bush was better because I stand up. I went to Bush in 1922, and I stayed up to '28 or '29.

If you load coal, you get so much a ton. More you load, more you make. Eh, sure, I liked it. That's why I stayed so long. I was by myself all day. Nobody but myself.

I got $1.25 a ton. Sometime I load six or seven ton. Sometimes more, sometimes less. All depend how many cars they give you, see? The car go on top the track, when it's loaded, they take them out, they dump it, and they bring it back. You get two, three car a day, all depends. The mules, they had them in Iowa. In Illinois, they had machines, motor.

They weighed the coal outside. They pull it up the cage, on top the scale and weigh, and the car come down and the coal dropped down in the flat, the railroad flat. Yeah, we had a checkweighman in Illinois. In Texas, too. If you got the union, you got a checkweighman. And the ones that's got the scab, like Colorado, I never was there but somebody tell me, they give you so much a day, that's all. Nobody to check.

The United Mine Workers was in Bush. Progressive Mine Workers, they come in, but they don't last long, and they weren't in Bush. They was way down west, in West Frankfort. They started in one mine. Back then, a lot of men work in a mine, you know. Six or seven hundred men. There was a mine there, in West Frankfort, there was over two thousand people.

There was the Ku Klux Klan there. Did you like 'em? One time we had wine. We was five or six men. We made wine. And these Ku Klan, they was look for the wine. If you make the wine you put it under the house, you take a piece of floor out, put the barrel down, to hide it. These Ku Klan, they went down with a sledge, break all the barrel. And it was the only time I make wine that year, and that's it. My wine was running in the street.

Oh, there was a lot of trouble down there. Herrin, Carbondale, all them places. Them people, they give a rough time, especially to the Italians, they don't like the Italians. They don't like the Catholic church. They don't like nobody. Finally, po', the government, he sent the army in Herrin. They quit.

Oh yeah, they killed some people. When they come in my house, oh yeah, they had a costume like sometimes you see on the television, a piece of cloth cover them. That's all. Eh, we was afraid, but we have to stay there. We just watched them. They ruin everything, they steal something, they look for money in the house. No, I don't think the Ku Klux Klan is there no more. There is some states they are there, in Indiana, I think.

In Herrin, they do a lot of damage, boy, in that coal town. They do a lot of damage. They killed a lot of people in that town. They called the National Guard up there in Herrin. But, what did they do? Nothing. Stay there and watch them, so they don't do no more damage. That's all. After that, they don't bother the Italian or the German no more. We can make the wine like anybody else. Take the permit from the county, you can make all the wine you want—for yourself. It was Prohibition at that time.

Oh sure, they drink, too. I can't prove that they drink, but they take the wine away, they take moonshine, because down there they make a lot of moonshine. You know what is the moonshine? It's the whiskey.

Yeah, they was tough. After you come here in Highwood, they don't bother nobody over here.

I saw the Ku Klux Klan myself. They go in parade. We watch 'em—from faraway!

In Bush, sometimes I was work a year straight, for two or three years, all depends on the contract they got with the company. I stay there 1922 up till '28. They make a strike, that's when they want to raise in the pay.

The mine closed because of the economy. The company had too much expense to dig the rock out, the dirt, because the coal was at different levels. And then they stopped the mine. Then, they got these strip mines. Down in Illinois close to Carbondale, before you get to Carbondale.

Oh, yeah, the contract, it was a good deal. At least we had a steady job. Up to that time, if you don't have the contract, you go in strike. That's why there was all these strikes. Well, me, I went there in 1922, and they just fixed up the contract at that time. Until 1928. Pretty good. Sometimes in the summertime, they stop the mine to repair the cage, different things, you know. For me, it was a good job. During this time, I never had no different job.

The mine that got the scabs, they don't get along too good with the union. Down in Colorado and some other states. Then they tried to put up the union, but they don't accept. In Illinois, it was pretty good. The scabs tried in Illinois but they couldn't get in.

There was a union in Texas. I worked there only a little bit, not too much. There was Lorenzo Santi from Pieve. He was a good man. And he helped us to get the union card. Because before you go down in the mine, you have to have pay the debt for the card. His brother, Amedeo Santi, he was here in Highwood, then he went back over there to Texas. This Lorenzo Santi, he's the one that made the contract to the company and to the working man.

John L. Lewis, he was the president of the national union. In the local, anybody can run for president. They had an election every year or two, all depends. Well, in some places there was Italians, like down in Texas, that Santi, he was from Pieve. He was pretty smart, too. He talked pretty good American. He was born in Italy. He came over as a pretty young boy, then he had a chance to go to school. Now, I don't care about the mines. Even ten year after, I never go back in the mine because they are too dangerous. And the guy that work in the mine, he don't think it's dangerous. But when you don't work no more, you think of everything. Think about the explosion, somebody light a match.

Lawrence Santi never lived in Highwood. An immigrant from Pieve-pelago, Santi settled in Texas, in an area that was a thriving coal-mining region from the turn of the century until the 1920s. Like many from his region of Italy, he first worked coal mines in southeastern Colorado between Walsenburg and Trinidad, after he immigrated there in 1910 as a seventeen year old. Later, he moved to Texas, where he was active in union leadership. He heard John L. Lewis and Samuel Gompers speak, and he attended the union's national conventions. In 1918, Santi became president of a United Mine Workers' local in Thurber, Texas, and later served as mayor of Mingus, where he settled after being run out of Thurber during a lockout by Texas Pacific Coal and Oil Company in 1921. Many natives of the Modenese Apennines were members in the local that Santi represented. Although he never lived in Highwood, he is connected to Highwood's inhabitants. His brother lived in Highwood for many years, before returning to Texas. In Italy, his father worked as a stonecutter, and then as a road supervisor, a *cantoniere*, a prestigious job in those hills, a position that entitled him to live in a red house provided by the state. Like others in Highwood, both of Lawrence Santi's grandfathers, Marco Santi and Lorenzo Benassi, were stonecutters. The names in Lawrence Santi's family are Highwood names: Benassi. Lenzini. Crovetti. Some have connections to my own family. His brother Vincenzo, a stonemason, worked in the stone quar-ries of Algeria with my great-uncle, Angelino Vanoni. This same Vin-cenzo married my grandfather's cousin. I would hesitate to invite Law-rence Santi to Highwood's table if he wasn't like needlework that graces one corner of the tablecloth—separate, but quite in harmony with the crocheted, tatted, and drawn-work that binds the cloth together.

I was between sixteen and seventeen when I came from Italy.
I come down to Texas from Colorado with three or four more fel-

lows that were working at the same mines up there. At the time that there was the last strike up there, I came in Texas as a union man myself. Up there in Colorado, the last few days everybody knew that the strike was going to take place and so on, and knew you couldn't get a job no how. That's what, we came down here in Texas, we knew some people, some of the people that I came with knew some people here in Thurber. And so we came down and we went to work here.

Five dollars a day was at the highest peak, because as I told you before, this was one of the hardest mines to make a living in so far as actual wages, although we had good working conditions. For instance, we had, you heard about this check-off—even the policemen in the city are trying to get now—the United Mine Workers' Union was the pioneer on that, fifty-sixty years ago there in Thurber, Texas. Of course, that was due to the efforts of the miners.

You bet your life I'm in favor of closed shops. I'm still at it, although I haven't been actively engaged in union work. I am still a union man.

At that time the wages, you must understand that in and around the coal mine there were a number of persons employed by the day. In other words, they were paid a wage instead of being paid so much per ton of coal that they produced. So wages at the time paid to these laborers, which amounted to only a small part of all those employed in the mines, were $3.00 per day. And when we closed on April 30, 1921, the wages paid to the same individuals that I have just referred to was $7.50. Again, I want to say that only a small part of those were getting that wage. For instance, you have the drivers, those that pulled the coal through the bottom and then to top, and those that would timber up where there was a certain dangerous place, or laying of the track on which the big cars would run. At any rate, the wages for the actual coal diggers was much below that paid to those that were paid by the day. But as I said, the conditions of employment compensated for the lack of wages made by the coal diggers.

The union started organizing in 1903. In '05, they made pretty much of a strike. They all moved away from the camp.

But let me go back to one thing—you didn't get it—before we forget it. Something which has not been made clear, they called this a strike in 1921, March 30. It was not a strike! Positively!

This is what happened. I'm just telling you. That was a lockout. We say lockout and there is no question about it because we had a contract with a coal company to run a year beyond that date. In other words, our contract with them should have been in existence until March 30, 1922. That was the expiration date of it. But the year prior to the expiration of the contract, the company sought to force a reduction which was very unreasonable. To show you that, the reductions that they were trying to force on the miners was just one-third of their wages, in spite of the fact that we still had a contract in existence. So that was a lockout, that was a strike by the coal owners, not by the mine workers.

I think this is very important. All the companies in Texas had a meeting, a confidence vote to themselves, secretly held and no disclosure made of their decision. But the evident facts show that they had this meeting, pre-arranged, to force the miners to take a reduction in pay. The very positive thing is this, on the part of the company, that they tried to force a reduction of one-third of what the agreement provided for in the midst of a contract period. In other words, the only contract we had with the company ran for a year beyond April 1, to '22, when everybody's contract would expire and then they would have a legitimate reason to try to force the miners to take a reduction, but not in the midst of an agreement that they had signed in good faith with the miners. That's an absolute fact. In other words, they forced, not a strike, but a lockout. They are the ones that turned to striking. They were trying to tell the people that the miners struck, which was an absolute falsehood.

That closed the mines until about the beginning of August when the company thought maybe that the miners were hungry and ready to go back to work by accepting whatever the company offered. In other words, those that were receiving $7.50, as per agreement, would have been cut down to $5.00. One third, in other words, 33 percent.

Finally, it was around '26 or '27, when the mine closed for good, I believe. You see they attempted, they endeavored to operate those mines with strike breakers. It was probably about the fall of '21. Incidentally, I was the second man to be chased out of there. See, we lived in a company property, and I got notice to get out of there. Of course, they didn't use very much diplomacy.

There were two local unions, that's right. Well, I'll tell you why. The reason was that there were so many from the old country that couldn't, in fact nearly all of them, couldn't speak English. They all, of course, the young fellows, pretty soon they got to learning and you know, and to be active, and they were conducting their affairs in a very businesslike manner, in other words they were pretty

stingy with their money, and the consequence was that their local
dues were a little smaller than the other local. So, our local union
group, they called them the "Italian local," but of course we had
more American-born in our local than they had in the other. But
that's the way it was. They had the privilege, in other words, these
two local unions had jurisdiction of seven or eight mines that the
Texas Pacific Coal and Oil at that time operated.

It was really astonishing to see so many different races represented there and being able to get along as well as they did. We had
at one time—talk about Italians—we had eleven hundred Italian
coal diggers alone up there, not counting children and women and
so forth. Polish, they were the next largest representation there. I'd
say about, Polish, there was about between 20 percent and 25 percent. There was Welsh, Anglos, and a few Prussians. No Japanese or
Chinese.

Well, the observation is, not because I'm of Italian extraction, that
I found that the workers we had in Thurber, the Italians in particu-
lar, were one of the best bunch of men I ever saw anywhere, and
I've been amongst all kinds of coal diggers, including Japanese.
Really know how to work and they put their willingness to do a
job.

The mines closed properly for the Mine Workers Union, miners
left on the last day of March, 1921. First day of April we were out.
March 31, 1921, they chased me out of Thurber, but they couldn't
chase me out of Mingus.

Most of the other miners scattered, went all over. Some to the old
country, some to California, Indiana, Illinois, everywhere. No, they
didn't have any warning at all.

Eritrea Pasquesi, *la canterina* of the family:

I was born in Thurber, Texas. We went back to Italy when my
mother died here. It must have been about 1917 or something like
that. She died at age forty-two. She dropped dead. My father didn't
know what to do with four little ones. The oldest was eleven. My
father's name was Giuseppe, good old Italian name. He was born in
Pievepelago. So was my mother.

Where we lived was Thurber, Texas, and to go to the mine, the
miners had to go and get a train that would take them to the mine,
and these mines were Number One, Number Two, Number Three.
And I'll never forget my mother, she was so good, and she was so
religious, my father the opposite, you know, and every time an acci-

dent would happen in the mine, a whistle would blow and my
mother would go hide in the closet. You know, and pray for these
poor souls. In fact, I know a beautiful song, it's call "La miniere."
I'll see if I can remember it correctly. *"E nella notte un grido, si sente
un grido, e la mamma piange, 'Chi sarà? Sarà ed'mio, sarà ed'mio?' "*
"In the night, a cry. And a mother cries, 'Who will it be? Will it be
mine? Pray to God it isn't yours.'"

We lived in a mining camp, and my mother had, besides us, fourteen boarders who all were miners, and they had left their wives in
Italy and come here to work and send money home to the families.
And these poor men, they were at least fourteen and all they did
was work in this mine, I'll never forget that. And on Sunday, they
would play *bocce* ball, and then Monday, back to work. Those men
in our house, they were mostly Venetian.

Our house was a big house, ooh, it was a big, big house. There
was two great big bedrooms upstairs where it held all the boarders.
It was a company house. They were all company houses. And then
we lived downstairs and the four of us slept in one room, and papa
and mama in the other room, then we had three porches going
around the house. And lots of grapes, a lot of grapes. Peaches.
Beautiful peaches. We never ate indoors. We mostly ate outdoors. We
had these great big picnic tables, where all the men sat. My mother
cooked for them. It was a big job, with these boarders and kids. In
other words we were fourteen and six, twenty people in the house.

I know my mother got up really early. We would help her. She
used three great big coffeepots. Then she'd make all these lunches
for the miners. I can remember that. My two older sisters, they had
the job that when the men came with those buckets, to wash out
those buckets, lunch buckets. They stunk from the mine, and I, till
today, I was always very funny with my eating—even now I'm
very funny—and I never forget those poor things, and sometimes
they'd bring me, maybe, a peach back or some grapes, and my sister Vanda, she was the one, she'd eat it. Not me! I wouldn't eat it if
they paid me. It smelled like the mine. I couldn't explain it, but it
was a funny oily, oily smell, I couldn't explain it. I never smelled
anything like it in Highwood. Oh, it was terrible.

My mother ran the boardinghouse alone until later years, because
I remember later my father didn't work in the mine no more, I
guess he was starting to get this cough he had. But he didn't have
much of a cough in America, but when he went to Italy, the changing of air killed him over there. And he died of what they call now

black lung. Oh yes, I remember. He was in bed for two years, spitting, spitting, catarrh, catarrh. Yes, I remember that. My father died in Italy. In fact, like I told you, he was an atheist and he didn't want to be buried by the church. So it was on Corpus Christi Day, and over there in Italy they arrange flowers on the street in the morning. And in the afternoon, they buried my father. And they didn't want him in the cemetery because it was a Catholic cemetery. But the law said that he could be buried. So they buried him there, and we had to make the black drape, the church wouldn't even give it to us. We had to make it. Not me, but the aunts or uncles, whoever they were. And with that same material afterwards they made the four black dresses for the four little orphan girls.

In the mining camp all these houses were made by the company and they were all wooden shacks, you know shacks, well, I call them shacks now when we see what we have here. Of course, Texas is not cold, you know, it was always so hot. Oh, so hot.

My mother used to send us to the store. That was the only time I'd put my shoes on, to go downtown. Otherwise we never wore shoes. Downtown there was the stores, a few stores. There was an ice cream parlor. I can remember those fans like they have here now, you know, and there was a little red school. And what do you call it where they play the band—the gazebo—and on Sundays a band played there. My father used to take us kids.

The movie theater was there and us four, we'd always have to go the four of us, you know, my father wouldn't have let one of us go alone. Then we had shoes on, otherwise we never wore shoes. But I remember it was Charlie Chaplin, in what movie I don't know, because as I say I was only maybe seven years old. But it was Charlie Chaplin, I remember that.

I never forget us kids would go with the wagon, with the little wagon, when the train with the coal would pass, some of the coal would fall and every day we'd go pick it up and bring it home for our stove. Everybody with their little wagon, these kids, we'd go get this coal. I don't know where we got the wagon, because we had no toys. Maybe for that purpose, to go pick the coal.

The boarders were so tired at night that they would hang around drinking a few beers and then they'd go to bed. And then in the morning early they had to go get this train and the train would take them to the mining camps. The mining camps had numbers, Number One, Number Two, Number Three, Number Four.

My papa had a great big cooler where he would go down and get the beer by barrels and then he would, on Saturday and Sunday, they would open the barrel and the men would play *bocce* and drink beer right from the tap.

And we had a lot of squab. And on Sunday, it was many times, I, oh, how I can clean a pigeon. They'd make us kids do that. And then the men would go hunting, and they'd bring these little birds, and we'd have to sit there and clean these birds, and clean these birds. My mother would put a bird, a piece of bacon, some sage, and bread on the skewers and us kids would have to stay there and turn. Then once in a while we had some oil with a feather, we'd have to baste them.

My mother was the best cook. In fact, I remember I was told that she used to cook for these rich people in Pievepelago. Every night it was soup, and every night it was pasta. And meat. And vegetables. Whatever. Mainly it was soup and pasta. And they ate. Boy, could they eat after eight hours in the mine.

And I remember about the beautiful fruit. The peaches we had, and the grapes we had, and us kids used to go out and grab a handful of corn and just stick it in hole, and two, three days, up would come the corn. Hot. That's why I think I hate the hot weather. It was hot. Mosquitoes. They had no screens those days.

It was so hot, it was so hot. And my father always had this great big barrel with a tap there at the bottom, and at the bottom there was ice, and we had ice water all the time. And we'd come home and my mother, she wouldn't let us drink it because she was afraid it would hurt us that cold, you know.

And nowadays when they come from Italy, especially these last Italians, you have to go meet 'em at the plane and when they come in, *"Eh, in Italia avevo questo, in Italia."* "Oh, in Italy I had this." Nothing is good enough. They shoulda come when we came, then they'd find out what hard times were.

The boarders all played an instrument. One played a mandolin, two or three of them played a guitar. And my father loved music, that's one thing that was good about my father, he loved music. We had a piano. And not only we had a piano, Ribella and Vanda, they both played mandolin and guitar.

I played a guitar—I didn't get far in the mandolin—and I sang. And I sang a song and I accompanied myself. So every time somebody came we had to sit and entertain. And I sang and I hated it. Oh. You sit there. *"La mia monella, non ho più bacci per te."* "My little girl, I have no more kisses for you." And that went on and on. And "My Bonnie was over the ocean." That went on all the time,

"My Bonnie was over the sea." The man that taught me would say
"Do, do. Change! Re, re." I can still do it today. These *veneziani*
taught me. They all played. They all played instruments. I don't
know if it was by ear. But mine was by ear, naturally. Even today, I
know very little about it, and I've sang all my life. Since I'm that
high. But I have never taken music. I didn't have time. I had to
work. But I can tell a little of it, you know. I know how to go up
and go down. How to hold a note and so on and so forth, and
down at the senior citizens group I also sing now. But I was always
la canterina of the family, you know.

I forgot to tell you about how I got to go to other towns. This
Miss Mitchell that gave me that Bible, see I always sang, and I was
of course the envy of my sisters because she would dress me up
and pull my hair down, and my father wouldn't allow it otherwise,
pull my hair down and put a bow, and then I would travel with
her. She played the piano. And she would play the piano and I
would sing to all these doings in church and outdoors, too. And I
even slept away from home in the hotel. I couldn't have been more
than five years old. And at night she would make me say prayers. I
had never said prayers in my life. And then she would say, "Now
when you go home, you mustn't drink beer." And we drank beer
like men. Well, you know it was the keg beer. And so, alright. The
minute I got home I'd go for a glass of beer or a bottle of beer.

It was something like the Salvation Army, because I remember
this church, I can remember this, she played and I sang. What did I
sing? "If a little child like me loves the Christ in thee," something
like that. She had this little red house and that was on Sundays and
my father would let us go. And she taught us that the world was
made in seven days and about Jesus, the first day, the second day,
that sort of thing, I remember that. But it's the only time my father
would allow me to pull down my hair down. And to travel with
Miss Mitchell. 'Cause it was singing.

My father, see, he was the boss, you know. Men were the boss.
Oh, no, no, no, my mother never taught us any prayers. What little
I learned I learned from Miss Mitchell in this little red schoolhouse.
Then afterwards we'd sing, naturally, and then she would give us
little books to read, with pictures. My father didn't care because he
knew I was singing. As long as he knew I was singing.

In fact, this is a cute little story. My father didn't believe in religion but if I sang, well, he would come. So Christmas Eve there
was a big, big doing at this Protestant schoolhouse. And all the
boarders came. They all got dressed up, they put their hats on. And

they sat there on the benches and then they put their hats down. One of the children would recite. The other one would read about Christmas, and of course, I did the singing. I think I sang "Holy night, silent night," and well, they were all happy. But the minute the minister came out, and he came with a Bible and he started to preach, one by one, these men took up their hats and they all went home.

None of the men went to church, they were all like that. I hear there's a lot of them that came from Italy, and they went to the mining camps like Bush, Illinois. What I was told, that all these people, when they all came from over there, they all joined the Masons and my father used to belong to the Masons, and they're antireligious. I know my father never taught us any prayers. I learned my prayers in Italy. I learned them in Latin.

I didn't know what Catholic was until I went to Italy. When I went to Italy I knew. In fact when we got there, my aunt—I'm supposed to look like her, she was supposed to be the beauty of town—oh, they christened us all, they changed all our names, they named me Maria, in church I'm Maria, well, Eritrea, that's not a Catholic name, none of us have Catholic names.

My mother died in January and in September we went to Italy. In September my father packed and sold our ranch. Of course when we left, papa had to get rid of all the boarders and get rid of whatever we had. We had a horse, because my father had to go get the beer downtown with the horse. John Bagatti's sister took over our house. Bought it, or took it over, like I said, I don't know if it belonged to the company. His sister took over the house with some of the boarders. After a few years she went back to Italy.

And of course, my father brought us to Pieve because he thought that with the aunts and uncles they would help, but they had so many kids of their own.

I can remember my mother's funeral. She dropped dead from a cerebral hemorrhage, so they told me years later, in front of the stove. It was in January. We had this big belly stove, you know. So they put her in a casket and they emptied out a room and she was on a board in the casket. I'll never forget, it was all black and it had a glass where we could see her face, and four candles and ice all around, mind you, even in January, and that ice was melting. And then they came with this hearse. I'll never forget. Black. And we went to the funeral. Drawn by a horse and we were in the back. And, oh, my father took that hard. I'll never forget. And I remember my mother's grave, too. It was a custom, I guess, at that time, instead of bringing flowers, if you had pretty glass and it was broken, they would put it on the grave, you know, and my mother had two little daughters that died, both named Eritrea, that are buried in Texas with my mother. And we were all taught how to make roses, those garlands of paper roses, and bring them to the cemetery. There was no such thing as fresh flowers, except what we had around the house. You know that crepe paper that you can twist, and that what you knit with, a needle, and you go like that and you pull it and it would curl the edges.

She's still buried in Thurber. Thurber, Texas. And I hear there's no town at all.

"Da Carbonhill, Illinois, Stati Uniti d'America." I saw the poster on a wall at the Center for Migration Studies in Staten Island, as I was leaving in a hurry to catch a ferry because I was late. But I had to stop. First I saw the boldest line, "From Carbonhill." Below, a list of names of people and towns that sounded so familiar. I missed the ferry. Later, in Highwood, I showed Delma Muzzarelli a photograph of the poster. We sat on her couch in a narrow living room filled with plants. Did she know any of the names, I asked. It's hard to say, she said, it's such a long time ago, 1899. From Sestola, did you know of an Antonio Burchi? No, she says she doesn't know his name, but there were Burchi from Sestola that she knew of. From the town of Trentino in Modena, Lorenzo Pellegrini, I asked, what about him? Before I was married, she says, I was a Pellegrini. My father was from Trentino and I think this is his cousin, this Lorenzo Pellegrini. We read the list of names from her town, Serrazzone. Antonio Torricelli? No, but there were Torricelli from my town. There are two Muzzarelli here, I say, Cesare and Costante. Cesare, no, but Costante, my husband had a cousin Costante Muzzarelli from Serrazzone who died in Italy. A sweet corroboration, the result of a blessed fluke.

I was born Delma Pellegrini, the nine of September in 1894 in Serrazzone. There are a few families in Highwood from Serrazzone. Not too much, though.

At the time I left there was about five hundred people in Serrazzone. Now, maybe about fifty. They all disappeared. They all move away. The young people moved over here and the old people die. In one place where there was maybe thirty people, now maybe four people.

My husband, Joe Muzzarelli, was in the mine for fourteen years. He was from the same town.

When he first came over, he went to Carbon Hill. He had some cousin or friends in Carbon Hill. Then after, he went to South Wilmington, it's not very far from Coal City. Where the mine is. Then he went to Johnson City, Illinois. He worked for fourteen years in the mine. He was in the mine, it was rough work, that's all I can say.

When we came here, we didn't have nothing, nothing. We borrowed the money from his brother-in-law, he was here in Carbon Hill. We didn't have nothing. No money. No house. And then after we came my husband stayed for six months in the hospital in Chicago. He was told he had the t.b. It wasn't true. They found it was because he was working in the mine. He have a spot in here in the lung from the coal. And perhaps when he went to the army, they asked did you work in the mine. "Yeah," he said. "For fourteen years." But they don't make that spot an issue to do the service.

After they find in Chicago there was no t.b., they sent him home right away. But they told him, "You can work no more in the mine. You have to work outside." When we came to Highwood he worked for rich people, taking care of the garden.

We stayed about three years in Carbon Hill. I was working in a factory. Clothes for the men. Sewing. Sewing buttons. Every hundred buttons I got thirty cents. We was working piecework. You have to work kind of hard to pull up a hundred buttons at thirty cents. We made the living, that's all.

Tomorrow, January 6, is Mary Baldi's birthday. She will be eighty-eight. There is a surprise party planned for her. She knows about it. She figured it out when her daughter slipped up. She's hoping the kids buy her a new clock. She wanted one for Christmas but didn't get it. She's pretty sure she'll get one for her birthday. She wants the kind that you wind: "I don't like electric clocks because when the electricity goes off, then you don't have no time." It's a busy morning. The phone rings three times. Once it's a son calling. Once it's a daughter. Once it's the man who is coming to fix the front door. "Oh, that darned phone," she says. The man arrives to fix the front door. Then, there is a visitor, a friend of her daughter, who stops by: "He says he comes to check on the dog, but he really comes to check on me."

I was born 1898, January the sixth, that's tomorrow. Last night I couldn't sleep. I woke up. I could not sleep for thinking of this interview. Oh, I could not sleep. What have I got to say? Something nice, you know. So I remembered Casino, that's a little town next to

Pratelioni. My grandparents were in Pratelioni and we were in Casino. In the *Piemonte*. And like I said, the province is Torino.

I remember coming on the boat and I was trying, that's another
thing, I couldn't go to sleep last night. I had to remember the name
of the boat and that I cannot remember. And once in a while it
comes to me but last night I couldn't remember. So I got up and
read for a while. I tossed and tossed and my hand was bothering
me, so I said, "If I can only go to sleep." And I didn't want to wake
my daughter Vickie up. But I can't remember the name of the boat.
But I remember coming over. We were on the lower floor. Do you
know anything about boats? I think there are three floors, the lower
ones for the poor, the very poor, and the middle ones, and the
wealthy ones were up on the upper ones. And I remember they
used to throw money down from up there. They'd throw money
down and I used to scramble and knock everybody over and try to
get more than the rest. I think I was a really mean girl. I was only
six years old.

When I came here, I wrote a letter to my grandma and I always
remember my mother always used to tell me, "Write to your
grandma," and I put down, "Pratelioni, Illinois." I thought the
whole world was Illinois.

When we came from Italy, my father was in Dalzell, Illinois. We
were there four years. Then we went to Cedar Point, that's another
mining town. I guess they moved because they were making more
money or maybe he had lost his job or something. His brother had
moved to Cedar Point before we did, so he sent for him. My father
followed his brother all the time. Wherever he moved, we moved.

And we weren't there very long that my father passed away. He
got pneumonia. He died within three or four days of getting sick.

My mother didn't like to leave her mother in Italy. She had three
sisters. Her brother was here already. That's the one who died in
the Cherry coal mine disaster in 1909. John Compasso. He had four
children. That was in 1909. And my dad died in 1910.

There was very, very few people that could afford to buy their
own coal. They all went down early in the morning to pick coal
around the boxcars, the open ones. They fill them up so much that
when the train cars hit when they get hitched up, a lot of it falls
down. And, you know what the big gunny sacks are? We'd fill them
up and bring them home. On our back. Every morning. That is in
the summertime. We'd furnish enough coal for the winter. And
there were a couple of miners, they could afford it more than we
could, I guess, maybe like this one widow next to us, she had only

one son and he was a miner, well, she used to order her coal and they'd bring it right to the front door of her house. And they paid me a quarter to take it down in the basement with two pails. A whole ton of coal. And a quarter I would get. But that was good money. We never had any money. I don't know how we ever managed.

When my father, before he got real sick, he wasn't feeling too good, I guess the doctor told him he had to quit drinking wine, it might have been something maybe with his lungs or something but those days they didn't know anything, they called it pneumonia. They told him he had to drink milk. So we brought two cows. And, that's what we were living on. We were selling it. They put me in charge of the cows because my two oldest sisters were working. I didn't like to go to school. So my dad left it up to me. You either go to school or you're gonna herd the cows.

That meant take them out along the road, because we didn't do like here. Here you rent a place where a farmer had a place you can put your animals, and they're fenced in. There was no such thing there. We'd herd them along the road, they'd give me a lunch and there were a couple of other friends that did the same thing, a couple of boys and a couple of girls, so I was not alone.

Oh, we had picnics all by ourselves with our lunch. We'd find some old dilapidated building and we'd go in and play house, twelve years old, you know, what can you do? And then when I brought them home, I'd help my mother milk and I'd have my quart and we had our customers and I'd go out and deliver milk morning and night.

So, I remember a lot of time, because we had one cow—a Jersey cow—that gave a lot of milk. My mother would put it in the crock and put it in the pantry and she'd take that cream out. Oh, it tasted so good. I used to sneak in there and sneak some away.

And what you mentioned about eating, mostly *polenta* and soups. There never was no dessert. And salads, I guess in the summertime we had lot of vegetables. We had a garden, my mother and I, we took care of that. And as long as my father was alive, he always butchered his own pigs in the wintertime and made his own sausage and *prosciutto* and all that. I think we got along pretty good. We'd go to the farm and they'd kill them right there and bring them home. Each neighbor would help the other. Like today, one would do it, and tomorrow, somebody else would do it. This is late in the fall because it had to be cold. Made our own lard, I can remember that. Sausage, I can remember hanging it in the basement, hanging it, and then we made *coteghin*, *cotechino*, that's a kind of sausage. That's how we lived. Made all our own stuff. My mother would never buy any store noodles. Always made her own, she always made her own bread. She was pretty good. She had a hard life.

Dalzell and Cedar Point were just about the same. There were all company houses. You paid rent. And they had the company store. There was a few little stores in Cedar Point but in Dalzell there was one company store. Everybody had to buy from them. In Cedar Point, there was a few Italian stores.

My mother took in laundry in Cedar Point. They had no water in the house, they had a well. They didn't have detergents then. After you washed your white clothes on a washboard, there's two tubs. One is hot water, where you wash your clothes, and then you dunk them into this boiler and you gotta use your club, punching them down so they get boiled, too. You'd think it would have ruined the clothes. And then you took them out with the club and stick them in this cold water, that's where you would rinse them. And they couldn't be rinsed very good because you only rinsed in one water, where the machine rinses them in two or three waters. Well, anyway, that was the style then.

She did laundry for some of the business people. There were taverns in Cedar Point, there were shops, and I guess others who could afford it. She probably charged fifty cents a day. To her it was a lot of money. And to them it was cheap, rather than do it themselves.

All the work they had to do. I tell you I'm glad we don't have to do that anymore. And people are complaining you know, now they've got everything and they're never satisfied. Just think how easy it is nowadays and I remember getting on the floor in this place where I was working for fifty cents a week, scrubbing a floor with a brush, on my hands and knees at ten, twelve years old. It was a private home with four or five boarders.

My mother, she was a great Catholic, so she would send us to Sunday school, and for Christmas they always had packages for the kids, with oranges and candy or an apple, something like that. And that was they only time I ever had an apple, and orange or candies, and I remember a lot of times after that I'd find an orange peel or a banana peel out in the street, I'd pick it up and eat it. How many times I think of that. And now I could eat all the fruit I want. It seems impossible that people could have been that poor.

I don't think I felt like we were poor because I didn't know what it was to have anything. I never had anything and I remember putting up my Christmas stocking and finding a little piece of coal in it. That was it.

The last Christmas before my dad died, there was a store there, an Italian place. And I saw they had little dolls. So Christmas morning I found this doll. I said to my dad, "Santa Claus didn't come, this came from . . ." and I named the store. So my dad said, "Okay, so now you know, there's no Santa Claus, next year you're not going to get it." Next year he wasn't around anymore.

My brother Tom Mussatto, the one that was mayor in Highwood, was checkweighman for the coal mine. They had two checkweighmen that weighed the coal, one for the miners and one for the company. Naturally the company cheats. So the miners' checkweighman, he's got to see that there's no cheating going on. That's what my brother was.

The coal miners mostly all were socialist. I don't know if that word is around anymore. You don't hear that word anymore, socialist. You ever heard of it? Well, at that time, my father was, too. Never was a church man. But my mother was a church woman.

The miners didn't believe in the church. And after you're dead, they didn't believe in that. Socialism didn't have nothing to do with their work. I don't think it had anything to do with the union either. That was just like, one is a Catholic, one's Protestant—it's not a religion, but it's just that they were against the church. I don't know why. Maybe he came away from Italy when he was a young man and came to Dalzell, there was not a church and he got together with the rest of the guys that were socialist.

What happened to the mines? Well, Cherry burned up. Ladd closed up. Spring Valley closed up. Dalzell closed up. The mines just closed. I don't know if there was no more coal or what happened. A lot of people got tired of working in the coal mine even if the mine was still working. They knew they'd come here to Highwood and make better money. And lot of them, they put up a little business, or some of them made wine and sold it. Make a little business there. There was a lot of bootlegging going around here.

My husband had some friends working in the golf course in the summertime. And the mine wasn't working so good. So he came one summer and worked, and he liked it, so then he came back and went back in the coal mine. Through my husband, their friends would come and then they'd bring their wife and then they'd bring their relatives. There's the Baruffis. You know any of the Fiocchis? The Tamarri family? They came from Dalzell.

And then next spring, that was in 1920, we all came up in April. In the fall, we went back home and we lived with my mother in Dalzell until finally we came back to Highwood and made it our town. Our home.

Among advertisements for businesses like the Majestic Pool Hall and C. A. Mason Light & Heavy Harness listed in a 1913 directory from Bureau County, Illinois, is the entry: "Baruffi, Rosa Miss. Dalzell." Her name is listed because she was a schoolteacher. Even though she left the classroom in 1917, she is still a schoolteacher. When there is a question about a geographical location, she gets up from the kitchen table and consults the atlas. She refers to the encyclopedia once, and to the phone directory several times, checking to see if a person she mentions is still listed. During her lifetime, she worked at a dry cleaner's and managed her husband's stonemasonry business, in addition to running a household and home. It is hard to erase the image of the schoolteacher, though. She prides herself on her memory and command of details. "I was always good in math. I was always good in remembering names and dates and addresses and that came in handy when we were on the job," she says. She gives herself pop quizzes. Trying to recall a date: "Had to be in the twenties. I think so. I'm trying to think of an incident that I know just about, you know, contemporary. That's how I check myself." Her memory is sharp and her grade book is in order.

I am Rosa Fiocchi. My maiden name was Baruffi. I was born February 2, 1894, in Lizzano in Belvedere in *provincia di Bologna, Italia.* We came here in 1898. We came to Dalzell in 1902. I was eight. When I was six, I couldn't speak a word of English, when I started school.

My father came over in late 1896, but by the time he got here it was '97, and a year later my mother and we three oldest came over. She was pregnant when my father left. He came over with his brother and his mother.

When we came we got off at New York—by we, I mean my mother and we three, got off at New York and then we took a coastal steamer to Norfolk and then we went by rail to Blockton, Alabama. Blockton has been swallowed by Birmingham now. But there were mines there.

My father had gone to Arkansas first. Sunnyside, Arkansas. My grandmother said that the natives there didn't think much of them. They were hostile. There were other Italians in Sunnyside, where

my father went, who later came to Spring Valley. Their name was
Bernabei, from Bologna, too. Somebody had been writing to my
father from Alabama and so they went down to Blockton. That was
a coal mine. All of that happened between January of '97 and '98
when we came to the United States. And then the next May we
came to Spring Valley and been in Illinois ever since.

What made my father, what made them all come to Illinois from
Blockton, Alabama, was one day they brought out a car from the
mine, and there were a couple of roasted men on it, you know,
burned from an explosion. So that was it. So they took off and
came up here.

Back then, they had hats that had a hard kind of metal thing, you
know, so that they could hang their lamp on it for light. Before the
carbide lamps were oil lamps. And they looked like a coffee pot,
you know, they have a spout. And they had a wick in the spout
that they put oil in there. That was their light. So that was open
flame. They put it on the metal part of their mine cap and that was
the light that they had. And then the carbide. Well, that was different. They'd open something, had a little place where the gas would
come out and they had the carbide in it. Put water in it and they'd
have it lit. And that was nicer and it had a brighter light than
the oil.

In 1906 we came to Dalzell from Spring Valley. I was eight. My
grandmother called the shots. Grandma would find a house and
we'd go in it, until my mother took hold of the reins. Grandma had
been used to being the boss, the matriarch. And being raised in Italy and being all one family, she was usually the one that called the
shots. They all lived together, my grandmother, my uncle, my father.
But they moved to Oglesby, across the Illinois River from LaSalle.
They were there, and grandma had found a house for us all, a two-
story house, and sent word that we should get ready, that we were
going to move. My mother said, "I ain't moving." My aunt said,
"What are you going to do?" She says, "If you have to go, you
have to go."

"I'm not going," my mother said, "I'm not going."

"Well, what are we going to do about the furniture?"

She said, "Well, we'll fix that. I'll say the price and you take what
you want. The stove, so much I keep it, so much you take it."

That was my mother's chance to make a break and she did.

I went to school in Dalzell. And then there was a Scotch teacher
and she just plain ignored the Italians. Once, somebody didn't want
a part in the Christmas play, and I volunteered, and she just plain

ignored me, just like she didn't hear what I said. So, I didn't get it.
But that's what she did to all the Italians. They were second-class
citizens as far as she was concerned, and then Mr. Mason came.
When Mr. Mason came, it kind of eased up.

I did always enjoy school. I got it from both parents. When my
father came, he heard about night school. "Ah, that is for me." And
he went to night school and he did alright. And somebody needed a
letter written, they'd come to him. You know people, some of the
townspeople from Italy would have him write, even write a letter in
Italian, some of them would. They had some business to transact.
He got a notary's seal. But I think he did very well. The night
school was in Spring Valley. And he could have gone longer but
then we moved to Dalzell. That would be asking too much that
he'd go after having worked, to go to Spring Valley and then back.
Walking, too.

My mother read but she did not write. She started to learn English when we started school. When my brother started to school,
then we started talking English, then it didn't take her very long to
catch on. It didn't take my father very long either. My mother never
went to school. She had to go tend the sheep. A couple of sheep
they had. But our mother's mother had a friend who was a teacher
and she would give my mother an hour and she would get, say, *una
ventina*, twenty eggs, or a little cheese, just be paid in food. But she
was a good reader and she read everything.

My father started taking the newspaper, the *Chicago Tribune*, in
1903, but we got it the day after because it came in the mail. Never
bought an Italian paper. But my mother had a friend who had been
a teacher and she used to get the Italian paper, I don't know if it
was *Il Progresso*, and there was a continued story and she would cut
it out and bring it to my mother. And I would read it, too. I didn't
know how much I would understand, but I would read it. That's
why I can read Italian.

The school board were all Italians in Dalzell. I'm surprised how
the Scotch didn't get in that. Well, they wouldn't have had very
many Italians voting for them anyway. Then they wanted a man
teacher and that's how they got Mr. Mason. And Mr. Mason was a
very, very good teacher and he separated the men from the boys,
really. I'd hurry and get my work done, then I'd listen when he was
teaching the other grade. I was interested.

And then when he left, he went to Oglesby and then he got to be
superintendent of schools there and then he wound up in Congress,
representative from that district. I thought a lot of him. He was

Welsh. His parents were Welsh. I don't know if he was born in
Wales or what. But the reason, they were farmers, but he'd been a
little puny so they sent him to college.

I got good grades but he used to have to every week make a list,
you know, how many girls, how many boys, all their names and
absence and so forth. He gave me the job. Two years. And then he
used to grade us for deportment. I would have been ashamed to get
less than a hundred.

The Scotch didn't come up to the Italian students. They didn't
come up. Oh, yeah we mixed. My best friend was a Scottish girl.
Her father was the night boss. Simpson. I went to high school in
LaSalle. There was the interurban streetcar. The minute I got off the
streetcar in LaSalle, I think even the first day, they started talking
about dagoes. Can you imagine? I said nothing. But some of them
snickered. You know, that's terrible.

Of course, the few Scotch, they were the elite, they considered
themselves that. But that was as far as it went. But when I went to
high school the first time, there was an Irish fellow, and maybe he
was more than first generation—I wasn't even the first generation, I
was *the* generation, because I'd come over. And he started to talking
about dagoes. Now, well, the next morning it was the same thing.
Now was that the only subject? I couldn't hear everything he said.
But he got the word "dago" in there and that's all I needed.

But afterwards, I didn't feel crushed anymore. I knew that in class
I could vie with most of them. I could vie with the upper fourth. I
knew that. And that helped. I knew my father was up there in his
head with any of the Scotch. And he was bilingual and they
weren't. You know, I felt shrinking but at the same time I did feel
that I had something over them. Even that high school one that
started to talk about the dagoes. And I could speak two languages.
Not only the dialect.

I think I was the only Italian there for the two years that I went.
Well, the Scotch talked about the Italians all the time. They were
"We the people." It is a little crushing, but then in school I had the
satisfaction of saying, "Well, I know that." I was in algebra class and
a child had written "millage." And the teacher asked about the
spelling, and I said, "it should be 'm-i-l-e-a-g-e.' " And he com-
mented that I was the foreigner there and I knew how to spell it.
But the Scotch just kept it up.

But not only that, when I took my son Bob to Purdue, he had a
letter of introduction from the principal and he wrote something
about "Italian boy." He was born here, he's as American as much as

you are. What did he mean? To me if they say Italian now, it's a feather in the hat. But at that time I resented it.

It seems the Germans went through theirs, the Irish went through theirs, the Italians were straddling the turn of the century, I think of who's getting it now. Do you think the Asiatics are getting it now?

At that time, if you passed the examination, you could be a teacher. I went to Princeton, the county seat, and I passed! It wasn't hard for me. If you passed, you got your certificate. Well, you know, they all expected it of me.

I was the first Italian teacher at the new school, Number Five. And later I went to the old school, Number Two. I started teaching in 1910 but I taught after I was married, too. It seems to me when girls got around twenty they usually got married. I don't think they were being pushed out of the nest, like I wasn't pushed out of the nest. I married who I wanted.

We stayed in Dalzell a little bit until we found a place in Cherry and we went to Cherry and I taught there. Then I was working in Seatonville but that was a little hard because of the distance.

My mother had fifteen babies, but she had thirteen deliveries. She had two pairs of twins. So you tell me when she was idle. It wasn't unusual. The Irish had 'em, too. I think it's after the last war that the families have gotten small, the Second World War.

They didn't go to the hospital. My brother Louie was the second child born in Dalzell when it opened. And the midwife—well, she acted as midwife—her daughter was the first one born. Louie was the second child in that little town. And she had the willingness and the courage and she read up as much as she could and they called her for anything. And it seemed to be that she usually doled out aspirin. I don't know what it was then but she'd give them a couple of pills, I guess. That would tide them over. But she was not qualified by law. But what was she going to do when they called her? Like now you go to a doctor right away and he watches you all the time. The midwife would come for a week and take care of the mother and watch the baby and make it comfortable. For anti-sepsis, she would tear pieces of rag and then she'd put them on the back of the coal stove which was never very dirty, it was clean, but it wouldn't get very hot either and when it turned kind of tan, she would take it. And she would put that over the umbilicus where the navel is. She was Scotch. With all the brogue that there was.

My mother lost just one at birth. Second to last child she was in labor so long. It was born with a cord around it's neck. She was born alive but she died in about an hour. Yeah, they went through some hard times. Scarlet fever would make the rounds. That was bad because it left some bad hearts. Diphtheria. What's diphtheria now?

I don't think we were in debt so much. We kind of took shorter steps maybe and gave certain things priority. If you don't get a check now, it's disaster. I don't think it was that way. There was credit. What's credit now? You go shopping for food and you pay now. We usually used credit. It was just routine, you paid every so often. Maybe you paid every week. Somebody would pay every two weeks. But those that were really from hand to mouth would go get a book of coupons and you could get a five-dollar one and then they had different denominations. Five cents, ten cents, and so forth. But my mother never went for coupons. She did it with the pay. They would deduct it from the pay. It would show on your envelope.

In Dalzell, people had bought the houses. Some people moved, and moved their houses. Some went to Cherry. That was a new mine. You know, they'd put it on rollers and move the house. They used horses to pull it. And they would put a stake down somewhere and they had rollers that were big like logs, put it here and there and they put some ropes and then have a horse go round and round and he would be winding this rope, you know, and then they started putting them on rollers and they just put the house on with jacks and put it on and make their way slowly. But a lot of the Dalzell houses went to Ladd and to Cherry. They were made of wood.

The mine in Dalzell was working all the time up until about 1919. That's where my father worked. My father never was active for the union. No, he believed in rights, but he wasn't looking for any fights. Like we were entitled to the county road. That he fought for when he was mayor of Dalzell. My father beat out the incumbent, the first mayor of the town, my father was the second. The first was *piemontese.*

It was mostly Italians in Dalzell. And there were a few Scotch. And there were some Austrians and a few Polish. Not much more. I would say about 75 percent Italian. 'Course, the Scotch always got the high priority on everything. Well, the mine boss, the day boss, and the night boss were both Scotch. See, they had experience from the old country. None of the Italians knew mines. In Italy, no coal mines there. The Scotch were the elite.

The blacks were in Spring Valley and they called it the Location, they had a place where they had to live. That was the Number

Three mine. East of Spring Valley. And they called that the Location. If you said, "the Location," then that's where the blacks were. I don't know if any whites lived there, too, but no blacks could live out of there.

In Dalzell there was just the one mine, Spring Valley Coal Company. Well, the town looked like rows of streets. What they called the Number Five mine was in Dalzell and the houses were one block long. It was a long block. And let me think now, two, four, six, eight, maybe ten double rows, ten streets. The last houses weren't finished when we moved to Dalzell. They were under construction. Every four houses had a well. Ours had a windlass, a rope around, like, a log, and you cranked it up. But there were some that had a pulley wheel and they had the old oaken bucket.

In 1904 my parents bought the house we lived in. It wasn't big, it had four room. Is there a pencil there? Let me draw it. My proportions aren't good. One room was the kitchen, the other was living room, one door to a bedroom there, and one to a smaller bedroom here. This was the pantry. No porch. What's a porch? They looked like little shacks, little huts. I don't think they were bigger than twenty-four feet long, and maybe they were twenty-five feet wide. What was insulation in those days? There was an air space underneath the house so people would put a couple of boards and then get a load of manure and put it up. That would make heat. Then in the summer they could put it in their garden. It made awfully nice grass by the house though. Well, you just see how people coped.

Everybody coped, yeah, I had as much as you had, and you had as much as she had. Except maybe, well, the boss lived in a bigger house. And the night boss, well, they had a lot of kids, so they had to put an addition to their house. But that's all.

We didn't have a church in Dalzell then. We went to Spring Valley, and if we went late we'd drop in the Lithuanian one, that was the nearest one.

They built the church after, way after, we left. And it can't be too, too old, I would just estimate between twelve and fifteen years. But one time, after they built the church, my sisters and I went back to Dalzell because the church was having some doings. And they had *tortellini*. A desecration. They had *tortellini* with *soffrito*, you know what *soffrito* is? With spaghetti sauce. And they had *tortellini* with College Inn Broth!!! They had canned broth! That's why I call it a desecration. Now I don't make chicken broth only, I always have a piece of beef. It makes a better flavor. It tones that feathery, I call it feathery taste, it's the taste of chicken broth, but I don't like it. But I put a piece of beef in when I make broth. My mother used to do that. I think she did that to stretch it.

She had *pastasciutta*, that's noodles with spaghetti sauce. And we'd have noodles in broth. And then we'd have bean soup and we'd have noodles in that. Because the company store didn't know what spaghetti was. It was meat and potatoes with the Scotch. And my mother cooked Italian style. I think it was better. Because we got our protein anyway.

And then that wouldn't be all. She'd buy ten cents worth of steak, it was about like that, in those days, and we'd have that and a salad after the soup. Then she'd divide it and my father's piece was double that of the kids. He had to keep up his strength. But she was pregnant. But that didn't matter. I never thought of questioning that.

But we never went hungry, like my husband. I told you, he said, "This is the place for me," when he saw them cutting up soup meat for the chickens. You see, he had intentions of going right back to Italy. He had come to see what he wanted to see and he'd seen enough. And then he saw his boarding mistress outside with the soup meat and she was cutting it up for the chickens. "This is for me. Meat for the chickens."

I stopped teaching in 1917 after my second girl was born. Well, I wasn't going to teach anymore, but it was bad times. The mine wasn't working in Cherry then either. So things were pretty slim. The Dalzell one was closed. You know, it's kind of hard. We left it in June of the year Tulla was born—1917. And they closed a lot of those northern mines, Peru closed, Spring Valley's closed. When I lived in Cherry it was after the disaster. We moved up to Cherry in 1915. Then, we went back to Dalzell. I don't think the mine had reopened.

My husband didn't do anything during that period. Somehow, we lived, I don't remember really. It would be harder now, believe me, than it was then. People had their gardens, and like I told you, when I was growing up my mother'd have our soup, and ten cents of beef, and we'd have our soup and there was plenty of that. But we stayed there until 1920 when we came up here to Highwood.

Louis Baruffi thought he was the first child born in Dalzell, Illinois. But, his sister Rosa, whose grade book is in order, corrected him. Eight years his senior, she said, "No, when the midwife came over when you were being born, she had this little bundle with her that was Betsy Donaldson who had just been born." So he was the first *boy* born. He said of his sister, "And I'm pretty sure she's right, because she was there, you know."

We used to start in the mines pretty young down there. I worked with my dad for two years before I got my permit to work by myself. I worked in the mines for four and a half years.

I left Dalzell in 1919. Seemed like the mine was going to be closed down in Dalzell after the First World War and so we went to Detroit. We built a house in Detroit, things started going bad there also. Then from Detroit we went to West Virginia. We worked there maybe about year or two. Then from West Virginia we went back to Dalzell. Stayed there awhile. Then I come up to Highwood. See, my sister Rose was in Highwood.

When Dalzell closed, I think everybody knew it was coming. Spring Valley closed long time before that. Number One, Number Two, and Number Three. Ours was Number Five. Number Five and Number Six were both in Dalzell. Ladd was closed a long time before Dalzell.

Then I went to Detroit, Michigan. We had a friend that was working up there. He said things were going good in Detroit. Which they were. Then after a while, everything started going down, down, down. I worked on the Packard Company, making springs for seats for the Packard cars. Then I went to work for Stone and Webster as a laborer. It was the big company that was building United States Rubber Tire Company's building in Detroit. And we cleaned the lumber—got rid of the nails and so forth—so that way they didn't have to buy new lumber again. And I worked on that until we went to West Virginia, in the coal mines.

No, we weren't union in West Virginia. It was an easier life there in West Virginia because the coal was high. You could be union or nonunion and it would still be a hard life for the coal miner in Dalzell because in Dalzell the coal was only this high—that means you couldn't stand up, you had to be on your knees. About thirty-six inches, some places was a little taller. It was hard to make a living. Very hard, no matter how hard you worked.

Then when we come back from West Virginia, we worked in the Cherry mine. They had the Cherry disaster, well, you heard of that one? Well, the disaster, I think, it was in the second vein, and we worked down in the third vein.

I'll tell you what, you can be a good miner or you can be a bad miner, it all depends on the place they give you. You work on your knees, I'm talking about Dalzell now, I'm not talking about the central fields.

The Catholic church in Dalzell was built after we left. But they used to have a building on the corner—my dad got a company house from the coal company, gave to him or loaned it to him, and my sister Rose and another young lady her age would teach catechism there. And every once in a great while then a priest from Spring Valley would come up there. But Dalzell wasn't attached to religion too much. No, no, no, no, no. A lot of bigots. A preacher would come into town with a horse and buggy, see, then the crowd gathers around, and starts making fun out of him and tell him to get the hell out of town. You know, they're pretty hostile. And they cross the reins so when he gets back on the buggy, the horse would go the wrong way. All kinds of tricks. They were really mean, mean, mean, mean, mean. Thank God it's changed now. There's a lot of 'em in Italy, too, that are anti-church, a lotta church people and a lotta anti-church people.

Adele Dinelli, who sold her house, but lives there in the meanwhile:

We were living in France. My husband, he sent for the money in Italy. He still have money in the bank and we go to Centralia, Illinois. He got a sister in Centralia and a brother in Indiana, in Clinton. All mines around, that's all. We was at St. Mary in 1911. It was a coal mine and then we went to Nokomis, Illinois.

At the camp at St. Mary's was a mine and homes owned by the company. They make those little houses like soldiers have, barracks, you know, out of wood, all out of wood, with no cement underneath, and they just put a big post here and a big post there and then they build the house in top. And underneath, about that high from the floor, you make a hole in the ground and you put a pan of broth, you put a little pan with stew, because it was a little cooler than house because the wind go back and forth underneath there. That's where we kept our food, in a pan, closed. It kept it a little cold because we didn't have any money to buy the ice. Was misery around the coal mine. That's all.

When we came there was not work enough, there was strikes because usually in the summertime, they strike most of the time those coal mines. In the winter, they worked, but sometime they make seven, eight dollar, every ten or fifteen day. They don't much pay that time.

You know me, I was working when he was in Highwood for the summer, I went to work for two dollars a week sewing, two dollars a week, over there in Nokomis. I was work every day for two dollar a week. But I didn't make nothing. Was no money around. No money at all. No money in those days, even the time I was working.

Then in 1919, I came over here in Highwood because he came and worked in the golf. He came home and then he want to come back by hisself. And I say, "If you go, I come too. I don't stay home by myself." And I came over here and never moved because while he could not make a penny, I could go out and work myself.

There was no work for women. There was no work for the men, neither. The mines, the coal mines, sometimes, they stopped, and my husband was one of those men that liked to move from here, go over there, and while he was over there, he got tired, like to go over there. You know those men that like to move all the time? Mine was one. There was not work all the time because there was strike and they don't work for so long. If you stay, you work just the same like the others. You take the misery and the good.

My husband, he think to move around, he think he'd do better. And you never do better to move around. You do worse.

He came over here to work in the golf. Because after we came in Highwood, he want to move from here, too. I say, "You can move *ma* I don't move anymore. Me, I stay here because if you don't work, I could make my living." Because I was work for five dollars a day. Washing floors, washing clothes, wash ceiling, wash windows, all over around here.

CHAPTER

7

Burying a Fire:
The Cherry Mine Disaster

WHERE IN THE COLLECTIVE memory bank does a community store outrage, shock, and grief? Does the tragedy occur, only to have the memory
shrouded in black, buried and sealed in a tomb, recalled only when
citizens stumble upon the grave? Or, instead, does it have its own life,
remembered, paraded out in conversation like other memories — the
end of a war, the meal at a wedding, a particularly effective practical
joke?

My grandmother recalls when a certain letter arrived in Italy from
Texas. Her uncle, a miner in Texas, was shot, had been killed in a
barroom brawl. Relatives and neighbors streamed from their houses
to the home of the uncle. There was uncontrolled wailing and sobbing.
What does this child of seven do with this idea of the death of a man
in another world called Texas? If private disasters like this one live on
in memory, what becomes of the tragedies of a community? Emotions,
after all, do not stop at the county line.

In 1909, in Cherry, Illinois, a fire swept through a coal mine, killing
259 men. The Cherry mine had been considered one of the safest mines
in the country. The disaster, started when a lantern ignited a bale of
hay, still warrants mention in almanacs.

Like news of the death in the tavern, the message of tragedy left
town, county, and country, and traveled to stone houses, ambushing
the inhabitants left behind by men who had come to work in America.
Did the families of these men, from little impoverished villages all over
the European continent, stream out of their houses, wailing and sobbing
in shock over a disaster at a place called Cherry?

Nor is the Cherry mine disaster the only mine disaster in the memory
of Highwood's immigrants. The explosion in Centralia, Illinois, in 1947
that killed 111 took the lives of miners with relatives in Highwood.

And years before that, in 1913, in an explosion in Dawson, New Mexico, 259 miners were killed, seventeen from one town alone in the Modenese Frignano—Fiumalbo. There, on the border of Colorado, at the foot of mountains among lizards and dust, are buried men with names of the Frignano and names of Highwood: Luigi Biondi, Federico Brugioni, Giovanni Brugioni, Giuseppe Lauderini, Beniamino Santi, Carlo Santi, Domenico Santi, Egisto Santi, Geremia Santi, Luigi Santi, Pacifico Santi.

These disasters could not be left behind like a piece of ratty furniture discarded on a curb. It came with the immigrants and remained part of communal memory.

Louie Bernardi, the mechanic with his brother's ladder, recalled the Cherry mine disaster of 1909:

In the vicinity of Spring Valley, it was a new mine that caught fire, it was very few that got saved. About three hundred in that mine. Three hundred men. The mine caught fire and at that time I guess they didn't have enough prepared for that. They didn't expect that. So the fire began to grow too strong. That was in a little town called Cherry.

At the time that that happened, I was in Rockford. I had left the mine because our mine was shut down. No contract. And this other mine, Cherry, was working under a different company and I guess they had a contract, but they lost more than the contract.

Josephine Fiore was a child of ten when the fire occurred:

The news was all over. Everybody was getting those streetcars, they were packed. Just packed.

Everybody was going to Cherry. When we got there, we could see the ladies trying to throw theirselves in, you know, into the mine. So they put a stone there because they didn't want the poor ladies committing suicide.

Some, they have intuition that same morning. They kissed when they never did before. Husband and wife. Yeah, they had an intuition. Some of them didn't go to work.

At the graveyard you can see on the tombstones, the name of a young boy, the first time he went down, the mother didn't want him to go work in the coal mine and the father thought he'd take him. He gets killed there. The mother, the poor lady, never forgive that man, because he took his son to work that morning.

Several days after it began, the fire still raged and the mine, owned by the St. Paul Coal Company, was sealed up. The escape route was blocked by fire. An entire group of rescuers, lowered into the mine, was killed when the cage was consumed by fire.

The newspapers of the day carried the story on their front pages. The *New York Times* reported:

> The entrance to the mine has been sealed up in the hope of checking the flames. The building above the pit entrance was blown up to permit this. Despite the frantic efforts of the officials and the scores of volunteer assistants in the little town of Cherry it seems assured at 6 o'clock that only bodies of the dead would be taken from the mine.

Italian-language papers responded in outrage. *Il Proletario,* the newspaper of the Industrial Workers of the World, wrote ten days after the fire began:

> An immense grave is burning.
> A devouring flame consumes hundreds and hundreds of victims of bourgeois cupidity. Flesh and bone and fire and stone are one mass, horribly kneaded in a deep underground burning furnace. . . .
> Our civilization is in a hurry and cannot look after the fallen. . . . It cannot stop to dry the tears of the orphans. It cannot shed one tear on the deceased.
> As for the living, the superstitious grease with your blood the screeching wheel of the machine of capitalism that proceeds triumphal. Your sons are the human machine that will move, again, the gigantic machines of steel that produce the wealth and the joy of our employers.
> Tomorrow, in ten days, in one month, other arms will go and dig the coal in the mine where you died.

La Parola dei Socialisti, reporting from Chicago, wrote on November 27:

> One more time the men who descend into the bowels of the earth to dig riches were swallowed by the earth.
> History says with exactness how many soldiers die on the battlefield in defense of the flag of a lord; no one will be able to ever say how many men die in the dark, subterranean tunnels in defense of the pockets of the same lord.
> Always the same servants who die for the same bosses. . . .

Maria Manfredini, a young married woman at the time, was living in Ladd. She recalled:

I was living in a house where we had two rooms and the little old lady, her husband was working in Cherry. He come up from there.

Oh, but that was a disaster. And we went down, you know, we walked to Cherry. They put them in the casket, these people that was burned and they couldn't do nothing much. There was five or six caskets piling up when they start to take them out. To stop the fire, they have to close the mine. The miners couldn't come out any more. But you have to imagine and you have to see, it was something terrible.

Later, her husband worked in the Cherry mine when they reopened it.

The flukes of family history can be remembered too. Rosa Fiocchi, whose grade book is in order, said:

My father and I went the next day, but there was an explosion, and some of the rescuers were roasted in the cage that lifted the men up. My uncle and my great uncle were both working there in Cherry. But one had a cold that day and one had a cave-in in his place. When that happened the company men would come clean it out before they go back to work. So they happened to not be working.

Riccardo Zanarini, whose wife and children eventually moved to Highwood, was also saved by a fluke, in this case an oversight—he had forgotten his admittance badge at home and was not allowed to enter the mine that day.

Others were not so fortuante. Mary Baldi, who knows they check on her, not the dog, lost an uncle, John Compasso, in the disaster. She said: "I remember that day, because my mother was just hysterical. You know, he was her only brother and they had four children. I don't think my aunt lived long after that."

After eight days, twenty-one men emerged from the mine alive. They had been saved by retreating in the mine away from the fire. Two of the men who were among the rescued had relatives who settled in Highwood—Joe Pigati and Riccardo Zanarini's brother, Francesco, who, like his brother was born in Tellicardo in the Modenese Apennines.

Pigati was trapped in the mine with his brother Salvatore, whose wife, Linda, had been already left a widow when her first husband was killed in a mining accident. She eventually settled in Highwood where she owned the Del Rio Restaurant.

Accounts of the ordeal appeared in the Chicago newspaper *L'Italia* on November 27. Joe Pigati's account included a letter he wrote to his wife:

It is the fifth day that we are down here. I think so, but I'm not sure because the watches stopped working a while ago.

I am writing in the dark, because we already ate all the wax that was in our safety caps.

I also ate a handful of tobacco, tree bark and some parts of our shoes. Really, though, we could only chew it.

I hope you will see this letter. I am not afraid of death. Oh! Blessed Virgin, have pity on me.

I believe that my hour is at hand. You know the possessions I have. We worked together for it. It is all yours. This is my will and you must respect it.

You were a good wife. May the Blessed Virgin protect us always. I hope that this letter will fall into your hands and will tie you to me.

Here it is very quiet. I am grateful that I am with my companions. Goodbye until the sky is reunited again.

Joe Pigato [sic]

Frank Zanarini told reporters:

As soon as we discovered the fire and saw that we had no more hope of getting out, we retreated to a place where we could try to find water. . . . We didn't understand exactly how serious our situation was. In fact, a bunch of us started to joke, complaining that we didn't have a deck of cards.

Zanarini's work partner, Antenore Quartaroli, wrote an account of the ordeal. Born in Poretta, Bologna, Quartaroli wrote: "If some errors are found, it is because I am but a simple laborer and not a novelist. I assure you, I have written only the truth."

Quartaroli's account is dominated by the group's attempt to escape the methane gas, or black damp, and their attempt to find water. In order to find pure air, the miners retreated deeper into the mine. On the fourth day, Quartaroli wrote, the miners decided to build a wall to block out the lethal gas. They had been so weakened that they took turns working for short periods of time. For water, the miners dug into the side of the mines. The water they found was dirty. "Anyone who has never suffered thirst cannot understand how insupportable it is," he wrote.

By the sixth day, according to Quartaroli, Salvatore Pigati was the only man who had a working watch: "Salvatore Pigati, every once in awhile, was disturbed by someone to ask him what time it was. How could he tell the time in the dark? Salvatore removed the glass and feeling with his fingers would approximately tell the time."

The men were forced to choose between staying in a safe place with relatively pure air where they were dying of thirst, or going in search of water at the risk of breathing bad air.

Joe Pigati, Quartaroli wrote, "always insisted that it was better to die quickly by black damp, than to suffer as we were doing." So on the seventh day, the Pigati brothers left the rest of the group to search for water, carrying a lunch pail to hold whatever water they might find. The next day another group, including Quartaroli and Francesco Zanarini, went out to search for water. During their search for water, the trapped miners encountered workmen near an escape shaft. Had it not been for Pigati, Quartaroli wrote, the men never would have left to search for water.

Like the other survivors, Salvatore Pigati was awarded several hundred dollars in compensation by the company. With that money, he bought land. He farmed the land, which yielded little, and later he died of gangrene. His widow came to Highwood.

8

"Working for Some Rich People"

THE MINERS WHO CAME to Highwood left behind shafts, caps with carbide, and cavernous workplaces. They left towns that looked like industrial scars on the prairie and communities vulnerable to one mercurial industry. When they came up to Highwood they must have blinked, as they probably had when first facing the light after emerging from underground. All around Highwood the wealth was dazzling.

Highwood's links to Chicago's affluent and to the business interests of the city were forged early when Highwood grew because of its proximity to Fort Sheridan, a U.S. Army base bordering Highwood on the north. The fort was built after the Haymarket conflict of 1886, which came on the heels of citywide strikes for an eight-hour day at the McCormick reaper factory, at Pullman City, and at the meat-packing companies. A bomb thrown into a crowd of a thousand gathered for a mass meeting at Chicago's Haymarket Square killed seven police officers and eleven others. More than one hundred people were injured. Businessmen of the Commercial Club of Chicago, some of whom resided on the North Shore, feared revolution. They donated land to build the federal military post to protect their interests. Highwood has always been a minor stockholder in their investment.

From the turn of the century, the towns along Lake Michigan on the North Shore of Chicago grew from farms and countryside into the permanent homes of the wealthy, the people who energized Chicago's business. The North Shore's money has always been Chicago's money. Chicago was the city that worked, the city that moved, the hub of the nation. Its business has been the future—corn, wheat, cattle, hogs, railroads, machinery, steel, meat, stocks, bonds, building. The movers of merchandise sought refuge outside the city. At first they came to the North Shore temporarily, to spend a weekend or summer in the country.

In an article from September 9, 1920, *The Highland Park Press* predicted the growth of Chicago's North Shore suburbs: "If we could look forward to the next 25 years we would probably see the entire North Shore containing more splendid residential palaces, and country homes and estates, than any other portion of the United States."

This growth, the newspaper accurately foretold, would be based on the lush beauty of the area and the proximity to Lake Michigan—and the desire of affluent Chicagoans to leave the city. The paper assessed the city's handicap in attracting and keeping its wealthy in this way: "Chicago's great south side is put out of the running as far as residences are concerned on account of its manufacturing area; and again the dark cloud caused by the colored population. . . ."

"We cannot conceive a safer or better estate for rich men," the article concluded in its praise for Highland Park.

North Shore communities experienced tremendous growth during the nation's economic explosion of the 1920s. During that decade, Lake Forest grew from 3,657 to 6,554 people, Highland Park from 6,167 to 12,203, and Winnetka from 6,694 to 12,166.

Highwood, which would eventually grow into a prosperous laborers' town, more than doubled its population during this period, rising from 1,446 to 3,590. It was then that the Italians came in significant numbers to work on the North Shore. They came initially, as so many immigrants have told me, to "work for some rich people."

The first jobs which Italians took on the North Shore included work on estates, country clubs, and railroad lines. Highwood's Italians worked on the Lake Forest estates of Harold McCormick and Cyrus McCormick, Jr. Later, others worked for powerhouses in the Chicago business world, including Stanley Harris of the Harris Bank and Trust; A. B. Dick, Jr.; General Robert E. Wood, chairman of Sears and Roebuck; utilities czar Samuel Insull; advertising executive Albert Lasker; and the Swift and Armour families.

Country clubs on Chicago's North Shore—most built before World War I—were early magnets drawing immigrant laborers to the North Shore. The oldest clubs of the surrounding communities, including Onwentsia in Lake Forest, Exmoor in Highland Park, and Skokie Country Club in Glencoe, were founded before the turn of the century. In the years surrounding World War I, new country clubs serving various sectors of the growing affluent communities sprang up along the North Shore. The construction and maintenance of these new clubs offered seasonal employment to hundreds of immigrants. This included the establishment of Lake Shore Country Club in Glencoe in 1908, Indian Hill Country Club in Winnetka in 1915, and Shoreacres Club in Lake Bluff in 1916.

Highwood's Italians were among the first laborers to break ground and build the golf course at the Old Elm Club, built on the border of Lake Forest in 1913. The club was formed as a golf club "with a special view of accommodating mature men of affairs who have time to enjoy the sport," according to a local news report announcing its opening.

As historian Michael Ebner argues, these lakefront communities were developing their own ethos, their own sense of community built according to standards of wealth and beauty. In a 1913 newspaper ad, the local association of greenhouse businesses and landscapers wrote of this beautifying renaissance: "There are but few localities in the great middle west where there has been more activity shown in the way of beautifying the surroundings of homes than along the North Shore where we live—not only is this true of the large estates but it got hold of the man with the 50 foot lot. It's in the air and we are, all of us, the better for it and those following us will benefit still more—a result of the 'Zeitzeist' [sic]."

The growing affluent communities required servants and laborers. There were country clubs to be maintained and roads to be constructed. Skilled construction workers and gardeners were in demand by homeowners. Houses needed to be cleaned. Shirts had to be laundered and pressed. Limousines needed chauffeurs. Diners needed cooks. Highwood's Italians were not the only people serving the wealthy on Chicago's North Shore, but Highwood's livelihood depended on the wealthy needing service.

By the early 1920s, Italian-owned businesses were able to take advantage of this growth. In 1920 Highwood resident Charles Fiore, who hired many immigrants in his landscaping and nursery business, ran this newspaper ad: "Have you Traveled in Italy? I am prepared to draw plans for your garden and grounds after the Italian style, and will be glad to talk over such plans with the owners of North Shore property. I handle the work either on a time basis or by contract. No job is too small to have my attention; still I am prepared to handle contracts running into thousands of dollars."

Italian laborers also made their presence felt in the construction trades. Many immigrant men, especially those from the mountain towns of Modena and Bologna, had worked as stonemasons or stonecutters in Italy. By 1920, ads placed by Italian contractors began appearing in the local newspaper, such as those of cement contractor Sante Tazioli, who advertised: "I do an honest day's work at very reasonable prices."

Construction laborers worked as general laborers, stonemasons, bricklayers, plasterers, cement finishers, and carpenters. They worked on homes, schools, and public buildings, including the Morton Wing of the Art Institute of Chicago, the school of Holy Name Cathedral in Chicago, and the campus of Northwestern University in Evanston. When Highland Park's public library was rebuilt, more than 50 percent of the laborers employed came from Highwood and Highland Park.

Just as men found work on the North Shore, so did women. "Practically all of the Italian ladies worked," Everett Bellei recalled. They worked as maids, laundresses, cooks, seamstresses, and in dry cleaners.

The arrival of the Italian immigrants on the North Shore coincided with the move of the affluent away from elaborate Victorian households in favor of less formal arrangements. There was a constant cry by local residents of a shortage of domestic help as women chose more lucrative office and factory positions.

"Only the wealthy can keep up their domestic establishments on a pre-war basis and even they have their troubles," a local newspaper editorial said.

The Italian women, to a certain extent, helped fill that void, although they rarely became live-in domestics as their Swedish and Irish predecessors had. They tended to work for families whose wealth was newly acquired.

Not all employers were eager to hire workers from the newest immigrant groups, as local ads reveal. In 1913, a manufacturer in nearby Libertyville advertised: "GIRLS WANTED—for putting up Fould's macaroni and spaghetti packages, piecework paying from $7.50 to $10.00 per week. Only American girls employed." Or: "WANTED— By the day. Protestant girl to help with two children."

Indeed, the immigrants found themselves arriving on the affluent North Shore during a period of intense nativism in the United States. The suspicion with which the newcomers were viewed is suggested in a guest editorial by Congressman Charles M. Thomson in the February 18, 1915, issue of the *Highland Park Press*. Writing about a proposed literary test to control immigration, Thomson said, "Have we reached the time in our history when we should adopt some means of controlling the flood in immigration coming to us from across the seas: I think we have."

He continued: "Earlier in the history of this country those who came to our shores were from the north of Europe for the most part, Norway, Sweden, Germany, Ireland, Scotland and so on. They came in comparatively few numbers. Our nation awaited development. There was an abundance of room even in our centers of population. . . . Today the immigrants are coming in veritable hordes, or they were before the war and probably will after it is over. They are coming not from the north but from the south of Europe. . . . In justice to them, without regard to ourselves, it would seem that we ought to in some way stay this wild rush of people. . . ."

One business that employed Italian and Eastern European immigrants was the Moraine Hotel, an elegant establishment in Highland Park that once overlooked Lake Michigan. Sante Pasquesi was one of the first Italians hired there, following his employment at the Gonnella Bakery in Chicago. In his memoirs, he wrote: "The hotel catered to a high-class people and, especially in summertime, the grounds had to look their best." A column called "Moraine Notes" regularly listed the hotel's guests in the *Highland Park Press*. An entry from June 6, 1921, named I. F. Merceles, president of Montgomery Ward and Company; Mrs. Montgomery Ward; and Arthur Reynolds, president of the Continental and Commercial National Bank of Chicago.

The attraction to the North Shore for the Italian immigrants was work—and if there was work anywhere, it was here in these lakefront communities.

Working on the Estates

Tony Casorio, who planted roses from seed:

From Chicago, my stepfather, he came to Highwood, you know. He worked on the track on the railroad. Building it. Working on the stone, the ties. Because all the machinery at that time was all hand work. He had some friend in Highwood, come to Highwood to work on the Northwestern railroad, and he was living and working with Frank Nustra's father. He came here 1910, something like that.

Then I came this country. Chicago. I wasn't sixteen yet, you know, see, so I had to be sponsored and came right to Chicago. And my stepfather come right up and meet me at the Northwestern depot.

There was a friend of my father's who was working for McCormick, and he told me, "Tony, at McCormick, they're looking for boys to pick up the dandelions." You know, I was a gardener over in Naples, in a big park, right by the ocean. So I went up to see and I got a job there picking dandelions.

And he take me away from dandelions and put me in the garden, see? He give me a bunch of cabbage and a shovel. So I planted those cabbage, and he hit me on the shoulder and says, "You gonna stay right in the garden." I'm going up, up all the time.

And then 1917, when the registration for the army come out, I was working for McCormick and I went over and registered in Libertyville. So I worked for McCormick from '12 to '28, except of course those two year I was away in the army.

When I got married, 1921, McCormick sent limousine here to take me to the church. Limousine and a chauffeur, big machine you know. With the chauffeur he wait right outside until we get married then he pick me up and take me back. Then before I got married, they had a big party on the place, a very big party, you know, and invite all the people, maids and people who worked in the house, maids, so many in the house, so many rich people there, you know. And invite all the people and had a big party. About two hundred people. There was two machines, two cars, loaded with the gifts when they took me out. This was why I didn't like to leave McCormick.

I want to show you the pictures. This picture was taken up at McCormick in the garden, 1921, on August 26. We got married August 27. That's all subdivided now. It was a beautiful place. Great big man, you know. Her, too. You know, that's the Harvester company. Oh, they was nice people, the two of 'em. Wonderful people.

But 1928, this Charlie Fiore was after me just like that. Oh, I was good on those things, you know, and he had just bought a little land, he was landscaping a little, and he wanted to put up a nursery. And he was after me just like anything. He was a good friend of mine. And I said, "Charlie, I can't help you because I wouldn't leave McCormick."

But this Charlie Fiore was so after me and he offered me good money, you know, over there I was getting $160 a month and then he offered me $55 dollars a week. "Oh my," I says. That was good money then. And I had the kids, of course, and then I told the superintendent, I says, you know, "So and so and so, and I want the more experience, I want to learn the plants. I want to learn how to propagate." Then 1928, when I start, Charlie Fiore and I'm working and everything's alright and then Depression came.

From fifty-five dollars, we got cut to twenty-five dollars. In 1932 or '33. They cut it down, little by little. And '35 the things, they kinda picked up and I ask Charlie Fiore, I says, "Charlie," I says, "everything going up again, you know. I gotta have some more money, you know, everything's going up. Food is going up. And I gotta big family." I had five kids, you know. I says, "I need more money. I need a little more money." Because, and then, I see the business doing pretty good now. And he said, "Oh, the business is no good, this and that, still Depression."

Well, I says, "My golly, I see that things have been alright." I said, "They look pretty good, and now I need a little more money, that's all," I says. Shake hands with him, I say that I'm going to start tomorrow looking for a job.

And this friend of mine happened to go up to Fiore nursery, looking for me. Matthew, a Scotch man, we know each other through the American Garden Association, you know, it's got all the gardeners on the North Shore. So he's the one who got the job for me in Harris, the Harris Bank—the people had a big place, three-acres place.

And as soon as my friend got home he call me up. He says to me, "Harris, they look for the gardener." Next day, I went up there and I had a job. After I got the job, Charlie Fiore want to give me what I want and more. I says to Charlie, I says, "Please," I says, "I'm going to try those people. I got a job there. You know I hate to leave. If I don't like, I'm going up to work for you." So from 1935 up to '74, I worked for the Harris. Long time.

Nice people, you know. Every morning, I had to go upstairs to ask them if they wanted anything. Flower and vegetables. And it didn't make a difference how she was dressed, she say, "Come in." Because when I was halfway, I called up, "Mrs. Harris, it's Tony, can I come in?" She say, "Come in." Just like one in the family. Boy, they was nice people. He was nice, a nice man, too.

They wanted to fix up the place. "Well, you can't do it all at once," I says. So little by little, we got the place fix it up. Oh, they had a beautiful place.

I was the only Italian but when I needed a hand I used to hire some of those Italians, boys. Sometimes, I had my son, my brother-in-law, you know. Somebody else from Highwood, you know. I used to have some Italians working on Saturday, sometimes twice a week, sometimes three times a week. I used to have two man, three man, help me, Italian, always Italian, that's all you get in Highwood, was just Italians, very few Sweden, and that's all. But of course the Sweden, they had a different little jobs, carpentry work and that's all.

When my wife come here, she got a little job up in the country club down here, Exmoor, washing. And then after a little while she got sick. Two weeks. Then she was taking care of the kids. That's all I want her to do. I don't want her to do any work. Take care of the house. Take care of the kids. And that's all. And I, Casorio, done all the work, whatever I could do, just to get along.

I always had a job. I never been out of the work.

Louie Bernardi, the mechanic with his brother's ladder:

I went back to the mines one winter and then in April the mine closed again and I came to Highwood and I'm still here.

I was here in Highwood in 1910, and then I went back to the mine and then to Rockford. When I came back the last time here to Highwood in 1911, I knew a family in Highland Park, the Lencioni. And I called him. And Lencioni said he'd get in touch with a fella named Pietro that was working at McCormick, see. By golly, I gotta place working in Lake Forest for McCormick doing landscaping work.

So, I put two years up there, that was 1912 to '14. I worked for McCormick. One is Cyrus, one is Harold McCormick, and I worked for both of them.

The first year I worked for Cyrus. When they didn't need no help up there I went back to the mine. The mine was shut down again in April, so I came back here. And well, the superintendent was really nice, he said, "Louie," he said, "You shoulda wrote me a card to tell me you were coming. But anyhow, I'll get you a job." And he did. He took me over to the superintendent that was working for Harold. I worked for a year for Harold. So I worked two years for the two McCormick brothers. Of course, the people at the time were so busy, you didn't hardly see them. You had to do work through the superintendent.

I worked in the garden, doing everything. Sometimes helping the chauffeur. In the summer or the fall of 1915, the company sent over from England a truck. The chauffeur was supposed to drive it. But he was downtown in Chicago all the time, taking the people there. So the superintendent called me and asked me what information I had in the mechanical field.

"Well," I said, "Not much, but at home I used to fix the wagon!" And he said, "I'll tell you what. There's a place in Chicago where there are two Italians, they had opened a school, mechanical school." And by God, the superintendent he had me going through. I was going three days a week for a half a day. So I used to go to work up there in the morning and at noontime, I catch the streetcar to Chicago and go to school. On Racine. And so, I used to take two half a days off on the job but the superintendent, he paid me just the same. And I used to go on Sunday afternoon.

I learned how to drive and learned all about the parts. Of course, the drivers weren't there all the time, and when they weren't there they used to put somebody in charge. But the two fellas, DiPalma and DeOresta, they were two champions in racing cars.

So I went for three months, those three and a half days a week. Well, I learned enough to get my diploma.

When the chauffeur wasn't there, somebody had to drive the truck, that little truck, one cylinder motor, and you opened up, the old style. Well, anywho, the superintendent sent me back to school so in case he needed somebody to handle that truck, he'd have them there handy. After I got that diploma, I stayed there with him for a while.

Then I got a offer in Winnetka. Winnetka Garage. And I went down there just for curiosity. I had a little idea in the mechanical field. So, by gosh, his name was Brandt, German people, and he said, "By gosh," he said, "we need a fella like you."

That's the time I showed him the diploma, see, and when he see that I could drive, that was enough. Well, anyhow, the old man Brandt said, "Well, come down. You get board and room here too."

Can you beat that? So I went back, I had told the superintendent just what I had down there. I says, "They opened up a garage in Winnetka and by God that would be my line."

And he said, "Go ahead. Go ahead and if you need a job, just let me know. I'll help."

The old man Brandt didn't have cars but he had horses to go the station, taxi, to go the station and meet the people. That was his business. But I was the only one out of the old man and the other two fellas that could drive a car! Right away, after I started working there, they bought a car. The old man, he sent his son to Detroit and bought two Model-T Ford taxi cab, the small car but seven passenger—they had a foldover seat in the back there. They used to call them seven—passenger. And we went and took the people getting off the train.

The car was electric. At the time they had the electric plant right next to where the Brandt building was up. North Linden Avenue. The place where they recharged the battery. So, oh, there was nothing to it. Just showed me once and then I took care of myself. In that car you got seven button, you start in first gear and you go up as high as six. And then reverse is a different button. And the first car didn't come out with the steering wheel, they came out with that later. They just had a stick to steer.

I worked for two years for Brandt. Well, the passengers were whoever we could catch at the station. At first nobody wanted a ride. They were waiting for the old man to come back with horse and buggy. Finally, they were convinced that they were safe.

Of course, after a while the people begin to buy cars, but when I got down there, hardly nobody had a car. They waited for the chauffeur or the taxi driver.

Oh boy, I'll tell you, I may not gain a lot in my life, but lot of experience, though.

Julio Brugioni, whose coal-blackened face frightened his daughter:

I was working in Chicago and an old man, he asked me where I was working. And he said, "Why don't you work north?" I said, "What north?" He said, "Way up by Highland Park. They got a lot of work up there. They got a lot of Italians up there."

So 1924 I came up to Highwood. During the summer months. I came up before Easter because the work didn't start before. In the coal mine, you know where you work every day, but here, if you work for a contractor, it's one day here, then from here maybe you go to Lake Bluff, from Lake Bluff maybe you go to Ravinia. You had to have your shoes, your clothes ready. Them days you had to use streetcars. And walk. If the streetcar was close, that's all right, but if you went out west where there was no streetcar, you had to walk. You have to get up in the morning, four o'clock, get a little coffee and go. At seven you have to be there. I walked miles and miles and miles and miles. And at night, the same, coming home.

First job, I went with Boilini, a contractor from Highland Park. Making a big home out west. He used to come up to Highwood and get the men. I didn't work there long. He had a Model-T truck, then he used to pick us up in Highwood.

Yeah, it was the Italians who worked with stone. There was no others. The Americans didn't want to. And them days, it ain't like now. Now it's easy, anybody, even I, can do it. They bring the stone already nice and cut. All you have to do is take the stone and lay it. Them days, the stones, you had to come down from the top and chisel it yourself, square it yourself. Now they have everything cut up. It's easy to make a wall. Any damned fool can do it. Pieve had quite a few stonemasons and Sant'Anna and Fiumalbo. They used to call them *scarplini*. You take a chunk of stone, chisel it. All with points and hammer, ting, k-ting, k-ting, k-ting. They could make a frame, a chimney. They used to make door frames even. Instead of making the frame out of wood, they made them out of stone. And above the fireplace, they can make angels on there, they can make women—they were like sculptors. They got to know what they're doing because a little nick that you miss, you break it. Not everyone

can do it. It's just like if you make pictures. You have to be born for
that purpose.

Well, when I went up to some of these towns, I said right away,
that's where the money's at, yeah, but they figure they don't want
to give you the money. What they give you, four and a half, the
most, five dollars a day. And nine hours of work. They didn't want
eight hours. You know what I mean? Nine hours of work for four
and a half, five dollars a day. They had plenty of work but they
didn't want to pay you them days. And working on the construction, they pushed you. "Hey! Hey! Hey! Get on work!" If you
would drink too much water, they call you, "Hey! You drink too
much water. You lose so much time!"

And then, if it was raining and if you was working outside for
the millionaires, they send you home. If you work an hour or two,
what the hell you get? You don't make enough money to go back
and forth. You couldn't count on it. While in the mine you could
count on it. And then, to work outside here, in the wintertime! Jesus
Christ, twenty-five below zero. You know it's hard to put a man
through. Stay out all day, twenty-five below zero. You understand?
But I done it. Many times. Twenty-five below zero, you feel it.

I used to get off Saturday and Sunday, and I'd go work. Church?
Well, sometimes. But church in them days, I said, I better make a
few dollars. Because the church, I seen how many times I went, but
they never give me nothing. They want something but they won't
give you nothing. So, you know if I'm hungry and I go over to
church—but if I got a dollar it's different. So you gotta be smart.
Because the priest, he's nice and fat, so I like to be nice and fat
myself.

I worked in construction and I got out of that, too. And then I
went to a place up here in Lake Forest. There were lots of Italians
going to work up there in Lake Forest. Like Guido Paglai worked for
the Armours.

I worked right close to the graveyard of Lake Forest. I was the
second man there for a hell of a long time. We had a greenhouse
and seventeen acres. There was the son and the mother. The mother
had the house by the lake and the son had the mansion on his
other side. We used to take care of both houses. Mrs. Dexter Cummings. She was good, the old lady. So nice.

"Do what you think," she told me. I used to say, "I spend you
too much money. I have to buy too much stuff." She said, "If you
need it, it's okay." Bulbs, you know tulips and all of that, they're
high. The bill would come in, would be four, five hundred, a thou-

sand dollars. She used to come out and say, "Sit down, Julio. You work too hard. Sit down, sit down." "I've got to go, Mrs. Cummings, I've got a lot of work to do." "Sit down."

When you go through Greenbay Road in Lake Forest, it's nothing but multimillionaires. Homes that, Jesus Christ, you could put in fifty people and there's only one or two living there. And some people ain't got a place to sleep. You think they give you a basement, when they've got a basement long from here to there that they could put a train road in? It's empty. Why? So much for you and none for the poor.

It's like I was telling a guy that used to work with me. He was working on Greenbay Road and the big boss died, they didn't want him no more, not even the chauffeur, and they done away with the greenhouse, they done away with everything. So he came and worked with me. So I asked him, "He passed away, what did he leave you?" "Oh," he said, "that son of a gun, I've been working for him eight or ten years and he left me fifty dollars. And the chauffeur was there only a year, and he left him $25,000." "That's okay," I say, "who would you like to be, you or them others?" All day long, I kept it on, and he said finally, "If you don't quit asking me that question all the time. I'm gonna quit." I said, "Listen here, if you'd a been them others, you'da got $25,000 but being that you wanted to be you, you have fifty dollars." "By God, your right," he says, "it pays to be the others sometimes."

That's like me, if I would be Dexter, I would lay there in bed. Don't have to get up. Because I'm Dexter and I'm not you. I'm the others. But as long as it's me I'll have to run.

Working *nel golf*—at the Golf Courses

Domenico Lattanzi, who turned down Seven-Up, saying, "You drink. I gotta talk."

My father was already here working in Lake Shore Country Club, south of Ravinia Park, right on the lake down there. They start working there when they cut all the timber—was all woods in there. He was most of the time in Glencoe, then he moved to Spring Valley with the coal mine. He and his brother were in Glencoe, and in the wintertime they go over there in the coal mine.

When they started to build the golf, my father worked in there. My father says it was all oak trees and they cut a lotta oak trees, and by hands, you know, about forty, fifty men, thirty men, all by hands. They burned up all the stumps. Those days, no machine. They had horses. My father says in those days there was an Indian trail, you know, through the middle of the golf course. The Indians had pushed a lot of branches to make way for the paths to Lake Michigan.

My father was one of the first working there. And three or four from Highwood. One cut the grass with the horse. They had the pull-horses, you know. I made the bunkers, cut the grass, clean up for a couple of months in the spring, one month in the fall.

I worked on the tracks of the North Shore Line with another uncle. It was very good work. Then I came in the spare time in the spring and fall, I got the job over here at Lake Shore golf club. When I was seventeen.

In the wintertime you know how it is, not much job. Those days, no working outside. Now they got a chemical for the cement, for not freezing. Those days, they close up the road, they close up the golf, too. That's why a lot of men, coal miners from Iowa those days, Spring Valley, Illinois, you know, they went back and forth in the wintertime, then summertime they find road work, this and that.

I lived in Highwood twenty-eight days. My father, he says, "Maybe it would spoil my son to stay in Highwood." Those days it was bad up there. A lot of soldiers around. Some fooling, fooling houses those days, but he knows maybe, you know what I mean? He says maybe it would spoil me. Wild woman.

He was living down there in Glencoe because it was more easy to go to Lake Shore golf club. And walking, you don't have to spend five cents for the streetcar.

My father was the head. I stayed under his power. When I was working, I give all the money to him. I kept just the loose money. If I had a $1.99, I take 99 cents. If I had $20.99, he take $20. I got the small change.

When the people play golf, you stop work and don't make noise. And this guy passed down, he was Italian. He talk Italian to us. "Buongiorno. Come vai?" "Good morning. How are you?" You know. He got the pronounce like north Italy. His wife, too, sometime, stop, just to say hello. The boss says he's got a factory in Torino, a Borsalino factory, Italian born, but a Jew, you know. Down there in Lake Shore Country Club it was all Jews, you know.

I worked there quite a few years, I worked in the spring and the fall. I came in 1913, I started in the spring. I helped do the bunkers. Patch up the tee. Seed. They had the place where they grow the sod inside the golf course. Every year, you had to cut the sod with a hack ax. You go in the tee, go on the green, and replace the sod.

In the spring there is lot to do. They had a pile of black dirt in the back of the barn. You know, Menoni and Mocogni, they had the building materials company? Well, before Menoni had the horse, he delivered the black dirt, and we had to screen that dirt, nice. All the dirt was put on the green so often, on the tees so often, especially the green every two or three days. All fine. Then with a rake upside down, wood rake back and forth over the grass, it goes in, you know, the green.

In the spring we put sand in the bunkers. An open train car from the Northwestern, it stopped right in back of the barn. They called it Braeside Station, right in the back of the barn. There was a horse and a wagon. Then you come along the side of the course on a little road, and we wheeled the dirt to the course. Those days they didn't have soft tires like now. They used to cut the old hoses and put it around the wheelbarrow wheel with a wire, so it didn't damage in the course.

When I came I was a greenhorn. I didn't understand much. I couldn't understand what the boss says. One time, when I started to work there, he told me, "You go in the barn and get the blanket."

So I went in the barn and I take a blanket they put on top of the horses. And I brought back a blanket. Everybody laughed. The boss, he says, "What do you laugh for? He make mistake." I had to walk all over the course to the north end to get what he wanted—a "plank."

In the morning, especially in the summertime, a lot of times we play golf. In the morning before we started working. At three or four o'clock we go up there and play.

The boss give us the clubs. The members give it to him, and him, he takes the best but he gives us some. I was like to play golf. All the gang come from Highwood, just me and my father from Glencoe.

I suppose the members were pretty rich. You know what I heard one time? In Chicago, the business district had two stores, one close to another, and the boss told us, "Watch out, today's tournament they're going to play, today and tomorrow, and those two Jews bet the store."

I suppose the members worked in Chicago, because I remember we had the Northwestern train station down there, and before they don't make a stop. After they finish the golf course, they make a stop for the train for the members. When the train come, a man

from the clubhouse would go down with two white horses and a
buggy to wait for the train, to see if there's some member. Then it
ended because everybody used cars. Too much expense.

Adelmo Bertucci, dean of Chicago-area golf course superintendents
and an accomplished accordionist:

I worked before at Old Elm before they opened the club in 1913.
I worked on the foundation, the locker room, the basement. And
then in 1915 I got the job foreman and then I was going up to superintendent. I got to direct all the work. I got all the men to take
care of.

When we started we had about twenty-two men, then we went
down to fourteen laborers. Then come the machinery. And the machinery take care of another couple of men. They close the job.

In the summer you got to sprinkle to keep the grass green, green
tee. And besides you got to fight the diseases, fungus.

I know some poor people who came from Pievepelago and I tried
to give them the job. They didn't know how to speak nothing. So I
give them the job to work until they know about the language and
so on.

Louie Bernardi, the mechanic with his brother's ladder:

I had a place, Knollwood Country Club, west of Lake Bluff. Knollwood and Old Elm, there for a number of years I was going every
winter, overhaul all the mechanisms, all the motors, the truck, the
tractor, the lawn mower. Bertucci, he was up here at Old Elm. And
up at Knollwood, it was his brother. So he was a Bertucci, too, see.

Lot of time this Bertucci, even during the season, he just said—
something small, the drivers can fix it themselves, but if it's some
difficulty, call Bernardi. I take my little truck and run up there and
fix it up. Yeah, I had orders from the superintendent and all I had
to do was send him a bill. So they know me, everybody.

No, I never had time to play golf because I had the family to take
care of, the rent—I rented the upstairs—and I took care of all my
work. I didn't have no time to play golf.

The Hotel on the Lake

From *La mia vita*, reminiscences of Sante Pasquesi:

. . . In April, 1912, I was told that at the Hotel Moraine in High-

land Park they were looking for a man to take care of the hotel
grounds. I applied for the job and was accepted for a trial period.
After a week, the administration informed me that I could stay per-
manently. The salary was good and I didn't have any expenses. It
was a good job in every resepect: short workday, free Sundays and I
was my own boss.

The hotel catered to a high-class people and, especially in summertime, the grounds had to look their best. I didn't have to work
too hard, but I tried to be very conscientious because this was the
best job I had ever had and I didn't want to lose it.

Mr. F. W. Cushing, the owner and president, who every once and
a while came to see me to tell me what he wanted done, always
praised my work. This pleased me because it meant I wasn't in danger of losing my job. My new occupation made me forget the sheep
entirely and I planned to stay for four or five years instead of only
three as I had originally planned.

Philip Pasquesi, who still asks my mother if she likes America:

My first job was at the Moraine Hotel. It was beautiful. Rich
people used to come for summer resort. They were rich people.
They were from Chicago, mostly in Chicago. All these Jews. Was
people they got the stores, big stores, downtown. They had the
whole family and they come to the Moraine Hotel in the summertime because it was too hot in Chicago. That's what they used to
do. Was pretty nice.

Over there I was a houseman. I used to do everything. People
want something down there in the room and they call me. They always wanted me. They liked me so much. You know why they like
me? I had a passkey for every room, and these people they had cigarettes all over. They had whiskey. They had jewelry. And I was
smoking then. They had everything around there. But you know
what I used to do? I never touch nothing! I used to smoke my own
cigarettes. And they had cigarettes all over. But I never touch one.
Would you know, they know it. These people they say, "We want
Philip." They didn't want nobody else in the room.

The hotel had a lotta rooms, boy. They had the main building,
and then an annex on the south side and one on the north side.
And then they had a garage, that's where the help used to sleep. I
used to sleep on the main building. Right on the fourth floor. I used
to go and take a shower every night. Jesus. It was so beautiful at
the Moraine Hotel.

The guests had the regular apartments. They had two or three rooms, depending on the family. There was a dining room and they ate downstairs.

During the day, these people, they're businessman, they used to take the train and go down in Chicago. And the family stay up here. The family used to go down to Lake Michigan. Go swimming and things like that. Oh yes. They had it pretty good.

The one that started there at the Moraine Hotel was Sante Pasquesi. And he got us all the jobs after. Mr. Cushing, the owner of the hotel, found out that we're honest people and we work, you know.

That time they didn't have no elevator. When they bring the trunks in from Chicago, you know, they come and live at the Moraine Hotel. I used to go over there, you know, these trunks, that time I was pretty strong. I got a hold of a trunk on my back and I used to walk way up on the second and third floor.

After 1929, the Depression you know, all the people lost money and they were not getting so much business. So finally I had to quit the Moraine Hotel and then I went to drive the truck for a trucking business that my cousin Sante Pasquesi and his brothers had.

Chauffeur for a Time, and a Related Story

Henry Piacenza, who heard perfectly without the distractions of rock and roll:

My father say, "You want to go to America or do you want to go and get a job here someplace?" He said they're looking for some help at Castelnuovo. But, ooh, that guy was so damned rough: "Come on, come on, hurry up, hurry up, come on, come on, come on!" I worked there two days, making the railroad bed for the track that went up into the Rhine. So I quit and said to my father, "Now we can go in America." So May 1913 I came over. I'm oldtime here in Highland Park. Seventy years, you know, it's a long time.

I worked as a laborer in the beginning. I couldn't speak the language. You had to just get what you could. Wasn't like now. There was a lot of work. There wasn't very many Italian people in Highland Park. And we "bached"—we were bachelors living together. We lived in a basement down in Highland Park. There was twelve people down in one room in the basement. I used to have to jump over the cot to go from one place to the other. Boy, what a life. I'm telling you.

I did construction work a couple of weeks but then I got laid off

because I almost killed somebody! I was bringing some bricks upstairs. You know that thing that you carry the bricks in, I had that,
they used to call it the hod. Full, about twenty or twenty-five bricks.
So when I got upstairs on the second floor, I didn't know how to
dump it easy, you know, not breaking the bricks, so geez, I let it
down. The whole damn thing went down, almost killed somebody.
Can you imagine that? But then I got called in the army.

After the war, I was working for the Dodge people after I came
out of the war—1920 to '21. But they didn't pay much. I would say
about sixty dollars a month. I was a mechanic around the garage,
you know what I mean, I did a lot of driving for them, you know.
We used to go to Detroit, pick up cars because those days, they
didn't bring them there like they do now. They had to go and get
them either in Chicago where they got a distributor or, but if she
want the special car, like, you know, some other model they didn't
have it, then I used to go there quite a bit. Back and forth from
Detroit. All kind of weather. In the wintertime. Oh Jesus.

So the boss one day, he came down and said, "Listen, boys"—he
called everyone "boy," there were about fifteen men working there.
He said "Come down in the office, I want to talk to you boys." I
kind of thought I knew, because the business wasn't so good. So he
said, "Boys, I'm sorry but I gotta let you out because you can see
yourself there ain't much business. I know it's hard to take, Jesus."
He said to me, "I know you're in the worst shape because you just
got married and you building the house and you're raising a family.
So he said, "If you want to work, I'll cut your pay down in half."
So that would be thirty dollars a month. Not even enough to feed
yourself.

Then I went to work for some rich people down here in Highland
Park. I was a gardener, a chauffeur. And they belonged to a club
down in Chicago. The University Club. We used to go down quite a
bit, either movies, opera, or something like that, you know. I used to
drive quite a bit. I never got back till twelve o'clock, one o'clock,
two o'clock, something like that. Almost twenty-four hours, you
know.

So I said to myself, well, I'll stay here as long as I can but if I
find a better job, then I'll quit. Because you can always quit, you
know. You can't get a job any time you want but you can
always quit.

Philip Pasquesi, who still asks my mother if she likes America, and
who got out of a scrape with Henry Piacenza:

My cousin Battista Pasquesi come over 1914 from Italy. Sante, his older brother, sent for him and when he got here, he sent him to school. He was lucky. School here in Highland Park. And then after that he send him to McPherson Garage and he learned how to be a mechanic. He was a very good mechanic.

Anyhow, I was working at the Moraine Hotel and we had a friend, Henry Piacenza. He was driving for a fella in Highland Park. And Henry, he was taking him to the Northwestern station with the car, you know, he had a Dodge car. And Henry used to get him at night and take him home. Henry was tending the garden and he was driving the car. So one time this guy that Henry was working for went to New York.

So Battista, you know, he called me. He said, "Philip, can you get three girls?" That time over here, it was Prohibition. It was only "blind pigs," where they sold the illegal liquor. You could not go to a saloon, nothing. So we were going over to Wheeling. You know Wheeling, it was wide open. At night to the tavern. And there was dancing, you know. We were young. You know, at that time, we didn't care. Oh geez. I was working with Polish girls. Nice girls. They were really nice. So I asked, I says, "Mary, can you get two other girls?" I says, "You be my girl, and ask two friends of yours and we're going to go up to Wheeling."

So Henry's boss was in New York and Henry was using his car. We used to go over there and dance and drink, you know, we used to spend all the money. We used to come home broke.

One night we went to Wheeling. But my cousin who worked in the garage, he wanted to drive the car. Instead of coming home from Wheeling, it was late, about one or two o'clock in the night, instead of coming straight home, he went way down to Niles Center and then from Niles Center he come up on Waukegan Road.

It was a big storm. And we met the policeman. And the policeman, they know my cousin Battista in Highland Park from working in the garage, they know him real well, and they told him, "Pasquesi, take it easy, it's a bad night." It was lightning and wind. And thundering. We come up near Techney monastery. And all of a sudden, he was going fast, he was wild driver, my cousin Battista, oh Jesus, all of a sudden, he said, "Oh my!" We went right into the storm. A big tree was right in the middle of the street and we went right in it.

He took the top off of the car. He broke the crank case, two wheels. And the car was not ours. One branch of the tree, it split my coat all the way down.

So we were there stuck on the branch of the tree with the car. So here comes the policeman. He said, "I told you Pasquesi, you should of take it easy. It's a bad night." So you know what they did? The policeman took the girls and took them home to the Moraine Hotel.

And my cousin Battista, he went to call somebody. He knocked on the door of a house, it was two o'clock in the morning. The guy come out with the gun. He said, "Get out of here!" So you know where he went and called up? He went where they got nuns and she opened the door and said, "What is it you want?" And he said, "I would like to call up Highland Park to go and get the tow truck to get us." You know what time we got in Highland Park? It was daylight.

And you know what he did? My cousin Battista, he was a mechanic, and Henry Piacenza was pretty good too around the cars, you know, and they worked day and night. We went down, there was a place in Chicago, Wisoski, where they was selling all sorts of automobile parts. So they got the wheels, we fixed the car. It took about two or three days to fix it.

Would you know, the maid, she was saying, "Where is the car?" Henry told her, "Oh, I brought it to the garage to have it greased." The car was all smashed up! So just in time the guy come from New York and even the top, you could see that the car was repaired. But this guy, he come out of the house, Henry was ready for him to bring him at the station. He always reading the paper. He got into the car, he never looked at the car. He never knew that his car was in an accident!

The Work of Women

Adele Dinelli, who sold her house, but lives there in the meanwhile:

I went all over. At eight o'clock you be in a job and four o'clock you leave the job. You was home at five o'clock. Then you got the wash, with no machine, they're all in the tub, and cook.

When my husband was sick in the hospital, there was a lady— she was *la* supervisor—said to me, you seem "*così* lonesome, you want to work?" I said, "Yeah, I want to work." She said, "Come down in the basement and I teach you to wash the laundry in Highland Park Hospital." And that first day she gave me three dollars. I was a rich lady. Three dollar. I was rich. Very rich lady. I came home, then that day forward I never suffered hungry.

Then I work for the lady, she give me the job for fourteen year.
She was big in the hospital. One of the big ones. In the winter she
was pick me up and take me. At first, she paid me five dollars a
day. Five dollars a day was pretty good, then you make a good living.

I worked all the time. I meet a lot of women where I go to work.
I got a lot of friend. I got a lot of friend around in Highwood. *Ma,*
just the same, when we go to work and when we come back, we
had no time to go visit and talk. When I don't work anymore, we
make a gang and play cards. We was about fourteen. We start with
about fourteen. Now is nobody. You know, all passed away. We
played cards about sixteen years. We play *vint'un*—twenty-one—we
play about a nickle at a time. And the money we lose, we don't
keep it, not you, no me. We put 'em in a box. And when we have
about fifteen or twenty dollars, we went out to eat together.

Mary Baldi, who knows they check on her, not the dog:

My mother lived with us. I was going to work every day and she
was taking care of my kids. When I come home, I'd find my supper
made.

I used to take in washings after coming home. It was too much
for a man. Most of the time there was no work. I remember my
husband working with me at a millionaire's home. They live on
Sheridan Road. That's one of the wealthy persons that I was telling
you about. Jewish. And he'd help me. I think they gave him about
a dollar a day. Going down there and washing windows and doing
a lot of things.

Then it would only cost ten cents to come home on the streetcar.
Well, he wouldn't take no streetcar. He'd walk. And I remember,
one day, because he told it, as he was walking, the boss's son, the
oldest son, was coming along with a car. He stopped, he said, "Mr.
Baldi, where are you going?" And he said, "I'm going home." He
says, "Well, how come you didn't take the streetcar?" He says, "I
don't have a dime." So he says, "Jump in, I'll take you home." My
husband was saving that dime, walking. It's not a very far walk. But
still, at that time a dime was a lot of money. Like I say, I was working for fifty cents a day.

At the beginning we didn't have no washing machine. I always
can remember my husband after he come home, he'd go down and
he'd help me. But then we got a Torr, that was the first one that

ever came out, I betcha. I ordered a Torr, with a wringer, and I went to work.

Sometimes I even went in two places in one day, to keep up my customers, 'cause I liked them, and I guess they liked me. They liked my work. I was a hard-working woman and I still would be right now, except I get bawled out from my daughter, "Don't do this, don't do that."

I worked in Highland Park, in Glencoe, in Ravinia, and as far as Winnetka. They mostly were Jews. And when I think of all the money they had and they were so damned cheap.

The guy that met my husband, that I told you about, he said, "How come you don't have a dime for carfare? How much does my mother pay you?" And I don't remember what it was but it was very little. He said, "You mean to tell me my mother only pays you so much? How many are in the family." And he said, "Seven." Because my mother was staying with us, four kids, and us, too. So he went home and the next morning when my husband went in she called him in the kitchen, she said, "I got good news for you. You're getting a raise."

Most all the Italian women went out doing this. I told you about Letizia Saielli, how she got her leg cut off, riding that streetcar. Her and Della Dinelli was working at the same place. Very wealthy people. They were good, hardworking girls. At that time, it was hard to get anybody and there were all these Italian immigrants from Italy, didn't know how to speak, but still they knew how to work.

Not me, there wasn't any other work I could have done. I don't know about the others. A lot of them took in sewing, they took in laundry at home, and then later on they started making lasagne, manicotti, and all that, and selling it. And I don't know, I guess that was the main thing, cleaning house and ironing and laundry.

Teresa Ponsi is watching a soap opera in the living room while I interview her husband in the dining room. At the end of my visit I talk with her for a while, too. Her mother, she says, walked like a hare, fast, with strong legs. She has *poche storie*, literally "few stories," which doesn't mean she has no stories. It means she gets to the point.

I always worked with the *signori*. Always in the houses. One job would come, then another one would come out of that one. I always worked, you know, pretty soon I'll be eighty-two years old. I worked until I was eighty-one because before I went to the hospital this summer, I worked with this *signora* who lives near the Moraine

Hotel. I went there two days a week. But now I feel better. My mother never went to school, not even to learn to write, even at seven years she began to work for the others.

(from Italian)

Teresa Saielli, who defied the priest on the feast of Santa Teresa:

When I arrived in Highwood it was bad. The toilets were outside. The first time, I cried a lot. I cried. It wasn't because of my husband, because he wasn't mean. It took a lot of courage to come, though.

I went to work at Fort Sheridan, ironing shirts with the machine. There was a laundry. They paid very bad, I think ninety dollars a month. I don't know. And then I started working in my house, ironing, sewing, washing.

To clean houses I didn't go much, but one time I went to Lake Forest. Mary Zagnoli sent me to Lake Forest. She told me they would give me four dollars. At that time there, four dollars was a lot. I had to work eight hours, nine hours. I went to clean. Two floors, the kitchen, carry out the rugs, sweep them with broom. There weren't machines at that time. Then, when I went to leave, she gave me three dollars. Maybe it didn't go well enough, so I took the three dollars, that's all. A week or two later, Mary told me that lady wanted me to come back because "you a good worker." I told her to tell that lady to clean the house herself.

(from Italian)

Delma Muzzarelli, who linked the miners' poster with Highwood:

My husband came up from Carbon Hill in April 1926. He have some friends and a cousin. He start to work, and little by little he find a job for the rich people. Then we came up from Carbon Hill in May.

Then after, I started to keep some boarders. Well, I have to do something because the girls were small, so I couldn't go to work. I had to stay home, see. Then after, little by little I get rid of the boarders when the girls start to go to school. It's a bother. They're never satisfied. They complain.

Then I started working at Skokie Valley Laundry. Oh, there was lotta, lotta, lotta, lotta Italians. Oh, there were some Americans but mostly Italian. One year I worked at North Shore Laundry in Winnetka, '33 to '34. Then after, I went to work in Skokie Valley in

1936. Mary and Joe Lenzini were the owners. Brother and sister. I work in there for eleven years.

I started at twenty-eight cents an hour at Skokie Valley. I ironed and pressed. I used the big machines. Hard. Very hard work. It was heavy work, especially in the summer with those machines. The heat. It wasn't very pleasant. Then after I start to go work in the house, clean house. You was make money. See, those times it was all Italian. Now, it's all different. Now it's all Mexican.

Burns? Sometimes. Oh yes! Oh yes! Get some burns on the hand, especially when you're on the machine. Yes, yes! That's what you got to expect.

We start work sometime at 7:30, we work eight hours, sometimes nine. Depends on how much work there is. Especially in the summer, there was more work. I had steady work.

I worked until I was seventy-five or eighty years old. Then I quit. Did I wear a uniform? To go scrub? No! Well, it was better to clean the house because you get a little more money. Mostly I worked in Highland Park. Sometimes, you see, when you start in one place, and then after, they've got the friends, and they call, "Can you help me too?"

I didn't work for really rich people. The middle class. The most I got paid, ten dollars a day.

Now they pay thirty-six dollars a day to clean the house. They work six hours. And me, at that time, the most I got was ten dollars for work ten hours. Now they get good money.

When I go to Yole Bagatti's house, there is laundry in baskets on the porch. It smells like clean laundry, starch and the steam that comes from an iron. She watches over her husband. She wants to make sure he tells his best stories. She prods: "Was it a nice trip, John, in the boat?" knowing it will make him say how terrible the first voyage from Italy was. She interjects details he omits. He went to visit his sister in Florence before coming to America, he says. "She was a maid for the rich people," she adds. Then it's her turn:

Well, I worked in the laundry when I come over here. Then I have Gino. When Gino, he start school, I went back to work in the laundry. I work in Winnteka, North Shore Laundry in Winnteka. Then I work in Skokie Valley Laundry, then I got tired in the laundry, I went to do housework. Then I had my son Bobby. Couldn't go no more. Then they start to bring me the laundry at home.

I still do the laundry. I still have one lady, first she was living in

Ravinia, then she buy a house in Lake Forest, then her husband pass away, now she lives in Winnetka. It's thirty-four or thirty-five years I work for her. I hate to let her go now because she's old, you know. I don't like to drop her now. This other one, I got her about ten years ago. Well, I keep it because even in the wintertime it's so long, you gotta have something to do to pass time.

Massima Vanoni, who was always old for her age and remains youthful:

My friend Giannina was working for North Shore Decorating and I took care of her son. And then my daughter Linda was born, and then Liliana, and I didn't have time anymore to go around taking care of others. I had enough taking care of my own. Then when Liliana was about four or five I started going to work at the North Shore in the evening, from four, when your *nonno* came home from work and your mother, Maria Silvia, from school, I would leave then to go work from four, I think, until about nine in the evening.

I sewed. I made drapes and things like that. And they paid thirty-five cents an hour. When I could make five or six or seven dollars a week, it was a lot of money.

Seeing others with money didn't really bother me very much. Because at that time, there weren't the deluxe houses that there are now. Then, in a house, there would be linoleum on the floor. There weren't carpets. It was all plain things, like the curtains, plain curtains without anything fancy, in houses like I could have myself, like my other friends. So that didn't really bother me. Because I thought if the other immigrants, like I was, could do it, that maybe I could hope to do it, too.

What I found harder than anything was the language. Because I couldn't understand anything. The way of working in Italy, for example, you begin to work with a certain stitch. But I had learned the way that they taught me in Italy. And when I started to work here at North Shore, the work that I had learned, it was different, they did it another way. So, I thought, "I don't know if it's me that doesn't know how to work or if it's them." That's what I was thinking. But then, instead, I understood that the way they taught me was more fast, it took less time. And little by little, I got used to it and I liked more the way that they did it than the way they taught me in Italy. It was different in the way you started. For example, *un sotto punto*, the way you do it is different because you have to hold the material different in your hands, and that's why at first it seemed hard to me, because more than anything I didn't understand anything. To teach me, there was my boss, she was an old woman, very strict. She was German. At first in the evenings my friend Giannina came too, so when she was there it was easy because she taught me and she talked to me in Italian. But then she didn't come at night anymore, and there was another lady, who wasn't Italian, she was born here, but she was very nice, and she showed me if I didn't understand, she showed me just how to do it. That's how I picked up their way of doing it.

We made drapes, bedspreads, a lot of things, little things like that. I never saw anything I made in a house because usually—now it's different, even someone like me, for example, and like a lot of others—even they can go to North Shore and have work done by them. But at that time, they were people who had money. And in those houses there I never went.

They had electric lights, because when I first started there, I was working in the basement, there used to be a big long room, and there were lights over the machine so you could see. That's how we worked.

I was curious to see the things I made. And then, when I would go, for example, in the stores that sell things like that, in these departments where they have them, for example, the drapes, I would look and see how they were done, how nice they were, what was the material like, how they were. You see the difference right away, you can see which material is good, which isn't good, you see the difference right away when you work with it.

When we worked we talked and we made our comments. A lot of people brought material to work on that we wouldn't want to work on because it wasn't worth it, to do a lot of work on material that maybe wasn't good and wouldn't hold up long.

The customers came inside to bring the material. You could hear when they gave their directions to *la padrona*, what they wanted, things like that, you could see. They sent our work even as far as New York.

(from Italian)

Rosa Fiocchi, whose grade book is in order:

I worked for Parker's. Parker Cleaners in Lake Forest. I worked there from 1922 until 1925. My husband had had it. I hated to quit because I'd gotten a raise, and he wasn't working, well, winter, they didn't work in winter then. He got fed up. He said, in all of that time I didn't get pregnant. And then he said I should quit. Well, I felt that we could use that money. I was getting seventy-five cents an hour then. And that was good. So he said I should quit. So I did. Well, the next year I had Bob. I already had four, and then I had him in '27. December '29 I had Elsa. And in '31 I had Jean, and that was two years, too. I went back on my routine. Every two years.

At Parker's, I ironed. The fine work was on irons and they had the presser. A man would be handling that. There was an explosion once, but nobody got hurt badly.

What was making it hard for me was the washing at home, you know, elbow grease, the washing, and I told my husband I'd get myself a washing machine. He said, "Oh, a washing machine?" I didn't know what he thought so then I didn't pursue. Then one day I was in Chicago, anyway I went with a friend of ours, Mrs. Tamarri, she was looking for something, and I went with her in the Fair Store—it's no more now, but it was maybe around State. The Fair, they called it.

And they had washing machines, and the used ones, you put down two dollars and it would be two dollars a month. Well, I could scrape two dollars, I felt sure. When he came home, he wanted to know what it was. I told him. "Send it back. I don't want used stuff around here. Get a new one." I had wanted it before, and then it sounded like it was his idea. So I've had a machine ever since. I really thought I had the bull by the horns.

Judy Cassai worked in dry cleaners' shops for thirty-three years, starting in 1925. She worked for Parker Cleaners in Lake Forest for sixteen years.

I was an all-around girl. I was like a floor lady. Was the first one in the cleaners. And I learned the cleaning from a French dry cleaner's father who came in from Chicago. They picked me up at home. Six o'clock. We used to work from six to ten for twelve dollars a week. Ten o'clock at night. Then I went to fifteen. Then I went eighteen.

I was making twenty. Depression hit us. The French boss and his wife, they left here. And he says, "Well, Judy, I'll keep you working but I'll have to cut you to ten dollars." I was making thirty. They cut me to twenty. And I was one of the fortunate ones in Highwood who was working, because these women used to work in the restaurants and everything. They worked for seventy-five and fifty cents an hour during the Depression.

The union could never get in. Never get in, in the dry cleaning, and hasn't to this day. They never could get in the dry cleaning. You know why? Because, I think, I think they all got together and they wouldn't join, you know, all the bosses, because then, there was only one, two, three dry cleaners in Lake Forest. We were doing the work for the Armours and Swifts and all those big people. We didn't go out of Lake Forest. There was enough, you know, for the amount of help you could get in those days, and then we had, I, for one, we used to have to teach everybody, you know, how to do it like I learned, you know. And I don't, I never knew the reason why they never could get in.

We had a lot of colored people come in, too, you know, like on the press. You can't get too many on a press, you know, that's hot. In those days they didn't have no blowers or nothing. Used to get up to about 128 degrees. And then all that dampness, you know. That's where I got my aches and pains from, be sweated, go out, and then the lake breeze. You know how changeable it is around here. One day it's a hundred, next day, it goes down to thirty degrees.

A lot of these other nationalities, they used to go do day work for the wealthy people in Highland Park and Lake Forest, you know, that day work, washing and ironing and cleaning. A lot of my German friends used to go. And then they had the Exmoor Country Club. That's a very old club. Way back when, they used to go and wait on table. There was always work.

Eritrea Pasquesi, *la canterina* of the family:

I used to be a seamstress by trade. And then when times got bad, I went and did housework.

I went and worked for the A. B. Dicks in Lake Forest by the lake there. They're the mimeograph people, you know. It must have been about '40.

But I had already started in '35 for another lady. I used to go iron her laundry. She was in Lake Forest. I worked in Lake Forest until many, many years after. I went to work in Highland Park after one of my friends says to me, "Oh my, you're not making enough money. Come to Highland Park." So she got me a place in Highland Park. In fact I just talked to the lady this morning. I do all her fancy linen. Washing and ironing.

I worked for the A. B. Dicks three days a week. There were eight of us working there. Two gardeners, chauffeur, cook, upstairs maid, downstairs maid, and a nurse. I was the laundress. The cook lived there and the upstairs maid lived there. The chauffeur lived there. The gardeners did not live there. I was the only Italian. They were nice, very nice people.

Mary, the cook, she was Swedish. In fact, she brought me that beautiful vase I got in there from Sweden. Very good cook. I'll never forget her salmon mousse and on top of that she had made some kind of a sauce made out of cucumbers. And one time I had crabs, soft shell crabs. Of course we were not supposed to have it because it was too expensive, but she would swipe one for us, you know.

One time I had to do some linen for the dining room table. They were all lace. What in the world can I do with this. So I had the chauffeur, Matt, make me a stretching frame and I would put it out in the sun. So one time Mr. Dick passed by and he saw this contraption and he said, "Now, who in the world did that?" So the chauffeur said, "The laundress, Dorothy." Well, you know it took a little brains to do that. It would be starched and you don't have to iron it.

The Dicks had a summer home in Barrington, Illinois. In the summertime, they weren't home and I would take along with me some-one, because we did all the blankets while they were gone. And I would always have some woman from Highwood come up and help me. And they always paid, no question about that. It was a good house.

Boarders and Diners

Caterina Lattanzi, who says, "I'm the boss now, right?"

Sunday what was I doing? Used to wash clothes and clean the house and cook at noon.

I didn't like it, having boarders. You have to work for a little money. But I wanted a couple of boarders and make a little money. It helped keep a-going. When they come in the house, they wanna be boss—not you, the boss of your house. They want to command, "I want to eat this, I want to eat that." They said, "You cook this!" They give you forty dollars a month, and then you have to cook for them. You have to buy the food for them. You have to cook. And then you have to wash clothes. And then forty dollars, you think it's big money but it takes thirty days to do all of that work.

I have boarders for a few years in Winnetka. I have two men from Abruzzi, the same province where I come from. They were working in the garden or in construction.

They complain, they complain. They think you don't wash the clothes good for them. They say I spoil the clothes, or I don't use enough soap. Or I don't change enough the bed. You know, I change it once a week. Shirts? Well, you have to be limited to one shirt on Sunday. You can't wear two shirts on Sunday. It's too much. They give you forty dollars, they think it's a big amount, and it isn't a big amount for what you're doing. That's why I had to wash Sunday.

The boarders, they called it *boardo finito*—limited board. With *boardo finito*, you eat just like family. I cook for my husband, I cook for them, too. Some people buy the food themselves and then they give you less money. I did it both ways. I don't like either one, I'll tell you the truth. Because I have enough work with my family and the apartment. *Boardo finito* is a little better because you cook one thing and everybody eats the same thing. Otherwise, if for you I have to cook a different way, and for him another kind, and for me another kind, that's too many *patel'* on top the stove, too many pans.

In the morning before they went to work, they ordered, "Well, to-day, *bacana*, I want you to cook. . . ." *Bacana*, they called me. That's the name the boarders give to the woman in the house. It's not a bad word. It sounds bad though. When I hear the first time, I don't like it. They don't call you "Caterina." They just say, "Today, *bacana*, cook beans or *pastasciutta*, or make a *scorpella*." *Scorpella?* Let me say, like a pancake, really thin, like a crepe. Then you put something inside or on top. You know, they give too many orders.

Sometimes they start to play cards around the house and I wouldn't let them. Otherwise they don't stay in my house. Because I have small kids.

When you have somebody around the house and you need the money, you support some words. You don't like it. But you forget about it. What are you going to do if they go away? They're not going away because they need to stay there. And you need the money.

Everett Bellei was born in 1898 in Pavullo, the big city in the Frignano. His first business was an ice cream parlor in Highwood, the next, a grocery store just over the border in Highland Park. He is a serious man but he likes his jokes, jokes that he passes out like meat wrapped in paper, over a counter, while pulling a wax pencil from behind his ear to mark the price. His daughter-in-law can't stay for coffee. It's Memorial Day and she has to take flowers to the cemetery. He tells her he can make her coffee "to go."

My mother used to have her own twenty or twenty-two boarders. After she sold that big house to Ciro and Pia Gibertini.

My mother always made wine. And, boy, she knew what she was doing. Well, my mother made money on that. She had it fermented to a certain point. And, then, if it didn't ferment right she used to take brown sugar and boil it and put it in there and that brought it out. If she found out it got a little sour in the mash, sometimes it doesn't ferment quite right. My wife and I have no liquor of any kind. We never drank. Just didn't care to.

She had a house with a great big private dining room and she could have set fifty people in there easy. Her main house, before it burned down, was right in the middle of a big piece of land there.

Well, let's put it this way, see, Mother started out on a shoestring like anybody else does, and built it up. Then she had the hotel and all the people that used to come out there to work in the summer, and she had the whole hotel filled. And they used to eat there and room there. And that was a nice business.

The boarders got along very nicely. They were all Italians. All people that came to Highwood to work. You see, there's nothing doing in the wintertime. In the wintertime, they went away for a few months. Then, the spring, they came back to work, golf course and they worked in the people's yards, and so forth. And then there was quite a boom on homes.

Some painter from Venice painted the walls in the dining room. It was a landscape. European style. He done a beautiful job. She spent a lot of money in there. I didn't think she should have.

Having boarders was a lot of work. She used to make *tortellinis* and pasta. As far as a cook, she could cook anything. And she could bake anything. She had training in Europe. They had a hotel in Pavullo, and my dad didn't know anything about a hotel and it didn't take him long to lose all the money he had. In 1907 we moved to Oglesby, Illinois. You know where LaSalle is? Well, Oglesby is a few miles away from there. That's where the Portland cement factories are. And a coal mine. He was working in the mine.

Well, at the hotel in Highwood, Mother had help. There's a lot of Italian girls used to work for her. In the home, she had an average of twenty boarders. It was loaded. There were people from, shall we say, all states, *piemontes', veneziani*, from all states, but not from south Italy. We didn't cater much with them. I'd say a lot of them stayed all year long and some stayed nine months, then they went back to the coal mine for three months and then they came back again. Like the people from Mexico, they do the same thing here now. See, just as soon as the season's over, they go back home.

Pia Gibertini, who serves her guests with the seriousness and calm of a waiter at a fine restaurant:

It was all men. I would have liked to have a husband and wife but it was always these men who boarded, many who came from the city and many who came from the mines to stay here in the summer, and then would go away. Just think of the work! Three meals a day, washing, ironing, mending. Ten dollars a week. Now, it's ridiculous. When all the work was done, we ate.

They were all Italians, all nice, all people you don't have to worry about. Sometimes we got an ignorant person who caused problems. But my husband got them by the neck and threw them out. If they act nice, *va bene*, okay, if not—Ciro meant business. Then, they were all good, decent people.

The boarders called me *padrona*. Some called me *bacana*. Or they called me by my name, Pia. Eh, you find everything in this world.

When the boarders went back to the mines, we had fewer. Sometimes we had the same ones who came back, seventeen or eighteen always arrived who worked in town. Once we had about thirty boarders.

We had two big washings every week. And then the ironing. And all for ten dollars a week. When I think of how stupid we were.

Then, I had to give them their lunches because the boarders took their lunch with them. Some came home but not very many, those who worked close by. I gave them two or three sandwiches, fruit, cheese, whatever they wanted. We made the lunches. At four in the morning my husband started to make the lunches.

Bread, we didn't make. We bought it by the sack from the baker, Teodoro Minorini. Ciro would buy twenty, twenty-five, or thirty loaves. On the stove we had eight burners and two ovens. Then we bought an electric roaster. Pasta, we made in the house. *Tagliatelle, tortellini, tortellacci, pasta in brodo*, almost everything.

I used to go shopping at Bellei's grocery store almost every day because then there wasn't the Frigidaire. You had to go shopping every day. The Frigidaire made things easier. When you're there with the ice only, you can't keep things really fresh.

For me now it's like a dream. I can't remember very much, a lot of things, because I was so busy that I couldn't think about just one thing, I had to think about a lot of things because Ciro didn't want to take over them, I had to think about collecting, I had to do the shopping, all those things there, because he never wanted to bother with it.

You had to pay attention and serve them well, right away, because they were jealous of the customers from Ravinia, see, they thought that the other table ate better than they did. But it wasn't true. More than anything, I didn't have room to make a lot of different dishes, because we had one stove for everything with eight burners and two ovens, and so we treated everyone the same. I had to pay attention to not treat anyone differently, oh *Dio*, like those who paid more, for example, for dessert. And sometimes, if I had extra, I gave some dessert to those who had only paid for fruit. On holidays, I always did that. But the boarders had this idea in their head. They said, "Oh, you treat those from Ravinia better." They would say things like that without thinking of what they were saying. Because it wasn't true.

But those times were bad. Oh, how many times I cried, "*Dio*, if my mother saw me, what would she say?" Because she would never believe that I had ended up in a place like this. If she had seen me, I'm sure she would have said, "My poor daughter!" But I never wrote, I didn't tell her. I always said that everything was going fine. She didn't know that it was like this. She thought it was like a restaurant.

When we first got the business, the boarders played poker, but we made them stop. They played all night and sometimes they would fight. *Morra*, too! Bad business. Oh, too much noise, too much noise. They played two or three times. Then *basta!* Because they'd argue and they'd make noise that you could hear everywhere. We were trying to keep the house properly.

A lot of the boarders worked for McCormick. And even for the man who later on went bankrupt, Samuel Insull, he was a big millionaire. There were a lot of these men who stayed in my house who worked for him.

A lot of the customers who came to dine had been in Italy many times. They knew the food. Some of the names that used to come?

The Swift and Armour families came but they were always nice. Ten
o'clock they always left. They usually came on Sundays. Nice people. *Davano la buona mancia,* gave a good tip. They tipped the girls
who were working. Dr. Theodore Proxmire used to come very often
but every time he came, somebody called him with an emergency.

I never had Mr. Insull, but I had some of his friends and I had
many of my boarders that used to work for him. They thought they
were eccentric, and little by little they went broke. Everything so
very expensive. He had a bunch of men working. But I know that
he was a big, rich man. Very rich. He had, I think, the biggest
bunch of people working for him there.

Then three young men from Venice worked for Lady Astor, she
had a villa. But she was never there. She was a beautiful woman.
She came with some of her friends a few times for lunch. I was
glad when it was over because they would stay there for a couple
of hours talking and I wanted to get finished so I could start other
work, supper. But they were all right.

The boarders all came from around Ladd, Kincaid, near LaSalle,
places like that. Some of the boarders were in accidents, they were
lucky to get away. I heard them talk at the table, that's all. Probably
they did talk about politics, but I didn't pay any attention. Not because I didn't want to but because I didn't have the time.

What did I do for fun? I didn't know what fun was. I was happy
to get the work done in time to be able to pay at the end of the
month, to pay for the house, the interest, the mortgage. Sometimes I
would visit friends. If there was someone sick maybe I would go to
see her. You know how you do to visit someone when they're sick.
But the rest, forget about it. I didn't have time. In the evenings at
5:30 I had to have everything on the table, and at noon, too. How
could I have gone out?

I had women help me. Maria Scherzalati and Maria who came
from Ladd. That one, too, was a good woman. And then there was
another woman named Pepina who was a widow. They would work
in the kitchen, or wash, or iron.

When I stopped working, it was just like the world stopped. I
didn't know what to do. Some of the customers that were there for
such a long time couldn't believe that it was going to stop. But
when they saw that I was sick, then they believed it.

Oh, I never did care for that, being like the *signori.* Didn't impress
me. Because I thought I had just as much as the other people. As
long as you can pay, that you have no debt, that you don't have to
struggle for making a living. I thought we were lucky enough. I

never cared to get rich. It never bothered me. I was glad to have
what I had, that's all.

I still have some friends who used to come. I have this good
friend in Lake Forest. Mrs. Halsted. Her husband was a broker.
She's my age. She was such a beautiful lady when I first met her.
They used to come into our house all the time. At least two or three
times a month, they used to come. Her husband used to like to
come, too. It was nice to see them together. We write to each other
about five or six times a year. She sends me a package every year.
Sometimes, I send her *tortellini* because she didn't know how to
make them. And so she's so happy to get them because she likes
them, you know.

I can't call Mrs. Halsted by her first name because it feels like I
would be being too familiar, *prendere troppa confidenza*. In Italy we
are strict about things like this. If I go to a *signora*, I wouldn't use
tu, I would use *Lei*. I started out calling her "Mrs. Halsted" and now
I'm no good to change. I have a friend who bought a villa in Tucson, even she is "Mrs. Brown." She says, "Call me by my first
name." I try. But I can't do it. When you're born like that, when you
have that custom, I'm not able to stop for her.

(from Italian and English)

Maria Manfredini, "Maria from Ladd," went to work for Pia Gibertini
during the 1920s. She lived in Highwood until the Depression came.
Then, she and her husband moved to the coal mines near Scranton,
Pennsylvania. The time working at the Gibertinis was the best period
of her life. She shows me a sweater draped over a chair. "That sweater
there, Pia gave it to me. My niece, she took some old clothes back
home. I said, 'That, leave it there because Pia gave it to me.' "

Well, we have to do something about it when the mine closed. We
have to eat. And we thought we gonna go to Highwood. There was
lots of garden work for the rich people. One of my sisters, she was
up there, too. Her husband, he was working, too. My sister was
working in the kitchen of these rich people.

In Highwood, we was going to see if we find something better
than we had before. We go there and see if we find the job, you
know, it was these clubs where the rich people go play. And the
women used to work and I went to look for a job there. They said,
"Come back next month. Now, it's too early and there's nobody
here yet." It was in the spring.

And I told you before how I was working for Pia. When we come to get our room and Pia give us a room in the morning, she have a nice breakfast with us. And afterwards when it was through the breakfast she asked me if I was looking for a job. She knew! And I say, "Yeah."

She said, "I need a cook."

I said, "Well, you got the wrong one." I says, "I used to cook the Italian things, you know, I used to cook pretty good but for a small family, but if you need a cook for in a restaurant like that, you know, I can't do."

She said, "I'll teach you. We'll try each other for a month. You try if you like the job. And I try you if I like you. And then at the end of the month, well, we'll talk business."

I was there five years.

I learned to cook lots of different things. I used to make ravioli and another kind with spinach, they call it *tort'llacc'*. Lots of things was the way I used to make; lots of things was different. She had a cookbook, it was this high. Written in Italian. And she looked in there and taught me. I catch on quick. She don't have to repeat it twice. I never was tired; you know, my boss, Pia's husband, he used to say to the people, "We have a woman, she never say one time she's tired." Now, I'm tired when I get up.

I didn't have no time to know Highwood. I start working right away and I don't even remember if I liked it or not. I think I liked it. In Ladd I wasn't working much. I was just talking with other women. There, in Highwood, I don't have the time.

I liked it when I worked because it was all opera people who used to come from New York, you know, and they used to like to tease you. Nothing out of the way, you know, and you know one time they hear me singing a little bit. I wasn't singing good at all. You know what they did? They went to the flower place. They bought a bouquet. And they brought it to me. I say, "What for?" They said, "Won't be long, you're going to be one of us."

I have to leave because she couldn't pay me anymore. No money coming in. There was a big bunch of boarders when I left. And lots of them, they was drinking and spending the money, and when the Depression came, they couldn't pay. They used to give them the credit to eat. But they had to eat. Well, I was kind of expecting it because I could see there was no business anymore. It was less and less. It wasn't many customers either. I don't know if they was rich or what. They looked like it. They look different than the ones that was poor.

But it was the best time of my life, in Pia's place. I don't have time to think about nothing else but work.

The Construction Trades

Rosa Fiocchi, whose grade book is in order:

The Dalzell mine was closed, and Caesar had to do something so he came up to Highwood. He worked for the gardeners, but they worked nine hours, and that extra hour killed him. He just didn't like it.

So then he worked at American Can, laboring, American Can is in North Chicago. And he worked at Johnson Motors. But that was still laboring. So he labored until he found a place where they were building a stone entrance. It was on Greenbay, south of County Line Road. There was a man from Luxembourg working there, and my husband could speak some German and he could speak French because he'd worked in the Alsace-Lorraine and people are bilingual there. So they talked and they'd been in the same mine in Luxembourg and Caesar told him he was a stonemason. So he showed Caesar the plan, and then he left him, and he didn't come back all day. And Caesar started to lay stone.

He grew up with stones. His father was a stonemason and in Italy the mason chose his helper, paid his helper, his laborer. Well, his father didn't need any other helpers, he had his boys. His father would say, *"Cesare"*—*Cesare* is in Italian—"I want a stone for here." Caesar could pick the stone out with his eyes.

Well, I learned about stone, too. I didn't know how to figure plans either and I learned it. Well, you take a plan and you have your specifications that tell what you want, the kind of stone they want, the kind of material, then you take the measurements. The first time I took the measurements, my brother showed me. He took a chimney, and I said, "Oh, that's easy. Down below the roof, I take three sides and above it I take four sides, plus the height." Well, I was good in arithmetic, I considered that my dessert. I like number problems. I like to figure them out myself.

We got some stone from Lannon, a little town west of Milwaukee. But the stone came from all over. We did a job on County Line Road, west of Barrington, and that was Pennsylvania stone and it looked like petrified wood, you know, you could see that it was petrified wood. It was a green stone. And from Lannon we got most of it. We'd get some from the environs of Fond du Lac. Oh yeah, I drove up to the quarries. How else would my husband get there? He didn't drive. I drove. So we were together all the time except when he went to the tavern before supper.

I've had a busy life and I just feel now sometimes like I'm not producing anything. I try to keep the kitchen clean and my bed made and the rest, my daughter-in-law comes in on Tuesday and straightens up.

Until 1925, he worked for somebody else. He didn't have trouble finding work because there weren't very many masons then. When the business first started in 1925, I figured the plans but I wasn't driving then—somebody else drove him. I learned to drive in '28. We bought a lot just south of Route 22.

The first contract we had is a house in Waukegan, it's a beautiful house. The Stanley house. It showed up in a book of old houses in Waukegan. That was for the architects Anderson and Ticknor.

The first time he went on his own—he had been working for somebody else—and John S. Van Bergen had a house in Indian Hills, and he said to Caesar, "I'll give you so much a foot if you do the stone." So he didn't go through a contractor. The architect wanted him. So then we started to figure for him. If he had something, he'd call us.

One of the first jobs we did was on Central and Greenbay in Wilmette. And that was a job. It was a gasoline station.

And then we did—this is by Northwestern University, you know where Sheridan Road runs into Chicago Avenue, it makes a bend? There's a chapel. The Millar, I think. And that's a very nice building. Well, besides that, of course, we did some work on the additions of the different colleges. All the time I was sitting in the car. I was the driver and I sat in the car and I crocheted and I knitted and I listened to radio.

I'll tell you, my vocabulary certainly expanded. I didn't know what a benchmark was. I learned what "access" means when it's on a plan. And "elevation." "Cross section." He trusted me when I was first learning. I don't know why he did. But if I didn't know something, I'd find out.

We did a church on Devon in Chicago, east of Route 41. We did the school on Holy Name Cathedral in Chicago.

We had a lot of work when the Depression started so we didn't feel it right away. We had that job I mentioned before west of Barrington that was Pennsylvania stone—it was a *big* home. And we had the Turnbull in Lake Forest. It's just east of Route 43 and north of Deerpath, in there. And we had Dr. Orcutt's in Glencoe, which is west of the North Shore tracks that are no more. We had three houses and then we had a fence on Ridge Road west of Lake Forest, that had as much stone as a house would have. We had four big jobs. So we didn't feel the Depression for a long time.

We did the Cudahy house on the west side of Greenbay in Lake Forest. It's a kind of white stone. We did the servants' quarters and the greenhouse but then somebody else got it, it was coming into Depression, and somebody else with a sharp pencil got it.

Oh, we did a nice job at the King-Bruweart. It was the old maids' home in Lake Forest. See, the rich people that had to go to a home would go there. They would pay, but there was nice accommodations there. The architects, Anderson and Ticknor, were from Lake Forest. When the King-Bruweart home came along, it was Depression, really Depression.

I'm trying to think of other jobs. There's some stonework on the Lake Forest High School. The cut stone that's up on the front gable, that Caesar laid himself.

Well, we did the McBride, that's on Lake over by the lake in Lake Forest. And we did the Burry house. Yeah, it's funny how I couldn't think of one before and I'm thinking of a lot of them. We did a lot of work in Lake Forest.

Glencoe. Dr. Orcutt's in Glencoe. Wilmette, I'm sure we did something in Wilmette. Sure we did! We did one on the south side of Lake Street, around Locust. And Locust makes me think of the Hoerstman house. Can you imagine how they get their tongue around "H-o-e-r-s-t"? And I know we did some work on Woodley. I've forgotten some of those places.

No. I didn't want to live in a big house. I knew that most of that work would be mine. Because after I'd taken my husband around to the jobs, he would lie down, or else maybe go to the tavern and I'd get dinner, maybe fight with the kids to get the dishes done after.

Any social life? What social life? Coffee klatch? What was that? I didn't even know what coffee klatch meant. Now, I find myself with a lot of time but I don't feel like doing anything. And then I think, "Well, you're feeling guilty, you shouldn't." I have to talk to myself.

Well, when we came up here, my brothers came up, too, and in '22 they asked W. W. Griffis for a job. Griffis in Lake Forest was the rich people's carpenter. And they asked him for a job. Louie asked for a job first. And asked to be apprenticed. And they took him. And then Joe came up and they took him too. So that's why they're first class, you know, they worked for a first-class carpenter. We did some work, too, for Griffis.

The masons who worked for Caesar the longest were the pups that he raised, the ones that apprenticed with him. It would have been Minorini, Bartolai, and Galassini. Valerio Zagnoli was one of the first. We were working in Evanston when Zagnoli came to ask for a job.

There was another man that was kind of jealous of Caesar and he would try to beat him when they were working on the wall. But then I had only his side of the story. But according to his story, the two of them couldn't keep up with him. He had such an eye, I believe it. He had small hands. My father's were bigger. My hand isn't too big. Of course, it's swollen and a claw. And arthritic.

Sometimes I'd be worried about something and it would always turn out to be all right. I really had faith in the man when it came to his work.

I don't want to give myself too much credit but let's tell it like it is. I did the driving, I figured the plan, I gave him the quantities, he priced them. He'd look at the plan, too, and look at my quantities and say, "I think there's not enough" or "I think that's too much." Well, I'd go over it, and most of the time I was right. Caesar wasn't too good writing it down, but he had it here, in his head.

I don't know if his business would have done as well without me. Because he didn't know English. He didn't know the language and he didn't know how to write English. He knew how to read it. He would have had to had somebody else drive. He would have had to have somebody figure the plans—maybe he could do it himself, but it would take him forever. We made a good team. He could produce the work. But then there were other things that was, like dishwashing to do, I'm just saying, the chores of the thing. I didn't know how to type but I hunted and pecked, and I raised the kids and they're all friends and I'm proud of 'em.

Louis Baruffi, whose sister Rose set him straight—he was the *second* child born in Dalzell.

I tell you what, I got into the carpentry business just by accident. I went up to a lumber yard in Lake Forest. Lake Forest Lumber Company, it's no longer there. The lumber yard is still there but it's changed hands. I went up to ask them for a job. He said, "No, but why don't you try that shop over there, maybe they need somebody." So I'm walking over there. And I asked a fellow by the name of W. W. Griffis. And I said to him, "Mister," I said to him, "you need a laborer?" "No," he said. So I said, "Okay." I started walking away. He said, "Hey, young fella, wait a minute," he says, "how would you like to be a painter's apprentice?" And I said, "What do

you mean, apprentice?" And he said, "Paint, paint." And I said,
"Naw, I don't think I'd like that." He said, "How about being a carpenter's apprentice?" I said, "Okay." So I took it on. That's how I
got the whole ball rolling.

I knew absolutely nothing about carpentry. Then they put me in
the shop. They had a shop and a mill. I didn't learn too much
about the mill but what I did learn was how to glaze. They'd make
the sashes for the windows. Those days they used to make a lot of
storm windows. Now they've got aluminum windows with the
screens, but those days you had to take out the screen and put the
storm window in.

At that time most of the carpenters were Swedish. That's all right,
we come along. Never any problem, the Italians and the Swedes got
along pretty good. We got along with everybody. Every once in a
while you'd run into a jerk. It's that way in all things.

The apprenticeship was four years, then after, you become a jour-
neyman. But there's still a lot to learn after that. I liked it from the
moment I started. And I never, never, never, never, and never hated
to go to work. I always liked to go. Whether I was doing the regular
work. Whether I was the superintendent or whether I was general
superintendent. In Lake Forest I worked mainly for the big residen-
tials. One for sure, one that I remember, was for the Morton Salt
people, down there by the lake.

You asked where I worked. Well, number one—this was years
later—I was superintendent on a large factory building in Bartlett,
Illinois, for Carp Construction Company. And the All American Insurance building in Park Ridge. Then, on the Gateway Transportation Company building. At that time, 1968, they had the largest
trucking dock in the world.

Over the years we did a lot of remodeling in high schools and
grade schools in Chicago. One of them was Von Steuben. Then, we
remodeled the Schurz High School on the northwest side in Chicago. I was a superintendent there. That was for Rudnick and Company. See, after about thirty-five years, I left Carp and went with a
different company, Rudnick, which was in Chicago also.

I worked on a church in Chicago Heights, and the first two dor-
matories over here at Trinity College in Bannockburn. We did a lot
of remodeling work down at Holy Martyrs in Chicago when Pope
John Paul II came to Chicago. And then, over here at Batavia, Illinois, it was a testing laboratory for our government. The thing was
about thirty feet deep. Like a tunnel. It's all underground and it's
about a mile in circumference. We did that.

We did a lot of other remodeling work and a lot of new buildings.
I joined the union August the twenty-first, 1921. You can imagine
the jobs I been on.

I was an alderman in Highwood. Around 1949. 1950s. I forget. I
was in office under Tom Mussatto and also when John Frantonius
was mayor. A total of twelve years. Before Mussatto, well, there was
a lot of prostitution going on in town, a lot of gambling and everything like that, and we all got in and we really cleaned it up. And
he didn't stay in office for very long, for this reason, you see, he
was also a business agent at the time, for the labor union. And the
reason he wasn't in office very long—he wasn't kicked out or anything like that—there was pressure from the union, the big union
down in Chicago, to leave this person who was harboring prosti-
tutes alone. We had a suit against him. So they started putting pressure on Tom. So, before he would cave in, before he'd give in, he
quit. We were all at a meeting when he told us he was quitting. He
told us to go ahead and pick who we wanted to be our mayor. So I
nominated John Frantonius. So they all agreed and he was the
mayor. They were bringing a lot of pressure on Tom. And Tom
didn't want to go for that. Tom was an upright man.

I worked on the Labor Temple. A lot of labor was free labor but,
like me, I had to go there every day and I couldn't afford to not get
paid. My brother Joe—he was a carpenter too—was foreman there.
I hung all those doors on the front of the Labor Temple. And Joe
Ferrari and I—Ferrari was a carpenter also—we laid all the maple
flooring in the temple.

Socialists? You find that in any, in all the towns, people say that.
A name's easy to come by. I used to hear of a lot down there called
socialists. What does it mean? Well, overthrowing the existing government. And it would be like if there was a community affair and
everybody pitched in. Something wrong up there in the head! Socialist! Can you imagine everybody pitching in and doing a certain
amount of work, and everyone getting up in the morning and going
to work and nobody being a loafer or anything like that?! Everything's supposed to be equal and everything like that. Well, I don't
know if that's a definition of socialism. I'm happy the way it is.

One time in fifty-one years, we were out on strike just one day.
All the years, they struck about five years ago and it was only for
one day.

My favorite work? Telling someone else what to do! I think I was
very fair as a boss. I hope this isn't considered as bragging, let me
put it to you this way. I'm justifiably proud of myself and what I

did. These Italian laborers, the people that used to come from Italy, they'd come and ask me for a job and it just happened that at the time I had work for them. And I was able to speak Italian well enough to carry on a conversation. They worked with me. They got union wages. If they worked five minutes overtime, they got their overtime. I never, never, never, and never cheated 'em one penny. That's one thing I'm very proud of. I didn't take advantage of them because they were foreigners. And the conversation uptown, I'd hear, "We have a good foreman." That I was right with the men.

Each job is different. And it's all a challenge. Well, what gave me a little ego is to be able to build the largest trucking terminal. I was general superintendent. It wasn't a big crew. See you don't have to have a very big crew. You can have a lot of dead weight there if you're not careful. You're not going to have fellas standing around, and paying them fifteen-eighteen-twenty dollars an hour. You gotta watch that because you'll break your contractor. You break him, he won't stay in business and you don't have a job.

Another job I was very proud of was over here at Batavia. We had cement finishers, iron workers, plasterers, electricians. I got to coordinate the thing. You gotta know what you are doing. You can't fly blind. You don't call the plumber the minute you need him. You alert him, say, "I'll be needing you maybe two days from now," so he can schedule his men, too.

We're all entitled to learn the trade. Make your application, wait your turn, regardless of whether you're Mexican, white, or black. When people leave their country, it's not because they don't like their couuntry, it's because they have to. It's because of economic conditions. That's why my father come over here. He swore he'd never go back. He didn't.

I'd pick the same trade. I'd pick the same wife. I'd pick the same problems to solve. And I'd have the same children I have. My wife and I are at old age, and we're both happy.

My wife, you know, was a dressmaker. Her mother was a dress-maker. Mary Bernardini. She used to sew for these millionaires in Lake Forest and Highland Park, Glencoe and all those places. She had a good going business. And then my wife would help her with the sewing, do the hand work. And she was good at it, too. Then after we had a few children, we decided all her time should be home with the kids. So everything worked out just wonderful.

I retired when I was seventy-two years old. Well, like I said, you know, I always enjoyed going to work because I had a pretty good position there, too. I was retired maybe for about a year when I was called back by the contractor. He said that he had a job at the Lincoln Park Zoo at the reptile house and asked if I'd take that over. So I said sure. I worked a little bit more with him, then I retired for good. You look at the roof up there. We remodeled. Can you imagine passing those cages, those snakes! My men were working up there—of course I'd have to go on top, too—working on top of a regular cage, all wire cage, and we had put plywood on top. These big pythons, they were about twenty or fifty feet long! Well, they wouldn't stay way down there, they'd come up as high as they could go. Right up and underneath where we were working. If one of your legs went through, they'd have chewed up on you. But we had it covered up by wood. That was no problem.

Okay, what's the next question? I'm winded.

Domenick Linari, who doesn't get along with Nietzsche:

I always enjoyed, always enjoyed construction. I started out when I was a kid in construction. I always enjoyed it. But I don't know. Maybe I'm not a very smart man. I know I'm not. I enjoyed working in a mine as far as that was concerned. To me, I thought it was just a natural thing. So maybe I don't know what enjoying is.

Here, I was working for a William Mavor Company from Chicago that went broke during the Depression. After the Depression kind of calmed down, things began to work, I went to work for Caesar Fiocchi. And soon after, he made me the foreman. I was his foreman for eight years. Then I started on my own after the war. I had a partner at the beginning. Cory Linari. We're first cousins. Our fathers were brothers.

The first job I did on the North Shore was the Deerpath Inn in Lake Forest. I laid stone. 1928. I worked on the Cradle Hospital in Evanston. I did St. William's Church at Sayre and Wrightwood in Chicago. I did the library in DeKalb. Beautiful building.

We worked all over. We went as far as Rockford. I did a job, I took a gang of men—well, I got it started there anyway—then I left, in Oglesby. Oglesby, Illinois. And I did one in DeKalb. I did a couple, three jobs for a saw factory that was in business in DeKalb.

We got our stone from Crab Orchard, Tennessee. From the hills of Pennsylvania and New York, the bluestone. From Lannon, Wisconsin, up here, from Winona, Minnesota, and Blythe, California. Oh, I can name a lot of places. You might say the one I favored is the one that you can make a better dollar on. Now if it was for my own

building, like when I built this house, I put Lannon stone because
the wife, especially, liked it. I thought it was good.

I worked during the day, took care of my business at night and
Saturdays and Sundays. I must have done it for about five or six
years, then it got so the gang got too big and I couldn't work anymore because I was too busy taking care of the jobs. There is an
awful lot to do. Getting the job. Collecting the money, which is the
hardest thing to do.

Keeping good skilled men, that's one trouble that you might say
that you have all the time when you're in the building contracting
business. You could always use men that are skilled. And then
comes time, if you haven't got work, you can't keep them. And so
it's a rat race all the time. Good skilled men are not easy to find. So
everybody wants the good skilled men and everybody tries to hang
onto them. And unless they quit, most of them that you get to hire,
you hire the one that the other guy don't want. Because he's the
first one that he's going to let go of. Our superintendent's Frank
Bertagni. He's my son Edward's age and has been with us since
1946. That's what, almost forty years, thirty-nine years. We got a
black man from Chicago has been with us I think since 1955, I believe it was. He's been with us around thirty years. Heck of a good
man. He was here yesterday. He was a kid and I was looking at
him, he's getting pretty old, I told him, I said, "Jesus Christ, I'm
going to tell Edward to fire you. You're getting too old!" When I
hired him he was eighteen years old. I guess you could say, though,
that most of our men were Italian.

Well, maybe I was a funny foreman, a funny guy to work for. I
believed that they should not speak a different language if somebody else was there that didn't understand it. Speak a language
everybody understands, if possible. I had no restriction if people
could smoke, they could do anything they wanted to, they could
talk, they could do anything they wanted to on the job. But no wild
language, no dirty language, absolutely, that I didn't want. I didn't
allow it. And I got some good reports that my gang wherever they
worked, they were respectful. Because they can get pretty rowdy
sometimes. When I was with Fiocchi's, I started out little by little,
whenever there was a dirty word and so on and a little too much
swearing, I said, "That's enough!" I started to clamp down and I
succeeded, maybe all of them didn't like it, but they accepted it. It's
been accepted.

Viterbo Ponsi, who traveled to Italy at age ninety and says the trade
is in the blood:

When I was discharged from the war, they asked me what I was going to do when I got back home. I was going to try and find work as a bricklayer, that was the work I did when I went to Libya. In Tripoli, I worked with Zamboni Company from Bologna. A long time ago. It was in 1911 and 1912. You was born?! Now, I say to myself, I'm old man, eh?

I bought a car in 1922, my first car. The people here told me I'm crazy, I was a bum. I buy one secondhand. I bought it because I need it. You see, I saw that the job start to be west. Before, it was in the towns along the track, along the lake. After, they started building out west.

The last five years, I worked for Kendler developers from Lake Forest to Northbrook. There I did a lotta houses.

Before, I did quite a few houses in Ravinia. One on Pleasant Avenue. All bricks. Two-story square house. Me and my brother. I worked in Highland Park in the Woman's Club on Sheridan Road. Joe Cabonargi was the contractor. In '26 or '27. I worked for him eight years.

After the Second World War, I work down in a big subdivision in Northbrook. So many houses. I stayed there, I don't know how many months. The Bank of Highland Park, I worked on that. Was me and Ezio Biondi. We worked for DeBartolo and Medici. I worked for them about three or four years and then I was not in business anymore.

Well, I like to build, see. I build all over. Lake Forest. Braeside. Glencoe. Barrington. Now, my hands is so dry.

I worked in my way, I never stop, keep going, keep going, not kill myself, like some people, when they start working, they wanted to be ahead and beat the other because they want the others to say "Oh, he's a good bricklayer." I say that's a mistake. Go like the rest. There was one guy, a contractor, who was like that. But he could go home to bed and come back when he felt like it. If he stayed eight hours on the job he couldn't do that.

If I was to start again? I like the trade, yeah. I like the trade. I like it. *Ma,* I don't do it for a living. You mean for a living? No. Because it's too rough. Too rough. You suffer too much. You make pretty good money in the summer, but then in the winter you spend everything.

I told my son to work for the public service because that's less hard work, it's rough work, bricklayer. How come? Because in the summer you suffer heat. In the wintertime you're freezing.

The bad weather makes it bad work, bad job, bad trade. Because it's cold you gotta put the antifreeze sealant. In the summertime, maybe you lay four or five bricks, you turn your back, and the mortar is already dried up hard. It's no good. You can't make a nice job neither. Fall is the best for work.

(from Italian and English)

Enea Cortesi, whose follow-through in *bocce* is picture-perfect:

I come and I board with Germano Ponsi. It was me, one of his brothers that's still living at my age—Viterbo—and your *nonno*, Tony. We used to sleep there, the three in one room. Germano owned it. He was partnership on the building trade with Joe Cabonargi, that's where I was working at the time.

Then I quit working for this Cabonargi in order to work for a fellow from Lake Forest, Hansen and Wilhelm, a building company, and I worked for those people twenty-one years, then I got back trouble and I had to quit. I could hardly lace my shoes. Then I got the job as a business agent for our local, labor union, going around on the job. Find the people that didn't have the card, make them pay so much a week until they have the card paid up. It's Laborer's International Union of North America, AFL-CIO. Local 152. We're up here in Highland Park. On Temple Avenue.

We had to go out and look on every job. If you had to work, you was supposed to work here in this building and I was supposed to ask you if you have the union card. If you had it, you would just show me. Okay. If you don't have it, then I would ask you if you want to join. If you want to join, then you start paying ten dollars a week. That's what we used to make them pay. And then, when you have the card paid up, you used to come over and get sworn in. And you get all the benefits just the same if you get sick. Like your grandfather, he used to belong there. I took that job for two and a half years. Then I quit. I had a lot of headaches.

That time they were building the Edens Highway, then I had to go and walk north and south along the highway because the contractor wouldn't let us go through with the car.

Years ago, they didn't have no trucks. It was horse and wagon. Angelo Menoni used to plow the streets here with the horse. Sidewalks, too. Then they come up with the truck and he was selling building material. He was in business with Egidio Mocogni. They had I don't know how many trucks. People used to go and ask for the job. Menoni and Mocogni.

At one time, we had to mix cement with the shovel, by hand. At that time, there was no machine. Then, they came out with the little cement mixer, a small one. We had to load it by hand and I was one of them that used to handle one of those machines, but I had to feed it myself with my shovel. Then they came out with bigger machines and they load it into the truck and mix it inside there.

At first we didn't have no union local here in Highland Park. I used to belong to the local in Evanston. Then we pulled away and we opened up our own up here. De Santo—he was from the southern part of Italy—and my cousin Willie were union agents when I first came. He used to be one of the officers—secretary. Then before that there was another friend of mine that came from the same town. By the name of Romeo Minghelli.

The problem was you had to work hard, really hard, because if there was a job there'd be three or four or five laborers there waiting to get a job. Sitting, looking for a job. Like when you go out and see baseball, you sit and you look. Those fellows, they was looking for a job. They knew that the boss, if you don't work hard enough, would lay you off, and they'd get one of the fellows there waiting. At that time, they used to do that. The contractor, he had the right to hire and fire, too.

We was two Italians working for Hansen. But then I don't know what was wrong, if they fired him, or what. Then I was there by myself. There was all nationalities. They don't look at the nationality, but they look at how hard a working man. Negro or white, it doesn't make any difference. There were no blacks working for Hansen and Wilhelm, not a single one. German, Swedish, because he had laborers and carpenters.

I worked all over, all over, all over. Mundelein. Lake Villa. Barrington. Lake Forest. Waukegan. All over, wherever they find the job. Lake Forest High School on Waukegan Road. We built the school in Glencoe. All over Lake County.

There were strikes in construction, but not us. Not our local here. A lot of them locals down in Chicago would strike. When we asked for a raise, they give. But you gotta strike when you ask for a raise and they don't give it to you. If you go on strike there is no job so it don't do you no good. But when the food and everything goes up in price, the union's gotta ask more money for their work, naturally.

Giosue Brugioni, the "wild kid":

I think this area, I mean for the working people, especially with the building trades, it's the best. I think they claim it's the best place in the United States because something's going on all the time.

When I first came from Italy, my dad said as long as you work you stay there in Highwood, but if you don't work you go back to Bevier to see where you were born. So I went down there in 1927, just before Christmas. I wanted to spend the Christmas there, and stay a little bit. But when I got down there, my uncle, Gregorio Brugioni, said, "You stay here for the winter, I'll take you to work in the coal mine." So I did. I stayed there till the end of April.

Then I came back up here and I went to work for Mandel in Rogers Williams down by the lake. He used to own Mandel Brothers department stores in Chicago. I worked in the garden. They had a big house there. But I didn't stay there too long. They weren't paying but about three dollars and a half, a day. I asked these two guys, Marchetti and another guy, Angelo Bartolotti, "How much you get a day?" They said "Eight dollars. A dollar an hour." I said, "Jesus Christ!" Lots of money. I make three dollars and a half. I said, "Ask your boss if they'll give me a job." After a week or so, they said, "He needs someone, do you wanna come down?" So I went down there and I stayed there all summer until the end of October.

At first I worked here in the summer because in them days, there was no work in the wintertime. The only people that were working here, like your *nonno* Piacentini, see he used to take care of the horses at the Exmoor golf course. And in the summertime in the coal mines there was work only one or two days a week. So I said, "What the hell, I don't make nothing here," I said, "I'll go back over there, I'll work four or five or six months."

In the summer, when I came here, I used to work as a laborer for the union with the plasters and the bricklayers. The bricklayers I didn't work with too much, because I never got along, they were too *inculenti*, you know that word? They were uptight, pains. I was hot tempered, you know, in my young days—now, no—but I used to tell them to go to hell. I said, "Why don't you get it yourself!" One time we was working in Deerfield, one guy got me mad, he was standing on top the scaffold, I took the sledge hammer, I started knocking the scaffold down, he jumped on top of the roof. They called me the wild kid.

But then I started with old man Fitzgerald up there in Lake Forest. He was a plumber contractor. When I would come back from the coal mines in the summer, I would work for him. I stayed with the plumbing until 1936.

Then, I started working with Ziegler in 1936. We put in all them big subdivisions down on Waukegan Road in Northbrook. All the way to Sky Harbor. We worked there for about two years. I was running a crew, we were putting in the water pipes.

The Italians, but most of all, the foreigners, a lot of the foreigners, but the Italians and the Polish and the Swedes, they've always got the hardest work. Like the sewer work, stuff like that, most of them were Italians. The Swedes, they're for the concrete and carpentry and stuff like that.

Before I went in the service during the Second World War, I worked up at Great Lakes. We put in all new water mains, we took up the old ones because they were too small when they built all them barracks and stuff like that. A lot of Italians from Highwood, they were working up there at Great Lakes. See, there was no private home or nothing during the war, or even before the war.

I worked for Cabonargi when he worked on the city hall in Highland Park on Sheridan Road. There was no basement underneath. Cabonargi was the contractor. They raised up the building and then they put jacks underneath. Then we dug underneath. I was running the elevator to bring up the dirt. That was the only building I worked in Highland Park.

9

An Immigrant's Conceit

MY LEGACY FROM the grand opera is a suite, a bureau and bed, in the spare bedroom.

The headboard, a baroque wave, is crowned in the middle with a flower, a sconce, and wings. On its shoulders, carved candlesticks stand watch like palace guards. The curves of the bureau mirror drop languidly, like a canopy; inside the mirror is etched an arc that crests in the center and flows down the sides toward its finale, a string of crystal beads dropping in a chandelier strand.

The bedroom suite was not bequeathed to me directly from the grand opera. It came into my possession via my great-aunt, Teresa Saielli. It came to her because she cooked meals for a maestro.

Of the chronology of the inheritance, I am not sure because the principals are dead. The bed originally belonged to a patroness of the arts, a friend of Gennaro Papi, a maestro of the Chicago Symphony Orchestra. Either the patroness gave the maestro the suite, and he, in turn gave it to my aunt, or possibly, the maestro, upon learning that the patroness was replacing dated furniture with modern pieces, claimed the set for his cook.

This is how my aunt, an immigrant who took in laundry, came to have elegant furniture in her house during the Great Depression. I imagine she clung ferociously to this bed and bureau, and that she entered her bedroom more than once feeling smug satisfaction.

My aunt cooked the noonday meal for Papi. She spoke of him with the superior ease of a confidante: "He was from Naples. He had a daughter in Italy. But he was separated from his wife. It was his fault, he told me. He told me that his wife was a good and beautiful woman, 'but me,' he said, 'I am a strange bird. Teresa, I like only the dark and ugly, otherwise I wouldn't like anything.'"

Like my aunt with her bedroom suite, many Italians in Highwood and Highland Park have carefully preserved a memory of their face-to-face flirtations with the people of the opera. They show it off on occasion, a fancy article, an immigrant's conceit.

Olga Somenzi Pottker, a native of Highwood and reporter for many years at the *Waukegan News Sun*, reminisced in an article on Highwood about a linen purse she had stored in a cedar chest. The purse was the gift of a diva, Lucrezia Bori, to a star-struck little girl. Eritrea Pasquesi tells of Rosa Raisa, who in thanks for the loan of a baby buggy gave her five gold pieces.

During the 1920s, the height of grand opera's majesty and popularity in the United States, the Chicago Civic Opera Company brought stars to Chicago. And Ravinia Park, with a summer opera season at its outdoor pavilion, brought them to the North Shore.

The summer season at Ravinia led to a transformation in Highwood as musicians and singers came to town. Members of the chorus boarded with Italian families; the stars dined there. For ten weeks, Highwood came alive. *"Era più viva, più allegra,"* my aunt recalled.

The stars who dined in Highwood comprise an impressive cast: Claudia Muzio, Tito Schipa, Rosa Raisa, Giacomo Rimini, Lucrezia Bori, Elisabeth Rethberg, Virgilio Lazzari, Beniamini Gigli, Sonia Sharnova, Jose Mojica, Giuseppe Danise, Giovanni Martinelli, and even the great Caruso.

It was a time when women wore tiaras in all seriousness, when there was no shame in luxury, no embarrassment about hyperbole, when a reporter could write: "It is hard to imagine a more delightful place than Ravinia on a summer evening with its broad sweeps of lawn and its masses of bright blossoms, its stately trees and its winding paths, and over all the clear summer sky and as the darkness falls, the twinkling lights and gay lanterns of the pavilion open to the air and the evening breezes. . . ."

Could not a laborer aspire to the transformation that comes with standing at the edge of elegance?

"We'd pay to go in," says Eritrea Pasquesi, "and stand up and watch the opera. But if a boyfriend would bring me, he'd have to pay for a seat. You were really a lady. You came in with a Spanish shawl, you went all dressed up. And after the opera, we'd promenade. Highwood people, especially the men, they'd all be standing up there. They loved the opera. There was one fellow in Highwood, Enrico Floriani, he knew every opera by heart."

Most times, the immigrants stood and listened, Domenico Lattanzi recalls. "I never did go in there to sit down. There was first-, second-, or third-class tickets. We took the last one, the third class. Not first or second. That was all the big shots," he says.

Lattanzi was thirteen the first time he went to an opera, sneaking through a tunnel to avoid paying. "I saw my first opera at Ravinia," he recalls. "I saw *La Bohème*. Almost cried. Then we went back to see *Rigoletto, Traviata*. We heard *Il Pagliaccio*, the *Trovatore*. *Madame Butterfly*."

Tickets came to Tony Casorio through his employer, Harold McCormick, one of the principal backers of Chicago opera.

"In McCormick's over there," Casorio said, "they used to buy a big book of tickets and give them to the employees. At that time, there was all grand opera. And when I heard there was gonna be some Italian opera, like *Aida, o solo mio*, singing regular Italian opera, I used to go and take I don't know how many tickets. Oh, I was just crazy for it, you know."

Just as the laborers in Highwood sought out Ravinia, the opera performers sought out Highwood.

They came for the food. At a time when there were few restaurants in the area, the performers came to the private dining rooms of Italian women in Highwood, including those of Olimpia Fabbri and Pia Gibertini.

Pia Gibertini's guests included stars such as Giovanni Martinelli, Virgilio Lazzari, and Jose Mojica, a star of the 1920s who traded on his good looks and popularity to become a movie star, and then traded it all in to become a Franciscan monk. Giuseppe Sterzini, a chorister with the New York Metropolitan Opera, dined at the Gibertinis' frequently. This same Sterzini captured headlines when he was fatally stabbed during a rehearsal of the opera *Caponsacchi*. Cyrus McCormick, Jr., dined there with Ganna Waleska, an operatic prima donna who didn't have the voice to make it despite her marriage to the McCormick heir.

Mrs. Gibertini has saved newspaper clippings about her famous guests:

This is Sonia Sharnova. She had such beautiful clothes. And this is Lucrezia Bori. She used to come very often. This is Rosa Raisa, she was another beautiful singer.

This is Elisabeth Rethberg. She was serious. But nice. I missed her when she didn't come anymore. She married some millionaire. She was beautiful. Beautiful brown hair. And a beautiful voice. I went to the opera she gave—*La Giaconda*.

This is Jose Mojica. The other artists were jealous of him. Sometimes they made it hard for him. But he was always very content. I never thought he'd become a monk. But you could tell he was a very quiet man, that all that was going on for him, it didn't mean anything. He was so respectful and kind whenever he asked for a favor. I was sorry, and glad in a way, that he decided to become a holy man.

Perhaps the opera performers and opera-goers sought the same informality, the same intimacy, in Highwood that they found at Ravinia. "They were happy to come here," Mrs. Gibertini said. "There were more choristers living in Highwood than in other towns. When they had time off, they liked to pass time, it seemed to me, talking, singing. They used to say, 'working with the Metropolitan Opera, there's so many worries. When we come here, it's like going to the country.' "

Frequently, the choristers returned to the dining room late at night for a snack, *uno spuntino*, of prosciutto or soup. On special occasions, Mrs. Gibertini made *zabaglione*, a boiled custard livened with white wine or Marsala. Sometimes, Sterzini would sing from different operas, with the others joining him. Often, when the milkman arrived and the laborers were going to work, the opera singers would still be sitting in the dining room.

One Highwood resident who fell under the spell of the voices was a neighbor girl named Gloria Linari. A protégé of Rosa Raisa, she studied for years before taking the stage of the Lyric in Chicago and the Metropolitan in New York as Gloria Lind. Her father, Domenick Linari, says, "Gloria always wanted to sing. Even from when she was born, I think."

Mrs. Gibertini and her family were most attached to the members of the chorus. The singers joked with the laborers who lived upstairs. They played *bocce* in her yard. They were egalitarians, she says: Orazio Alfieri of Parma, Amedeo Mazzanti of Bologna, Guido Bertazzi of Trieste, Giuseppe Sterzini of Ferrara, and Castellini of Piacenza.

"The choristers were very democratic. They weren't arrogant. They didn't put on airs. Some of the artists thought because they were artists they were better. There were many choristers I preferred to artists. They were just as refined and educated but they talked to everyone," Mrs. Gibertini says.

The artists demanded more attention. And since she usually fed forty or fifty people, it was a strain.

Take, for instance, Martinelli, who ate at Mrs. Gibertini's house only once. Usually, he was a regular customer at Olimpia Fabbri's. One time he called Mrs. Gibertini for a reservation. She was full, but it was just as well she says. He would have taken up too much time.

"I didn't want to lose the others, and why should I, just because he's Martinelli?"

Maria Manfredini, who was a cook for the Gibertinis, also remembers the choristers affectionately: "One was Amedeo Mazzanti. One time, he made a dinner for a gang of them. But I had to help him out. We made lasagna. And he started putting in the pasta. I says, 'But you have to cook it before you put it with the sauce!' He says, 'Do you know better than the doctor?' I didn't say nothing anymore. You know what that pasta was like! They couldn't eat it. There was one of them, *maestro* Giacomo Spadoni, he ate a little bit, but the others couldn't eat it. The pasta was like a piece of leather. And Mazzanti gave me a dollar not to mention it anymore!"

Mazzanti, says Pia Gibertini, "could make even the saints laugh." Mazzanti was from Bologna. Like the hands folded in prayer, Modena and Bologna overlap in the Apennine mountains. The dialects of the provinces are different, but they are close enough, and, I imagine, Mazzanti must have found comfort among his countrymen from Emilia-Romagna.

The walls of Mrs. Gibertini's dining room were decorated with murals. I can only conjure up these paintings based on a couple of blurry photgraphs. They were pastoral scenes, where colors bled into one another creating misty backgrounds, an imitation of the ambiguous landscapes painted by the Venetian masters.

The artist, the story goes, boarded with Arcisa Bellei before she sold the business to the Gibertinis. Perhaps he figured he could find a patron on the North Shore. Maybe he thought he could pick up day work at a golf course and continue painting. In either case, he found his credit was good at the boardinghouse and preferred a life of ease, that is, neither painting nor laboring, until the proprietor, a hefty and imposing woman, said, "Pay up or get out." Then, I imagine, he talked fast. "My dear Mrs. Bellei, I'll tell you what. As a way of paying you back, I will paint murals in your dining room. Beautiful scenes of Italy. Everyone will envy you." I wonder if, as his boardinghouse brothers hoed, he hummed: "I am like Giorgione, a mystery artist, the immigrant Venetian, paying off debts with my paintbrushes." This is how I imagine a Venetian muralist came to paint misty landscapes in Highwood, a laboring town.

Highwood had a reputation as a rough town. But still the opera-goers and opera stars came to Highwood. "Those people loved Highwood," says Mrs. Gibertini. "Some people thought that it was a town where there were more poor people than rich people. And the opera people didn't think nothing about it."

Perhaps they sought in Highwood an evening of intimacy. License to relax. And the immigrants, who treasured a bed or a purse or a coin, perhaps they needed tidbits of fantasy for their souls, an item to set them apart in a world of laundry, mortar, and soil.

10

In paese: Uptown Highwood

To THE OUTSIDER, Highwood is composed of two streets: Greenbay Road and Sheridan Road, both of which run north and south. They are separated by the Northwestern train tracks. If Highwood is known to outsiders, it is because of the taverns and restaurants on these streets. In reality, both streets have had other names: Railway and Waukegan avenues. At one time, during the World War II years, those streets were lined mainly with taverns. There were nearly forty of them, catering primarily to the servicemen passing through Fort Sheridan to the European theater.

Now, like many other ethnic pockets, Highwood has gone upscale. The taverns are now bars where food is served. Patrons come to dine. Restaurants are pricey. Everett Bellei's grocery is a restaurant with valet parking. The Del Rio, which fifty years ago served a hearty dinner to laborers like Enea Cortesi, is now known for its veal dishes.

In the 1920s, Italian immigrants began to outnumber the Irish, Swedes, and Germans, and became the dominant ethnic group in Highwood. Mexicans and immigrants from other Central American countries have now taken the place of the Italian laborers. Highwood has two Mexican restaurants, and the building that once housed the Highwood theater is now a Hispanic grocery store.

In the early days, say before 1920, Western Avenue was the western boundary. Beyond it were fields where families went for picnics *in campagna*, to the country. Men went there, in packs, to hunt and play the games men played: *bocce* or *ruzzolone*, a game where a cheese-shaped disc is rolled along the ground. And straight west, at a clearing in the farmland, was Half Day, a cluster of taverns that shimmied its way through Prohibition.

But *in paese*, uptown Highwood, was the place for business transactions and social interaction. At the corner of Highwood Avenue and Railway Avenue men met in the morning to share gossip. Uptown was where the Modenese Society met. *In paese* was St. James, the Catholic church, and where social clubs like the Dante Alighieri Club and the *Cuore d'Arte* met.

In paese there are landmarks which help you find your way around a story. There is the location of the *para* house (does that translate "power house" or "repair house"—I have heard both) where the streetcars for the North Shore Inter-Urban Railway were housed. The line, which no longer exists, used to take laborers and maids to their jobs in nearby suburbs. As Adele Dinelli recalled, up by the *para* house is where Letezia Saielli lost her leg when she slipped and fell under the passing train.

There was Santi's building, a big brick structure on the corner of Railway Avenue and Highwood Avenue that housed a grocery and a dance hall. The demise of Santi's bank still causes people to take sides about the immigrant proprietor, Casper Santi, whose business transferred money to Italian banks and made loans to immigrants. When banks all over the country collapsed, so did his. There are those who say he helped build the town up; there are those who say, "What did you expect? You gave the money to Casper to hold, and he held it."

In paese, there were the grocers, each boasting the best butcher to a clientele with strict standards. There were bakeries, including Teodoro Minorini's, whose bread left Rosa Fiocchi, an articulate woman, unable to find the right words to describe it.

"Where are you going?" the wife says to the husband as he walks out the door, jingling coins in his pocket. *"Dove vai?"* says the husband to the wife, her pocketbook making a hollow sound when she snaps it shut as she drags it down to the crook of her elbow. *"Vado in paese."* I'm going uptown.

Gina DeBartolo, whose mother killed a snake to protect her nest:

This is something that might interest you and that everybody doesn't know. My grandmother Santi came over here in 1906 and you know there wasn't any Catholic congregation. And a priest used to come over from Techney monastery, and he would come and say Mass in the City Hall. He must have come on horseback because there was no other way he could come.

This would be Mrs. Santi of the Santi brothers that had the grocery store. My grandmother came over in 1906 with her youngest son, Domenic Santi. He was called Frank.

Frank actually died in 1918 with the flu epidemic. He died in the Highland Park Hospital, which had just started. The flu epidemic of

1918 was so contagious that they wouldn't take any of the patients in the hospital. They opened up Exmoor Country Club and put them in the country club. He died about November 10, 1918. We had the wake on Armistice Day.

I'll just give you little pointers that you might be able to work in some place. My father's building at 314 Railway Avenue, or you know, Greenbay Road—that had been the old stagecoach station. The horses and the coaches were downstairs and the inn rooms were upstairs.

My grandmother Santi's husband had preceded her to America. He died in the mine, in an accident in Pueblo, Colorado, and she was left a widow in Pievepelago, Italy.

My father married my mother in June 1901. And I was born in June 1902. After my parents came to Chicago, my father sent for my mother's brother Sante, who was fourteen years old. My father let him work in saloons and he lived there with them. Then my mother's brother came up here looking for a job. He was one of the first hired at Exmoor Country Club.

So, Sante came up here and established himself in Highwood and then he sent for his mother and the youngest brother. Then they sent for my mother's other brother, Casper, in Scotland where he was working in an ice cream parlor. Well, having been in the ice cream parlor business, they first opened an ice cream parlor on Waukegan Avenue. Then they decided to go into the grocery store business. Then they started a bakery. And then they moved to where Sante Bernardi had his store. I think there's a thrift store now. Then, from there, they bought the corner of Highwood Avenue and Greenbay Road and built a new building about 1915. So my mother was a Santi of the Santi Brothers Grocery, Bakery, and Market.

They did a lot of business with Fort Sheridan. That's where they made all their money. The second brother, especially, was such a salesman. He would go up there and sell groceries to the commissary. The groceries would come in on the Northwestern and they would unload them on the platform. And Railway Avenue wasn't even paved at that time. It was so muddy. They had an old truck and it would get stuck there. And they'd have to deliver all this meat up to the commissary. So the Santis were a real old family in Highwood. Casper Santi, the oldest, I guess he sponsored almost everybody here in Highwood for their citizenship.

Most all the old settlers were discharged soldiers. They married local women. At that time was mostly Irish and German, and a

number of Swedes. There was a little Lutheran church on the corner
of Oak Ridge and High. The Methodist church was where the
American Legion is. And there was another little Methodist church
down where the Labor Temple is now.

Well, remember we had bought a farm in Indiana. But my mother
always wanted to come to Highwood where her family was, so my
father sold the farm and he came up here to Highland Park looking
for a farm. He found one down in Highland Park where Bobolink
Golf Club is now. But before he bought it, he talked to this Bertucci.
"Oh," he said, "you'll never make a living on that farm. It's all
wet." Because it was slough. And so my father didn't buy it. He
bought a house in town instead.

My father went to work for the Catholic church in Highland Park.
And then, he bought a little ice cream store from Giannetto. I
worked there, which I hated. And probably that was one of the reasons why I married very young. We didn't have anything but high-
schoolers. We never had a lady customer come in. You don't just
send somebody to a Catholic school and put them in an ice cream
parlor—which is a hangout.

By the time my mother got here in 1918, there were a lot more
Italian families. But in 1906, there was the Lencioni family. Joe Ori's
family. The Mordinis. My grandmother lived upstairs in the old
Charlie Mordini house, which is the American Legion now. Then,
Mrs. Scornavacco and Mrs. Phillips were here. They were railroad
people. They worked on the Northwestern. I know Reilly was an
old family. And Severson. And the Llewellyn family. The discharged
soldiers did like the Italians did with the railroad—when they were
discharged, they just stayed.

And you know, of course, the land for Fort Sheridan was donated
to the government for the purpose of—well, Chicago was growing
and they had riots every once in a while and so they stationed Fort
Sheridan for protection of Chicago.

Then, there was another great big old house down on Oak Ter-
race, that was the chicken lady, *La Gallinaia*. She raised chickens.
She was an English woman. And she would come up to the store.
She just loved to talk to my Uncle Casper because he had been in
Scotland. She thought he was about the smartest man she'd ever
met. And one time, there was some kind of a doing and he told her,
"Why don't you come to this dance?" And she says, "I think I will."
So she went to the safe deposit box. She said she had been engaged
to some English something, and that she had all the jewels and she
could use them as long as she lived. But she couldn't sell them.

She'd have to return them to the English estate. And she wore all
her jewels and she had one of these fancy dresses. Of course nobody would have anything to do with her because otherwise she
was just down there in old clothes taking care of chickens and I
think they finally ran her out. I think all those old places had their
interesting characters, don't you think?

One time I went up to a garden shop. My husband, Alex, was
looking for something. I was looking around and I said to the man,
"Do you know the Santis from Highwood?" And the man said,
"The one that curled his mustache all the time?" I said, "Yeah." He
said, "I used to sing songs in the tavern in Edinburgh with him."
There was a Scotch colony in Lake Forest that the millionaires
would bring in. They brought in these little Scotch cattle, and then
they would bring in Scotch people to take care of them. And they
would trade at my uncle's store. They thought it was so funny because he had a Scottish brogue. Because he learned his English in
Scotland. But I'm talking to you about myself and I'm still trying to
think about Highwood.

Guy Viti, born 1898, made a good living *in paese*. The son of an
immigrant from Guarcino, a town near Rome, Viti and his family moved
to Highwood because that's where most of their contracting business
was. As a married man, he later switched to real estate and insurance.
As a successful businessman, he became a benefactor and built a
sanctuary in Guarcino. A former school board president in Highwood,
he has given careful thought to what he wants to say in the interview.
He makes a presentation, topic by topic. At the end, he eyes handwrit-
ten notes lying on the coffee table. He has covered the territory he wants
to cover. He has been very precise, although the crack in his voice
when he speaks of progress and age is unrehearsed.

My family lived in Chicago before moving to Highwood. We were
there for seven and a half years, see. We came from Italy in 1913.
Then we were contracting and we had our labor mostly from Highwood, so my father thought we'd move to Highwood from Chicago.
We moved in Highwood May 1, 1921. And then I married in 1921
and we have quite a family. Then my wife and I came here to Wilmette when we couldn't find a house in Highwood.

We found this house in Wilmette, and we've been here ever since.
And we've been here, happy, because we have a nice location.
We're Catholics. We have the school and church right here. And St.

George's High School, where the boys went, is not very far. Everything is convenient. We're still here.

I changed from contracting to real estate and insurance. When I saw a lot of children coming, I thought possibly that would have been a better trade for the children, you see. I began insurance particularly because insurance is something which is renewable. You sell the house, you are through, you have to keep on getting other houses, you see. Our office first was on Railway Avenue, 226 Railway. We still own that. And then we moved. We built our own office then, you see.

I came to the United States when I was fifteen years. I graduated from grammar school but I didn't go very far in high school. My father wanted me to be a banker. So I went to work for an Italian-American bank in Chicago. I worked there not long because I didn't like the family. They were paying me very little, but nevertheless, they were paying me. They had two sons there. Just bums. I was saying, "I'm not gaining anything by this association with these people here."

Then I began to work in water and sewer construction. We worked from Wilmette up to Highland Park. We put up pretty good-sized jobs in Highland Park. 'Course what I'm telling you doesn't help you about Highwood. I don't want to make a big story outside of myself, see?

You see, Highwood, talking about Highwood, when I came to Highwood there were some Italians here. The Italians were just coming at the time. Most of the people, they were Swedes. Scandinavian. This would be 1921. Well, it was funny for me not to see Italians. The Santi brothers, Sam and Casper, had a grocery store. They really were the pioneers of Highwood. They made themselves. Well, they began with the store, and finally, they were successful. Then we had all the others, mostly laborers. What you have is still there now, the sons of the immigrants and so on. Most of the stores in Highwood are Italian, see, but the Swedes, we had a tough job there in order to begin.

I felt bad when after a couple of years we were there in Highwood, we thought, first of all, as soon as I saw that most of them were Scandinavians, there, well, I called on a lot of these Italians, so we organized the Italian American Association.

We had a man, Aurelio Ori, I'll never forget his name. He was a nice fellow, working as superintendent at one of the local golf courses. Well, he ran for alderman. He got three votes. It was a shame for us. Well, as I said, it might have been about 1925; he was a nice fellow, he deserves to be an alderman to represent the Italians. All the others are mostly Swedes, you see. And the mayors. I thought, sooner or later, we're gonna have these Swedes changed to Italians. I mean, I really had that in mind. And it happened. Right now they're, most of them, Italians. You see?

But I also visualized the political war between the Italians themselves. Which, it happened. We had the two Italians one against the other. We always tried to prevent it. They look whether you are from Modena or Bari, and so on, you see? But we were all Italians. Because when we had the organization, we had most of the Italians from Highland Park and Highwood in this organization. They knew each other well and we had dances and all that, you see. And it was nice. I liked that. Young people coming up, they knew each other.

Charles Fiore, Egidio Mocogni, and Joe Menoni were in the Italian American Association. We got all the laborers in our association. Then, we had the Highwood Business Association. That's where the businessmen were. Very few Italian businessmen then, see? But finally, most of them are Italian now. We helped people a lot, you know that was the purpose of that. Not only in the language, but also the poor people. Oh yes, the main thing in there—the Italians were not poor—good labor is not poor.

And I think it worked out over there, because in Highwood the people that buy property in Highwood, they stay there. They own their own home. Before, you know, if it looked like a shack when they bought it, after five years, it's not a shack anymore. They are proud of their house. Their home and their family. And that's a success, what I'm talking about. There's not much more than the family, because that remains. I was twenty-four years old, now I'm eighty-five years old. Time goes on, you see, and my children are getting old. You see, that's what it is. You see. And we're happy. I am. And I'm happy about my children, that each one of them is married. And have a family and what can you want? But I'm not talking about Highwood again. That's what the proposal was.

What we did, we had to, first of all, get these Italians to become citizens. Now, through our association, we got assistance to do it in the county, Lake County, judges and clerks and everybody. They needed us because they wanted to be elected, so they helped us to get these people to become citizens. I prepared, myself, two hundred questions. You see, when they got up there, they ask you a lot of questions. How many senators, how many representatives, the president, how many years and all that stuff. We passed them out to all these fellas so that they could study. I thought we should really mean it. Not only talk.

And we succeeded, really. Because we made a lot of citizens. And we were witnesses for them. Sometimes I had to leave my job to be a witness. But then you were happy when this fellow became a citizen. All the citizens of Highwood, we made them at the time. Soon as we begin to have the election, well, we succeeded because we got aldermen and we had the justices of the peace. All Italians. Which is its reward.

I'm happy every time I go to Highwood. I see the names of all the businesses there. Now, we're beginning to see attorneys, Italian descendants, which I had something to do with their fathers, they came in here as laborers, now they have the sons who are attorneys. I'm happy. We have accountants. We have well-educated people. At that time, very few.

Myself, I say that the Italians worked together and got where they are now. We have a beautiful city hall. And the mayor's an Italian, you see. They had a chief of police, also an Italian, for quite some time. Then you see, when you expand, then you don't think anymore of them as Italians. Because it's mixed in there. You want it to be that way. Before, they didn't want us to walk on the sidewalk. The Italian was secondary when we went to Highwood. I didn't like that. We're no better than anybody else, but why should we be under everybody, see? Now, we're equal. The Italians are just at par with the others.

Highwood is not the same Highwood now, you see. To me, it's a pride to see nice buildings. When you know that they were shacks and now they're nice buildings. But Highwood, the people in Highwood, they're more refined. They're more educated because, we're not talking about the old fellows, now, we're talking about the young people. In Highwood there's a third generation now. And they all go to college.

Right now we have Italian judges in Chicago, the best judges in Chicago. We have Italians who are the presidents of boards. Iacocca. You know, the head of Chrysler. Well, I say the father of Lee Iacocca, possibly, was a laborer. I had some feelings that this fellow Iacocca will be called upon, maybe vice president or something like that. See, and he's got the brains, see, no question about it.

But now the Italians just get best, whatever they do. And I like that. See, because they deserve it. They worked for it. The Italians are really growing.

Zeffero Pacini, still a *giron'*, perhaps, despite using a walker:

C'era la miseria. There was misery. In those times, it was hard to get even a piece of bread. There was nothing there. After I came in America, then there was something, when I came in America.

I went to work as a gardener in Lake Forest for McCormick, for one of the brothers. My cousin worked as a mechanic. From there I went to work in Highland Park at a small business. I had friends there, and then, the boss had a lot of workers, and he was looking for a trustworthy man. He liked me. Between the fifteen or eighteen working there, he liked me. This was at Zengeler's Cleaners.

See, when I was at McCormick, his foreman had a cleaner that was looking for men. There were a lot up at McCormick, fourteen or fifteen, but they picked me. Dumford, the foreman, was a cousin of Zengeler. When he retired, Zengeler sold the company to me and two others together. I didn't even know how to speak English yet. The business is still in Highland Park. There were a lot of Italians working there.

The customers were all Americans, Jews. They were all *signori.* No, we didn't clean our clothes there because it cost money. Not like today, but it cost. I learned how to clean. I stayed in the business.

Someone from outside wanted to buy my business, but I never sold it because it fed my family.

(from Italian)

Everett Bellei, a butcher who passes out jokes like meat wrapped in paper over a counter:

In those days it was nothing but Irish and German and Swedes. We had a lot of Swedes because there used to be a lumber camp and the Swedes are great to fool around with lumber. And the Irish used to work on the North Shore. There were not too many Italians when we came here in 1907.

Well, my mother backed me up to start out with. But after a little while I didn't need any help. Then, I went over to the grocery business and made enough business out of it to carry on. And when I sold the business, I got quite a bit of money out of it. I went in business when I was sixteen years old. And I didn't miss the school at all.

Where I got my start was selling ice cream in Santi's building. That was a beautiful building. We had sketches all over the wall in the ice cream parlor that were done by Dante Bonetti. He was a good painter. I had the ice cream parlor from 1917 to 1921. You learn the business as you go along. If you have the vision to go into something, you learn.

We had forty thousand soldiers up here in Fort Sheridan. The town was all young people. We were open until eleven or twelve o'clock. I had to give it up because I never got home until late at night, and I thought I'd go into something that wouldn't take up so much time. So, I got into the grocery when Everett, my first son, was born in 1921. When I was a young fellow I had worked for Santi Brothers grocery, so I knew all about the grocery business. When I opened up, I hired two professional meat cutters and that's where I learned my trade. And I had two trucks running delivery.

I had enough money to buy the building and the grocery store. A fellow by the name of Hemmler had the grocery store and Fritsch owned the building. Years back Fritsch used to have a store when there was their old settlement of German people.

We had a good start until the Depression came along, and that hurt. Depression hurts small and big.

There was no grocery chains. We were the chains then. We bought meat from all the big packers in Chicago. Oscar Mayer. Wilson. Swift and Armour. It used to be the Northwestern that brought up all the meat, and we had to go over to the station with a truck, pick it up and bring it in the shop. Later on, when they build the roads, the big business people bought trucks and gave you service. And at first Pasquesi Brothers transported produce to me. And boy, they missed the business when some started to do their own delivery.

I used to make Italian sausage. I couldn't make enough of it. When you make sausage you got to know what you're doing. I thought I knew the meat business a little better than the majority of people. That's why I had too many customers. Now, your pork loin should be about ten pounds. When you go over twelve pounds, you'll get in trouble. It's the age of the hog. The older they get, the tougher they get. See?

Giangiorgi Grocery came in after the Depression. There was Gandolfi Grocery, was in before that. Santi was a strong competitor, but I went after different business than he did. I had trucks running all the way to Ravinia. I went after the big business. I had a lot of them in Lake Forest. I even had Albert Lasker, you heard of him?

People that had money—their businesses were in Chicago and the labor, they just took care of the town. And there's been a lot of

building going on for many years. And even Lake Forest. It took a
lot of manpower to build all those new homes they built. Lake Forest has always been taken care of. There's always been building
going on. Deerfield was a little hick of a town. And believe me,
Deerfield is some town now.

The Italians are all hard-working people. They don't fool around
much when it comes to work.

Adeodato Fontana, a mountain boy who took to America like a fish
to the sea:

When they start building, the people working as carpenter, labor,
they didn't like the Italian too much. Most of the people didn't.
There was no sympathy for the Italian, very little. They were kind
of jealous or something. After that they got mixed. Then it was all
right. It's a big change between now and then. Oh, Jesus. Now it's
friendly.

I used to walk from here to Evanston and come back with the
streetcar to find a job. You'd go down and see if they need any labor. "No!" That's all. I have to go back. Oh, it was hard time. After,
when they started working and work come out, then they got more
friendly, more independent because everybody was working.

Our first grocery store was on Deerfield Avenue in Highland Park.
There was a fellow there, he was Italian, a Pasquesi. I had a bad leg
so it was hard to walk, and I said, "I'd like to buy that little store
there and he wants to get rid of it." So I asked, "How much you
want?" So and so. Alright. Hundred dollars. In those days it was a
lot of money, you know.

We used to sell ice cream to a lot of kids. A lot of kids I have at
night especially. And pop, oh boy! There was a big porch, you
know. It was full of kids. They all make me mad. Oh boy, I used to
sell a lot. I was busy. I used to do my business mostly with the Jew.
Nice people, some of them are very nice.

It was a brick house. There was a porch in front. Shelves and a
counter where I used to sell the ice cream. Oh, I used to sell a lot of
ice cream. The kids would come back from the golf course, the cad-
dies. They used to buy pop, you know, they used to play with the
pop and *sshhhh!!!* Oh, they made me mad!

Highwood's changed a lot. Before, they was against the Italians,
you know. Now, they're all friendly. Before, you go and ask for
work, they'd say, "No, you're Italian." I can remember a lot of

times. Little by little, it was more friendly. Now, there's nothing to
it. Now they marry each other, mix, you know. It's a lot of
difference.

During the Depression, it was bad, it was bad. It was bad. Friends
and family, they used to come in the store all the time, asking for
the charge. Who say no? Nobody pay. I lost a lot of money.

If I go back in business — cash and carry.

Leonardo DePalma, who plays *scopa* at poolside and ate butterscotch
candy while discussing Mussolini:

I started working in construction. They was making the waterhouse in Waukegan and I worked there about six months. Then we
were working in Mundelein. I worked on the church, on the bridge,
everything, all the construction, a waterhouse. They were all big
jobs. It was 1921. We worked as laborers. Laborers. A lot of Italian
people. We had work until then the Depression came out. Jobs was
pretty scarce to get.

We lived on Prairie Avenue three years. I move in this house the
week before Christmas. But it wasn't complete, you know. I had a
lot of friends that came and helped me out. Everybody was feeling
sorry when we had four kids! Yeah, sure, I helped them on their
houses. My wife, you know, made dinner for all the people that
come and work here and drink together. Before, there was not a
lotta money, you know. Now everybody got money, see. But before,
they have to come over and help each other. But now we don't
help. Before we all depended. Now all independent. Everybody on
his own.

Well, 1937, I went to work for the city of Highwood. I was superintendent of the street department. Until 1943. Nineteen forty-three,
I was in partnership with My Favorite Inn. In the tavern business.
And I stayed with that one year. And after the year, I went on my
own and I buy the Tower of Casino from Milani on Highwood Avenue. Then 1952 I sell out.

How did I get my job with the city? Through politicians!

Well, I was finance secretary of the local union. The Labor Union
Local 152, so these politicians, they knew I was finance secretary of
the union, figured they would get some votes, see? And they come
to me to support them. Yeah, Italian politicians. So finally, you
know, I helped them out as much as I could, and I got the job for
the city. And I worked ten years for the city as superintendent of
street department.

You know, the businessman, he had his own union, too. The labor's got his own union, and then they get together and agree on the wage, how much they're gonna pay, things like that, see.

There was Tony Rossi. Onoratello Dorini. Then Tom Mussatto come in. He was the business agent. The recorder/secretary was Louie Diasparra, I was finance secretary, Ruffolo was a trustee, and Peter Mazzetta was a trustee. Tom Mussatto was from north Italy. So it was a mix.

Most of the roads in Highwood had been built by 1926. At that time I did mostly repairs and things like that, sewers, streets. Then they built the water works at that time. We make a lot of new sewers. See, until 1926 the only paved streets were Highwood Avenue and Prairie Avenue. The other ones were all mud roads. Even in town. Waukegan Avenue was all brick. The rest, Railway Road, all mud. Planks here, planks there.

When I first came there were not very many cars, but there was a few. Most of the businessmen had cars. Most all the class people that worked in construction, all rode either the Northwestern train or the North Shore electric train.

You'd see, in the morning, on the corner of Highwood Avenue and Greenbay Road, most all the class that worked—you had the car, take five, six with you in the car for transportation. Now, everybody got the car. In one family, three or four cars! Before it was different. All together. There was no radio, no television. Nothing. We get together at night, you know, the families all together, play a game of card, have a little drink, a little coffee, things like that. One time over your house, next time, my house.

I was glad I was here. Because was not *fasciste* yet in Italy in 1920, you know Mussolini come in power in 1921, 1922, see, but I'm glad I was here because I no like that party anyway because he doing the dirty work all the time. You have to join. If you don't want to join, he'll kill 'em and things like that.

Massima Vanoni, who was always old for her age and remains youthful:

At first *nonno* made his own wine. Then finally I said, "Enough!" There were always those little flies would come in the basement even if you kept the windows and doors closed. Finally, then, he stopped making it and bought wine.

How did they make it? First they bought the grapes. They went to buy them in Chicago. Sometimes he made wine with Angelino Grandi. The grapes came from California. And then they washed their feet and stepped into this barrel, which was called a *botte*, and they stomped on the grapes. And as the grapes were pressed, the juice came out. And it had to stay there for awhile. And then they put the juice in smaller containers that were called *barili*, little barrels. Afterwards they added some more grapes and then water and made another kind of wine that was called *mezzo vino*. It was lighter. And then when the wine was ready—they knew when it was ready—they put it into bottles. It took, altogether, between making the wine, the *mezzo vino*, adding the grapes, a good month.

Was it good? For me, it was awful. Too strong.

(from Italian)

Enea Cortesi, whose follow-through in *bocce* is picture-perfect:

I used to go a tavern owned by a friend of mine. The Del Rio, now, they call it. The friend of mine, when he first opened, his name was Billy Biagetti. He married a widow. That lady Linda, she was a good, hardworking lady, I'm telling you. We'd go to eat there sometimes, especially on Sunday. We used to eat a little late, one o'clock or so. But I didn't want to be late to play these games with my friends. *Bocce*. Or we played, *ruzzolone*, they call it—cheese-throw.

The *ruzzolone*? We used to play with a disc that was about ten inches across, and you wind a string around it two and a half times. And you hook it and get a hold of it. And then you throw. You had to throw fast but you gotta have control, you know, to throw it on the street, not off the street. Because if you throw outside the street—no good. That's tough. You throw it on the ground, naturally. We would start from here, say, and then go along the road there, and we used to pick a point and we see how many throws it takes to get there. And whoever goes there with less throws is gonna win the game.

We had a fellow, Aldo Piacenza, he used to be crazy about it but he wasn't any good. He used to own the ice cream store on the corner of Highwood Avenue and Greenbay Road. That fellow was crazy about *ruzzolone*. He wanted to stay with me for partner. There was a fellow by the name of Egidio Piacenza. Was a big young fellow. He had a lot of speed but no control. Osvaldo Rabbatini was pretty good, and another fellow by the name of Pepe. Your mother's father, Tony, he used to be pretty good. He wasn't strong enough but he had control.

That game, it come from Italy. They used to play with cheese on

the street. With the round cheese, naturally. Then, they started making them out of wood. We used to make it ourselves. You gotta have
good, hard wood and seasoned, not fresh. Walnut, any kind of
heavy wood. Make from the stump of a tree. This Aldo Piacenza
used to make them. He made four once. Oh, boy, he was crazy
about it.

You know what happened once? We was on O'Connor's Road
playing, and it was me, and the fellow that I was playing against
was Jimmy Bartolotti. He used to have a tailor shop in Highwood.
And Jimmy was ready to throw after me, see, and a car was coming. And I told Jimmy, "Wait a second, there is a car coming." So
the car came up. He stopped and I guess he saw me when I was
throwing. The man asked what kind of game it was. And Jimmy got
up and says, "Watch me, I'll show you." He start making three or
four steps and before letting go, he fell down. Those people in the
car, it was a man and woman, they started laughing. They said,
"That's a heck of a game! I don't want to learn!" Everybody was
talking about it. But we used to ask Jimmy, "Show me how the
game is played!"

Oh, I was one of the best. We used to go up by Fort Sheridan,
just north of Fort Sheridan before you get to the Sacred Heart
school, there is a road that comes down to the lake and there used
to be a dump. We used to play there. Even the officers from Fort
Sheridan used to come over and look. Then, they closed it, and
from there, we used to go out west here on O'Connor's Road. There
was very few cars. West of Deerfield. There was a few cars going by
there. Nobody bothered us. The owner of the property used to be
O'Connor. He says, "Go out and have a good time." Every once in
a while we used to buy O'Connor a present. He used to own a coal
yard up there on Highwood Avenue.

Last night I went up to Highwood to play *bocce*. There was about
twelve ladies playing. I play every afternoon and every night. But
on Friday night the ladies go up there. They've got their own team.
Some of them play good. In the afternoon until four or four-thirty
we play, and at night around six or seven o'clock, they open up until midnight, all depending if there are people playing.

No, we got a nice place to play for the old people. You'd be surprised. What am I going to do here now? I'm here by myself. I take
off, I got my car. Take off. I go out for lunch every day. I go here
and there. McDonald's, and sometimes it's too crowded, you can
hardly go in, it's packed. And after I get through, I go up there and

play *bocce*. There's always somebody up there. Who don't like to play *bocce*, they play cards.

Louis Baruffi, the *second* child born in Dalzell:

We were Gonnella's soccer team. When Gonnella sponsored our team, there was a fellow by the name of Gino Capitani, he got the route of delivering bread to the Italian families in Highland Park, then pretty soon it started growing, and pretty soon all the stores in Highwood and Highland Park were taking Gonnella bread. Well, we were the ones that started it. Because they sponsored us. And how they sponsored us, John Ugolini used to be secretary of the Italian Chamber of Commerce in Chicago, that's how he got to know the Gonnellas. So he asked them to sponsor our team. They bought the uniforms. We used to play the Italian-Americans, the Swabians, the German-Americans, the Swedish-Americans, Luxembourg, and the Maccabees.

You bet your tooten it was a good team! A championship team! We used to take 'em all. Oh, yeah. This was many, many years ago. The thirties and forties. I played center half. See, I come from a coal mining town and we learned to play down there. And then there was Mario Sacco, he had played down in Mark. And then George Bivatti, Mark, too. Then Ray Paghinelli and Dino Paghinelli, both from Mark. Then Nello Piacentini. Then there's Art Amedei, he owns the garage. Then Emedio Amedei, his brother. John Peradotti and Peter Peradotti, they both come from Mark. And John Pacini, another guy from Mark, the one that owns the bowling alley. Then Robert Magnani, he comes from Mark also. There was a bunch from Scotland and two brothers from Kansas City. Then Frank Dinelli, I think he come from the mines also. And then there was Joe and Guido Gualandri, and John Ugolini and Domenic Ugolini from Italy. John Ugolini did all the organizing. He played center forward. Nello Piacentini played goalie. He was a good one. I'm gonna tell you something about it.

We went and played Marengo, that's on the way to Rockford, and that's a game we should of lost but your grandfather played so good that day, he seemed to be there, every place that ball went to that dang goal, he was there. And he saved the day for us. They should of beat us. That day there, they shoulda taken us. But, old Nello was there.

One time we had won the championship here in Illinois, well, there was only teams in Chicago, and we won the championship there, so we went up to Wisconsin. We played the third Wisconsin state champion and beat them. But afterward they said, we'll let you play our first team if you beat our second team. Well, old John Ugolini went back and he said, "No, we'll play your first team!" And we just beat the heck out of them. We just did.

Philip Pasquesi, who asks my mother if she likes America:

It's kind of funny, Highwood's boundary, it's very, very funny. You know Caringello's store on the corner? It's true, half is in Highland Park, half is in Highwood.

We couldn't go to the beach, we didn't have no beach in Highwood. You know behind Walker Avenue? You know Lake Michigan, it was all owned in Highland Park. So finally, I don't know, they complained to Washington, now we got the right of way at Walker Avenue, we're entitled to that piece of beach there. See, the beach, that's for Fort Sheridan, they've got a little bit of Highwood, and then the rest is all Highland Park. That was a funny, funny thing.

My cousins, Sante Pasquesi, his brothers, and my brother were in a trucking business. So Santo said to me, listen, "We're all one family, we're in business. To leave you out, we don't feel good."

So finally I hadda quit the Moraine Hotel and then I went and work on the truck. For fourteen years, I drove a truck from Highwood way over to South Water Market in Chicago. At that time they didn't have solid tires on the trucks and every bump you hit, ooh, and they were hard to steer. I'll tell you, when I come home at night I had enough.

We used to deliver from Evanston all the way up to Lake Forest. It was all private groceries at that time. No chain store. We used to charge them so much a package. We used to make good money.

But 1929 we went broke.

I come here 1920, I never once went and ask for a job. They called me. Would you know, that one time, I had the Santi Brothers, they call me up every night and I was delivering bread for Minorini. Gonnella Baking Company, they wanted me to deliver bread around here. And I had Skokie Valley Cleaners. It was 1942, I had three people that wanted me to work for them.

In 1942 I went to work for Santi Brothers Dairy. And that was the best move I ever made. Then I was a shareholder. Bought Santi Brothers out.

I was one of the best milkmen around. Everybody in Highwood bought milk from me.

Mary Baldi, who knows they are looking after her, not the dog:

I was working for these Jewish people, and she said to me one day, "Mary, why don't you get a bunch of your friends over to your house some evening and I'll come over and I'll bring the food, and I'll show you how to cook American, because the Italians make rich food, you know." So, well, I was there that night at this place where we were dancing, and mentioned it to my friends and I said we could make it as a sewing club, you know, we'd meet. And we sat down and we said, "Okay, I'll tell you what we'll do. Next Thursday"—this was on a Saturday night, and next Thursday, I guess I wasn't working that day—I said, "Get a few of your friends. I'll get some of mine, us three together we'll get a few ladies and we'll talk it over. We'll see what we'll do." So we got together. They came and we decided it would be a philan—how do you call it, philanthropic—yeah, we would do things to help the poor, the sick, and that's what we did.

Well, we were looking for a name, then, and in Spring Valley where I worked there was a club, they called it a prosperity club. On Sunday, the miners would take their wives over and they'd sit down, have a glass of beer—that was the only place they could do that and it was called prosperity club. And this was in 1929 when a Highwood bank went broke. And everybody was saying, "Oh, prosperity's around the corner." So I said, "Let's make it 'Italian Women's Prosperity Club.' " They were saying prosperity was coming back or something. So that's what it was. Italian women. Only Italian people could join. And that's what we're doing.

There were eleven of us. So we all got a job. We put Mary Somenzi as president, because she was the one that had more nerve, you know. I was very shy. She was the president. Lena Gualandri was vice president. I was the treasurer. Mary Bernardini was the secretary.

Eritrea Pasquesi, the *canterina* of the family:

We used to dance in the street. I remember Adam Bernardi played the saxophone and he had an orchestra. Then we used to go on Sundays and dance out at Diamond Lake. We'd go out in broken-down Fords or what-have-you. Say, five or six of us in a car, and we'd dance there in the afternoon. You could go boat riding and you could dance. Oh, we had a good time, I'll never forget. One time it rained coming home and with one of these open Fords and I had a beautiful big orchid hat and the rain ruined my hat.

We used to go down to Sunset Park in Highland Park on Thursday nights. It was ten cents a dance. The men had to buy tickets to dance because they had to pay the orchestra, you know. And for Highwood Days, they would dance in the street. And that was ten cents a dance, too. I was very popular in the dancing department.

But I had to learn the English way of dancing, you know. In Italy, in fact, they were more modern there than they were here at that time. We did the fox-trot and the tango. But it was a little different here. Over here, they had the two-step, it was just a little different, longer steps and so on.

Every Saturday night there was a different orchestra. And good orchestras, too, here in Highwood. There was the street dance. And then, you know Santi Brothers Meat Market, that corner there? Upstairs there was a hall, they called it Santi Hall. This is where we went to dance. You pay fifty cents to go in. There was no air conditioner those days, and boy, was it hot up there! There were no Italians at those dances. They were Swedish or German, or whatever they were.

I remember just one song, "Tie Me to Your Apron Strings Again." "I know there's room for me, upon your knee." That's all I can remember. "Sing to me a song and then take me back in your apron strings again." They played "Yes, we have no banana, we have no bananas today." And then what was the other one? It was a waltz. It was very pretty. "Three O'clock in the Morning." "Oh, it's three o'clock in the morning, I dance all night with you." That was so pretty.

My brother-in-law Aldo Crovetti played the accordion and he would go and we had two, well, there were quite a few of these houses in Highwood where they would serve liquor. One of them was named Quattrini. *Quattrini* means "money," and he took me and my sister Svezia along. And there were all men there. There was no girls, just Swannie and I. And they would sell those men the wine that they had made, or what did they call it, that bathtub gin. They would sell wine at a dollar a bottle and they would invite these girls over because the men would come if they knew there were some girls there. But I didn't know what it was all about. We just sat there and just listened to my brother-in-law play the accordion and that's it.

Then, years later, I was one of the first presidents of the *Sacro*

Cuore. It was religious, you know. We went to communion once a month and we went on pilgrimages. Once we went to Holy Hill and we went to Chicago for some big doing at Solider's Field before the war. It was a peace thing.

I was president of the Italian Women's Prosperity Club for two terms. And then I was in different social groups. One of them was the Dante Alighieri Club. We gave plays and dramas, not heavy dramas. Variety shows. And we'd give benefits. One was a benefit for Oak Terrace School in Highwood. Another one for Elm Place School. Silvio Muzzarelli and I sang.

We had a regular orchestra. Mr. Aldo Biaggi was director of the orchestra. And he had a band, too. On Sunday afternoons, there was a little gazebo where they would play. In fact, he wrote a march, it was called the "Dante Alighieri March." He was smart, boy. He was a smart little man. He looked like a real musician. With this long hair, *svelto*, oh boy, he was a corker. He had a tailor shop in Highwood. Just before he died, his hair was all white. He looked really like a *maestro*, like one of those old time *maestri*.

At the end of my interview with Giulia Mordini, we dicker. She won't let me take her photograph. "Why?" "Oh, no, no, no." "Just one." "Oh, no, no, no, too old. *Troppo vecchia*." Finally, we reach an agreement. I am not sure how. She poses sweetly.

One time, they danced more than now. There were parties more often—picnics, things like that. People had more fun. There was the opera. I went many times to the opera. To Ravinia. I went even to Chicago to see *Aida*. All these fun things.

In my family, everyone, everyone, good musicians. In our house in Italy there was always entertainment, really. It's true. If you came into the big room, there was room enough for dancing. There was little to eat but we had more fun. My brother Delmo played the accordion—*ma proprio bene*. My brother Domenico, who was younger, played everthing. He played the clarinet, everything. One played the guitar. *Tutti suonatori*, all musicians. What did I play? Nothing. I danced. We were poor, but we had fun, really! When he was young, Domenico played the organ in church. He was good. How did he learn? By himself! *Macché* teachers! He learned himself. My brother Delmo played in America, too, when Biaggi had his band. But they were all *suonatori*, my brothers. And good, too.

(from Italian)

Caterina Lattanzi, who says, "I'm the boss now, right?"

When I move in Winnetka, then I have some friends in Highwood. Mrs. Marsilla Mazzetta. And there was Cristina Mazzarossi,
she come before us. And Mrs. Gardarella. All from the same town
in Italy. All *abruzzes*! I used to take the train, the North Shore line,
to go to Highwood on Saturday or Sunday and stay there with Mrs.
Mazzetta.

Well, we eat, cooking, have a little picnic with the kids. Everybody have small kids. It was like a little family, you know, because
come all the same time.

In our town, the twenty-ninth of June was the feast of San Pietro.
We had a *festa*, made a *ballo*, a dance, you know. In the summer,
especially, in the night. Dancing, the accordion, and rent one room
someplace. Polka, mazurka. *Ma* me, my mother was so strict, you
know, I can't go. You know, I didn't have no time to think about
missing the *festa*. Because I was too busy and in a new country, it
was so different. Big change, you know. Big change. In the Fourth of
July, when it comes the Fourth of July, we go to the parade. Go
home and cook and eat. A little different, that's all. That's the *festa*.

No, I didn't feel like anyone was better than anyone else, because
I have much contact with the *toscani, modenes'*, or *bares'* or *calabres'*.
I respect the same. I'm that way. Some people say, *"modenes'* is
good," or *"bares'* is bad." I don't grow up that way. It don't bother
me the colored people. I'm not that way. I still hear them now, they
don't like the colored people. For me, I say, it's people. It's colored.
God, he made them that way.

Teresa Ponsi, who, like her mother, walked like a hare:

On Sundays we always had picnics *in campagna*. Always. Some
women made *tortellacci*, someone else made this, someone else that.
The men played *bocce*, cards. For us, it was a lot of work making all
the food. We made *polenta*. And when we went away to a party or
something, always with the kids—we didn't have money to get a
babysitter. There was such confusion.

(from Italian)

Viterbo Ponsi, whose says the trade is "in the blood":

The Modenese Society had a wooden platform for years and
years. On Route 22, before you get to Half Day, there were some
woods. Now, it's all houses. And then we went on picnics even at
that monastery up north of Libertyville. There was a big place and

the Modenese went up there a lot. We drove up there with the cars packed.

(from Italian)

Teresa Saielli, who defied the priest on the feast of Santa Teresa:

We danced until we were tired, until the morning, in the basement, in the houses. We even danced here. Bertucci played the accordion. Life was different. People kept themselves happy. Well, now, it's a different thing. It's better that people are better off, no? It was bad, but it was good, those times there. When you're young everything's good, no? *Tempo passa. I figli crescono, la mamma imbianca.* Time passes. The children grow, the mother grows white.

(from Italian)

CHAPTER

11

Bad Press:
Highwood as a Tavern Town

"HIGHWOOD ALWAYS HAD a bad, bad, bad, bad reputation," says Philip Pasquesi:

In fact, we had Fort Sheridan so close, and when they opened up the taverns after Prohibition, the soldiers used to come in town here and every night they had some kind of a fight, you know, between the soldier and other people. It was pretty bad. Soldiers and the Italians. You know when people get drunk. It's just like somebody, they used to call them "wop" or a "dago" or something like that and they start to fight. And then there was a time here when we had the soldiers, they used to get the girls. Not from Highwood, but used to get girls from outside. And they used to do business with the soldiers. Used to come from all over the North Shore. They used to come from all over. And not Highwood girls. Highwood girls, they were very, very good.

From the beginning, it seemed Highwood was destined to get bad press. Local newspapers from the teens and twenties record episodes of drunken brawls between locals, soldiers, and the Italians. As late as 1965, community leaders were still struggling to shake Highwood's reputation as a rough, tavern town. A headline in a *Chicago Tribune* magazine piece reads: "Weary of the reputation of Highwood, Illinois, as a saloon-saturated square in North Shore circles, a small group of businessmen is determined to drive out indifference and instill a Continental atmosphere."

The installation of Fort Sheridan on the shores of Lake Michigan was the first step in giving Highwood its reputation as a rough garrison town, and for many years, even before the arrival of the Italians,

Highwood was known as "Whiskey Junction." Highwood was report-
edly called "the toughest town in America" by Theodore Roosevelt.

During Prohibition, Highwood had a reputation for being a town
where the thirsty could procure a drop of alcohol, and where gambling
and prostitution went on. "Highwood really was, well, Highwood was
known as a tavern town. They come in here and then they do a lot
of things in Highwood. And not only gambling," says Guy Viti, an
Italian immigrant and Highwood businessman.

The reputation of Highwood as a rough town predates, certainly, the
arrival of the Italian immigrants. Sprinkled through press reports in
the years preceding their arrival are calls to uphold and improve Highwood's reputation, to uplift the town's "sanitary and moral conditions."

Since its early days, Highwood has struggled to gain respectability
in the eyes of its more affluent neighbors. In his book on the North
Shore, Michael H. Ebner calls Highwood a community "out of place"
on the wealthy North Shore. Indeed, this working-class town, with its
longtime reputation as a saloon town, was an awkward aside for neighboring communities that had vice under control. During Prohibition,
tough women were bootleggers and certain private homes sold liquor
illegally in blind pigs. Highwood was one of the few spots in a stretch
between Chicago and the Wisconsin border where liquor could be had,
a lapse on an otherwise sober shoreline.

The arrival of Italians in great numbers following World War I became
very closely related with Highwood's tarnished reputation in the minds
of many people. In particular, the Italian miners who came to the North
Shore in the spring to work as seasonal laborers were singled out for
harassment by the residents of Irish and Swedish descent.

The crime reports in the Highland Park newspapers were studded
with the names of Italians at a time when Italian names appeared only
occasionally in the newspapers, and then usually in advertisements for
contracting and gardening businesses.

"Stabbed in Fight—Soldier May Die," read the headline of a story
from September 5, 1912. The soldier, according to the report, was
stabbed during a street fight in Highwood: "No trace of his assailants,
said to be Italians with whom a group of soldiers had been having
trouble earlier in the evening, has been found. The men engaged in
the brawl were all, according to reports, in an intoxicated condition
after a nights [sic] carousal in a 'blind pig.' This is only one of the cases
through which a few men catering to a lawless element gathered from
all parts of the North Shore are putting Highwood's reputation back
to the place where it used to be in the days of the wide open town."

On February 19, 1919, a story ran under the headline "Two Italians Held Here for Murder—Supposed to Have Killed Man at Northfield." The men, charged with the crime in Northfield, a town more than ten miles away, were from Chicago.

The issue from February 12, 1920, carried an account of a "quartet" of Italians arrested for carrying concealed weapons. The article went on to say that at the time the men were arrested the police believed "the four men were implicated in some sort of crime on the north shore, but nothing could be proved against them, so they were not held longer."

An article in the *Highland Park Press* from November 18, 1920, documented a perception by local residents of an "epidemic of crime which infests the north shore towns at the present time."

A letter to the editor printed August 19, 1920, showed well the tensions between different groups in Highwood that crystallized during Prohibition:

> When laws are made, why should they not be enforced? In the village of Highwood there are three "blind pigs" kept by a low class of Italians. One might ask, "How do you know, if you have never been in a place of that kind?" Seeing is believing when you see men go into a place, see them under the influence of drink, and see them lying in the woods. I understand that it is known to everyone in town except the mayor.
>
> Highwood is beautifully situated. It has a good school, good churches and would be a good community were it not for those few evil places. . . .
>
> The excuse of having a little wine in the house for one's friends should not go. The men who frequent those places pay for what they get. Otherwise they would not go there. Wine or beer which causes some intoxication must have some kick in it.
>
> I would suggest that the mayor take action to compel these law-breakers to obey the law, or deport them. The better class of people in Highwood will stand by him. . . .
>
> One Who Knows

The reputation of Highwood was so bad, recalls Helen (Gibertini) Cadamagnani, the daughter of immigrants, that girls attending Barat College in Lake Forest during the 1940s were threatened with expulsion if they were caught in Highwood. She remembers being confused: Would she have to chose between going home and being expelled by the good sisters of the Sacred Heart? Later, she was assured by a nun that it was acceptable to go into people's homes in Highwood, just not into the taverns.

According to the mayor, Fidel Ghini, who himself owned a tavern for many years in Highwood, the highest number of bars in Highwood at any one time was thirty-seven. This was during World War II. As late as 1965, Highwood had twenty-eight bars. Today, with a population of about 5,500, Highwood has issued thirty liquor licenses, the majority of which are held by restaurants.

In my own family, enough information has passed through the sieve of family censorship to let me know that my Uncle Bob Saielli had a tavern for a few years during the war. It was an ill-fated business whose end is a mystery and involves a mortgaged house and bad debts.

When I asked my aunt about my uncle's tavern business, she scoffed. She said: "A tavern is no good for nobody. That's all."

Philip Pasquesi, who asks my mother if she likes America:

They closed all the taverns during Prohibition and you know what happened, they was selling, they called 'em bootlegger. And these ladies, they used to get one dollar for a bottle of wine.

Pasquesi Brothers, we used to get carload of grapes right on the tracks here from Chicago. And then these Italian people, they used to come and buy the grapes and make their own wine. And some, they used to sell it. But then people from Waukegan, from the county, they used to come down and arrest these people. It was Prohibition. It was dry. You could not sell alcohol. It was prohibited by the law.

At that time, most of the people that were here in Highwood were men that had their wife back home in Italy. They stay here three or four years, and then they used to go back, and then they come back. They used to live in a rooming house. They used to eat and sleep in one house, you know, and then when it come to Saturday night, they used to go to these, they called them blind pigs. That's where they used to sell.

And these people that had the blind pigs, they used to make money. But they had to be careful because in come the law from Waukegan, sometimes they get arrested.

People used to come to Highwood here from outside Highwood. Most of them used to come here and gamble, too. They used to play for big money, too. Oooh. They used to have roulette, they used to have everything. It was just like what they have in Las Vegas now. It was not legal, but they used to pay whoever run the town.

Enea Cortesi, whose follow-through in *bocce* is picture-perfect:

When I first started going up to Highwood, I used to walk from
here, my house in Highland Park, to Highwood in the evening. I
used to go to the blind pig for a drink, they used to call it blind pig.
They used to sell during Prohibition. Whiskey, wine—some—they
used to make their own beer. It was against the law. This was in the
private houses. There were a lot in Highwood. Then they started to
open the taverns in Highwood after the Prohibition. During Prohibition, there was an old lady, a widow, I guess. She would sell liquor,
wine, beer, that's all, make coffee. It was mostly the Italians that
was selling. And another lady, she used to sell a lot, too. Then she
opened up a tavern at Half Day. After they opened up the taverns
again, they stopped selling here. There was a tavern at Half-a-Day,
they used to call it the White House. Me, I used to go there.

At night, when they used to close the taverns here in Highwood,
we used to go out west. I went to Half Day a lot of times on Saturday night. Sunday we were off, we weren't working. There was
one, two, three, four, five taverns for sure. All Italian. And they was
making money! On the weekend especially. The place was packed!
They had slot machines. And we used to play sometimes, not much
because, you know, we didn't have much money. I don't go in the
tavern now.

We used to play *morra* at those places where they were selling
during the Prohibition. We used to play on the weekends, especially
Saturday and Sunday night. But they wouldn't let you play *morra* in
the tavern—too much noise, that's right. They shout.

Well, this is how you play. You gotta guess how many fingers the
people you play against are going to put down. If you put down
one finger, and I put down three, and I call four, I win. But you
gotta call before you come down. And if I say, "THREE!!!" and if
you call three, too, then it's nobody's point. When you make twelve
points, that is game. Some people, they get in fights. Not me. But
they do.

I used to play together with Battista Zanotti, and he would get
mad because someone tried to cheat. If you play the right way,
there's no harm in it. But some of them, they don't call the numbers
right. Some, they try to come down a little late. Some, instead of
calling *otto!* or *quattro!* they say, "TTO!"—say it so you can't understand. You don't know if they say *otto* or *quattro*. If it adds up to
four, they say, "Quattro! That's my point!" If it's eight, they say, "I
said eight!" But they didn't say neither one. It was in between.
That's why a lot of time they have arguments.

Gina DeBartolo, whose mother killed a snake:

The ladies who ran the blind pigs had very interesting lives of their own. You know, because their husbands were exiled for blind pigging and they remained here and raised their families. See, they couldn't get married because their husbands were in Italy. And they were here and they lived with men because when they ran a blind pig, they needed a man around as a sort of protection. If they had this man, no one else would annoy them.

One woman who ran a blind pig, she was a great big woman, and she would go over on the tracks there and pick up a tie, one of those railroad ties, one under each arm, and carry it to her house and they'd get them sawed for cooking. Her husband was this little skinny guy, a little one. She was quite a woman. She's the one that made the money.

Pia Gibertini, who serves meals with the seriousness and calm of a waiter at a fine restaurant:

The opera people, they loved Highwood. They didn't think nothing about, like some people thought it was a town where, well, there was more poor people than rich people, you know. But sometimes they were more honest than the rich people. And they didn't think nothing about it.

Well, some people, they put it in their head that Highwood had a bad reputation. But to me, I know if I like the people, the town has got nothing to do with it. I didn't think so, and either did the people from the opera.

Well, at that time—they said it was just like it was here in Arizona in those days when they had all those cowboys—the town had a bad name because it had saloons. But to me, it didn't matter, as long as they don't do anything wrong. Of course, if you give too much to drink to a person, you can't expect him always to be nice.

To me, Highwood is just as good as any other place. You know, those things are all over, even worse in some places.

Leo DePalma, who plays *scopa* at poolside and eats butterscotch candy:

I left working for the city because I wanted to improve my condition. I rented the My Favorite Inn building from Bruno DeBartolo. And then from there I went to Tower of Casino—the owner was Geno Palmieri.

It wasn't a hard business to get into. It was for sale, you know, they ask the price and you offer whatever you want to get together. Same thing when I sell out. I'd been there for nine or ten years. And I was kind of tired, and I sold out.

1947. 1948. That two years was good. Most of the business was from Fort Sheridan with the GIs. Because they came off the discharge, see. After the war. Most of my business was from the fort, but even from Highwood, too.

Oh yeah, oh yeah, I had to break up a lot of fights. Them days. My son, you know, always when I asked him to bartend—and my son is a very quiet boy, he doesn't like fighting—and I told him, I says, "You realize, you no sell ice cream, you sell liquor!"

People getting crazy. There was a lot of trouble. Then my son got married. I wanted to give the business to him. He didn't want the business and so I sell out.

I had to call the police a lot of times. There was the city police taking care of the city people and the MPs taking care of the GIs, see? That's the way it is.

It was open until one o'clock in the weektime, and two o'clock in the Saturday.

Sometimes my wife came and washed the glasses in the morning. And I had the clean-up man in the morning. And my daughter, she helped too in the afternoon.

I had regular bartenders at night. Oh, yeah, sure, I was there, too. The bartender relieve me about six o'clock, then I come home, stay a couple hour at home, and then I stay the rest of the night. Meet the people, talking, things like that. Me, buying drinks. You, buying drinks back. And things like that. The business way.

Then I got tired, see, tired to be that kind of life, coming home three o'clock in the morning. You know, you close one o'clock, two o'clock, until you come back home, you was so tired, that you go in bed about two or three o'clock in the morning, every morning, every morning.

We were open every day. Every day. Sure, Sunday, twelve o'clock.

I had My Favorite Inn only a year. I was in partnership there and every profit, you gotta split. I liked better being by myself.

When I had my bar, there was a lot of taverns. Santi was one. The Rainbow was the name of Michael Lomorro's. At that time there was—I forget all them damn names anyway.

All the rest of the territory was all dry, see. And all, they came in Highwood. Just like now. Maybe now Highland Park sells the liquor, but before they never sold the liquor. They all came in Highwood.

And Lake Forest, the only bar was beer only. Not liquor. And most all came in Highwood, see.

They had more fights in other places than in Highwood. Well, we had a little arguing, you know how it is. Nobody got killed, nobody got knifed. Nobody got nothing. You had a little fight once and a while. That doesn't mean nothing anyway.

Highwood? Not a bad reputation. But the point is like I said before, you sell the liquor, people get crazy, see? They have a little fight, so what are you going to do? But the people came from Highland Park, Lake Forest, Deerfield, Fort Sheridan, all came to Highwood to drink. For all that class of people that came to Highwood, we had a good reputation, not bad at all.

12

The Great Depression:
La miseria, Again

THE MEMORY plays tricks.

Nowhere, in the process of writing this book, have I felt as tentative in recording and creating images as with this chapter on the Depression. In collecting and assembling items from each corner of the attic, I realize they are images derived not exclusively from the words of the people interviewed. Can I say, with certainty, that my telling has not been influenced by other images, images that are entirely separate from the experience of this community? That in writing this, I have not superimposed Dorothea Lange's famous photograph of a migrant mother, head propped by hand, her young face overrun by lines and the vacant look of exhaustion? Or, that *The Grapes of Wrath* has not unduly influenced the tone? There was no dust bowl in Highwood, yet I have seen hands like the broad, gnarled hands of the farm woman in Russell Lee's photo.

I am confident of one story that emerged, because my grandfather Tony Vanoni told it, and because it came not from Farm Security Administration photographs or a college reading list. He spoke rarely about the Depression but this is what he said: "How many times, I can't tell you how many times, I walked down Sheridan Road, to all the mansions, and rang the doorbell asking if they had some work. Just to rake leaves, anything. I'd walk all the way to Evanston. In the winter, too. *Ma beh, ma beh.*" Then he would look down, shake his head, and stop talking about it.

Though this chapter is constructed with the images of the immigrant generation, I have been influenced also by the words of their children, Depression kids in lumpy wool socks. These images have to do with *ceci*, chick-peas, a staple on Depression dinner tables, and *lesso*, boiled meat, the remnants from soup, too valuable to be wasted. ("Yah, yah," my grandfather Tony said, "and today we give the soup meat to the dogs.")

The Depression was a great divider. It divided a community into those who took government jobs and those who wouldn't, those who proudly recall they didn't take "government handouts" and those who sought help from *la contaia*, the county, from its hospital and food lines. It separated families who buried their dead in private cemeteries, and those less well-off, who buried their dead at St. Mary's Cemetery in Highland Park, where handmade headstones written in Italian can be seen today.

How well one got by or didn't get by during the Depression set a tone: whether you would save twine and buttons, or whether you would make sure to have a roll of bills in your pocket to pick up the tab. After the nattiness of the 1920s, the Depression would seal attitudes about bountifulness and frugality, where one drew the line between luxury and necessity. The Depression influenced whether one eyed the future warily or whether one was confident of it.

A Polish researcher who was working at the University of Minnesota's Immigration History Research Center at the same time I was seemed unconvinced of the value of oral history. "I don't trust memory," he said. He is quite right. Memory is maleable, it can be manipulated and it changes over time. Certain memories are pulled out and displayed, refined, retooled, while others are placed in steamer trunks and left to rust in a damp basement.

The value of memory is limitless as long as one realizes its limits: It is not a concrete Truth but a collection of thoughts, emotions, sensations that we consciously and unconsciously manipulate for our own reasons. Our construction of memory—the images singled out from a lifetime's collection—deserves scrutiny. Perhaps the selection itself tells as much as the content of the tale.

My grandfather Nello never spoke to me about the Depression. He was fortunate—he had work throughout it, a steady job that paid little, but paid regularly. He even worked through the winter. A miracle. He tended to the ice for the curling lanes and skating rink at Exmoor Country Club. During the war years, he was offered a more lucrative job at a defense plant but turned it down. He felt too loyal to the club, my father says. Philip Pasquesi tells another story about the Depression that involves my grandfather Nello: "Your grandfather and I, we got married the same year. You know what year? 1929. Oooh, that was a great year. But we didn't care. We were in love."

Viterbo Ponsi, who traveled to Italy, alone, at ninety:

Until '29 it was pretty good. I even went to Italy. There was work. When I first came here I didn't have any troubles.

No, no, there wasn't much work in the Depression. Me, I go around. I work in Barrington. You know why? Because those farmers, they sell the land for cheap. And the rich people buy. During Depression time, they fixed the houses and build new barn and stuff like that for nearly half the price because it was Depression. Maybe I was one of three or four bricklayers that got pretty good in the Depression time.

If you took work for a week it was a miracle. I got work in Kankakee in '34. We worked making the house of insurance man. He wanted an addition with stone. He lived along the river, southeast of the town. By the Kankakee River. The name was, a German guy, Snyder. We went there because Frank Parenti knew a salesman, a stone salesman, Wisconsin stone. Anyway, this salesman says the owner wanted to see a house before he buy the stone, to see what it would look like. He came to Wilmette, there was quite a few, and he just picked one that Parenti worked on! That's what the trick was. Synder, he say, "Well, I like very much this kind of job but I like to have the man in Wilmette." Then the salesman, he called Parenti. Parenti called me and asked if I wanted to come to Kankakee. "*Ma* sure, *indemma fin a New York.*" — "I'd go as far as New York." That one, I made a miracle more than any other during all the Depression. We had a contract. We had a birthday party for my son Frank, who was little, in the basement at Mocogni's.

Ooh. This was '34. We was working for one summer. I come home every two weeks. We make pretty good, we make a dollar an hour. You not find nothing for a dollar an hour, Depression time.

I worked at Fort Sheridan. I worked for fifty cents an hour, but not the trade—working on the track. The streetcar was going in Fort Sheridan at that time. Then we have so much a day, three day, you had three day to work, to give a chance to everybody. Then the other gang, move the track to the other side. Just to keep them busy. It was the government job.

The worst jobs I had, I think, were in the Depression time. They pushed you.

When I would work, if I could do it for one day, or two, oh, I was happy. How many times I would leave here, there was Boilini, too, Tina's husband, on foot, we went as far as Glencoe and then even to Winnetka, to see if there was work. Just to dig ditches. Nothing, nothing, nothing. *Macché,* they didn't give anything. There were six years, terrible, maybe more, seven or eight. But how many houses were lost. Then came the war. After the war came, *ecco, è venuta la guerra e tutto lavoravano*—see, the war came and everyone worked.

I remember that I worked with this Parenti in Oak Park. At that time there in the Depression I had taken work for two days.

At the World's Fair I worked for Charlie Fiore to build a nursery. He had made a show. I made a beautiful little stairway, a platform, all bluestone, where he put all the plants, flowers, little trees. Me and two others who are dead did it all. That was in '32. Something like that. How long did I work there? A year?! *Macché*, sure, a couple of weeks. At that time there wasn't any work, *macché*.

I don't know how many *signori* killed themselves here in Lake Forest. One here in Ravinia Park. He had a huge house. One from Lake Forest killed himself. Tonight be millionaire, in the morning, zero, nothing. *Niente.* The big Depression. Disaster.

Pia Gibertini, who serves meals with the seriousness and calm of a waiter at a fine restaurant:

After the crash, it wasn't like it used to be at Ravinia Park. The people from the opera, in that last summer before they all left, they called to see if I could take them.

And then, there wasn't work for the boarders. The work in the mines slowed up, too. So, then, a lot of them didn't return. There was no work. They worked in the gardens, see. A lot of people had built a lot of homes, you know, and then, those people couldn't pay for gardeners anymore.

Some of the boarders worked in Highland Park. Those that had a job, even if they made little, were happy to have it. They held onto it tightly to be able to work. It gave them honor.

Very few boarders had work. We lost a lot of money. We let them owe two hundred, three hundred, four hundred dollars. The boarders always paid as soon as they worked but the work never came. My husband said we couldn't keep them there. And I said, "What are we going to do if we send them away?" They would always say, "Oh, pretty soon I'm going to have work here, work there, and I'll pay you right away." Instead, *questi lazzaroni*—these thieves—forgot about it.

Then came Roosevelt and they started to work those jobs. There were some who were very good, even if they gave me ten dollars at one time, once in a while, I saw that they were honest, that they wanted to pay. But there were very few like that. Bellei lost a lot of money, too.

During the Depression, people were very, very—how can I say it—they were feeling bad, because they were waiting, waiting for the work and it never came. It's for certain, they weren't happy and gay. You saw poor people going around in old clothes, old cars. There was, you saw it, *la miseria.*

Instead when the good times came back, like now, everyone had nice clothes. Even those who before had dressed poorly when there was work, worked. But when there wasn't work you couldn't be happy. Things were bad.

There were two or three of these big millionaires who committed suicide when they went broke. It was ugly to live in those days. But you went on and waited for better times.

We never wanted to eat. You had to know how to economize in those days. A lot of things that you would make today, you couldn't make in those days. But you went forward. There were many poor people who had little children to raise and they suffered. It was horrible to see the people who had to go out poorly dressed. But what could you do? You had to always wait for prosperity. Prosperity was around the corner. But it took it a long time.

Menghina Mocogni, who pours coffee as she was taught in Florence:

When we arrived, we stayed a while with Rosina and Aldo Piacenza, I don't know for how many months, because Giosue wasn't working. You could count on only a few dollars. Then, too, it was an awful winter. There was ice. Then, later, we took in laundry and wash.

There was no help from the church. They weren't interested. *Macché,* nothing. There was nothing. Instead, today, even if you stay home, you get a check from Waukegan. Instead, at one time, there was nothing. I went to Bellei's grocery, and there, instead of paying ten dollars, you could pay only five. See, they were good during the Depression.

Then, there was an office down in Highland Park where, if you made application, they gave you things, for example socks for children, little sweaters, all children's clothing. One time when Cassatari was a policeman, he said, "Menghina, they're giving away blankets at city hall, so see if they'll go give you one." They gave me a *quertina,* a little cover for the bed, that's all they gave me. There were people without food, and others throwing it away. *Non è mica nice*—it wasn't nice.

When I came here, I went to see Stella Pichietti's mother and Francesca Sassorossi, and, oh *Dio*, I thanked the Blessed Virgin that I had come to America. I was happy to be in America. I was overjoyed even if I didn't understand anything, I hoped to make it in some way. At least, my family was together.

Giulia Mordini, who protested, then smiled sweetly for her photo:

C'era la miseria. There was misery.

There was nothing, nothing. You lived very poorly. You had to spend everything you made in the summer. Very little, too. It didn't go well. *Va mica bene.* The men did nothing. They went around with the other men. That's all. With friends. That's all. *Faceva anche lu'*—even my husband did that.

What was there to eat?

Very little. *Poco, poco.* It's true.

Everett Bellei, who passes out jokes like meat wrapped in paper over a counter:

We had a good start in the grocery business until the Depression came along, and that hurt. Depression hurts small and big. We survived. There were a lot of 'em went broke. I was in there for fifty-five years. I had a nice living out of it.

I lost an awful lot of money in the Depression. I lost a lot of money among the Italian people. That's unbelievable. When they once get a habit of getting over the shame of not paying a bill, they just forget about it.

1930 and '31 were the worst years. I had courage. I had courage. I said, "We'll fight it out." When you're into something you don't want to lose courage. Well, we got stuck with two banks. That's why the government is backing up this big bank in Chicago, Continental, because it doesn't want that to go under. It cost the government a fortune.

Enea Cortesi, whose follow-through in *bocce* is picture-perfect:

Oh, nobody was working in the Depression.

When I came from Gary, I come over in Highland Park, as I told you before, worked for a friend of mine, Cabonargi. But during the

Depression, we used to walk, me and one friend of mine, with a shovel on top of our shoulder. Walk down until Evanston sometimes. Alongside the railway tracks. Looking for jobs. Was hard to get it. Every once in a while we'd have a job for four hours, sometimes one day or two. Nobody was working in the Depression.

Jane McNally Floriani, kindergarten teacher at Oak Terrace elementary school, when asked if mothers worked:

Well, honey, that was the Depression, they had to, they had to work, honey. It was a necessity. And many of them worked but there was always somebody, usually, very seldom you would hear of a child not having a *nonna* to go home to, to have lunch. Or coming of the grandpa to pick them up at school if the folks were working late, honey. But it was a necessity. It wasn't easy. It was hard-going in the Depression.

Domenick Linari, who doesn't get along too well with Nietzsche:

I was working for a construction company, William Mavor, from Chicago, and during the Depression they went broke.

During the Depression, I picked up a little here, and a little there. But we lived, made it, we didn't suffer any because the wife worked. She took in laundry, worked day and night, and I helped her, of course. I worked in the daytime whenever I had a job, whatever I could get, whatever it was, it didn't make any difference what I got. We had to make a living so we made a living. We made it just the same. And I went to the authorities because they'd send somebody to work. They'd have a job like at Fort Sheridan or someplace, WPA, so on, I wanted to see if I could go get a job sometime. "Are you on relief?" I'd say no. "Well you got to be on relief to get a job." "What the hell," I say, "I'm not going to beg. I don't care what it is. I'll go steal it before I'll beg." So I didn't get to go on WPA or anything, I had to support myself. But we made it anyhow.

My wife just started taking in laundry. She happened to get one in Ravinia, then from there it began to spread out and she always had more than she could handle. First she had one washing machine. And then we had two of them because one didn't keep up enough. I used to do the mangling. You know what the mangle is? Where you run it through the rollers and irons all the straight pieces, the sheets, the hand towels, the pillowcases, and so on. You just put them in there and the thing grabs them and there is a roller under here and a shoe that's red hot that irons it. So I used to get that for her and help do the washing. So we made it just the same. In fact, during the Depression we bought a new car. So they always talked that Domenick had a lot of money because we bought a new car.

Gina DeBartolo, whose mother killed a snake to protect her nest:

Most of the development was between 1918 and the crash of 1929, when everything was crashed.

In fact, my Uncle Casper, everybody would bring him their savings. There were so many single men who didn't know what to do with their money. They were boarding with families, living in a group and they didn't have a safe place for their money. So they started bringing it to my Uncle Casper, who had the store on the corner. And he began to get so much money from different people that he didn't know what to do with it. So, the Highland Park bank said, "Why don't you open a branch bank in your office, accept these people's money, keep the books on 'em, and pay 'em the interest." And he started lending them money.

In fact, that's what was the biggest cause of their bankruptcy. Because then the families, after 1920, after World War I, the families started coming over and they would go, "Oh, Casper, I wanna buy a lot." And then when they had a little more money, "I wanna buy a house. Where can I borrow the money?" And he gave them what he had and almost everybody had a mortgage from Santi's. Then when the Depression came and they didn't have any money, they tried to draw out their savings; he had it invested in all these homes. And when he went bankrupt, well, they sold those mortages for not all what they were worth. And he had to give up everything, even his house on Palmer Avenue, which was Mary's little grocery store.

Julio Brugioni, whose coal-blackened face frightened his daughter:

There was no work during the Depression. No work. You couldn't hear nothing. You couldn't hear a hammerhead pretty nearly.

There was no work at all, everybody was out. They used to give to the families the rotten bacon. The government. The salty bacon. And you have to wash it and put in water for twenty-four hours before you could eat it. It was so poor here in them days. It was poor, I'm tellin' you, in Highwood, too. The families used to go in

line and get a loaf of bread. The government give it. You had to
wait for whatever they give you and sometimes they didn't want to
give it them people

If you go down looking for a job, they run you off the property.
The rich man. They don't want you. They want to cut down, see,
and the poor they want more money, yeah, but you wait and see if
they give you the money.

CHAPTER

13

The Smoke of the Train:
Allegiance, Identity, and Food

THIS IS A STORY stolen shamelessly from my father, recounted verbatim to him by his father. There was a man who boarded in their house. He had a tremendous appetite. He couldn't get enough to eat. He would eat anything in sight, anything. So voracious was his appetite that he'd even eat the smoke of the train if he could: *"Mandia' anch' il fum' di treno."*

This story belongs to a table set in a crowded dining room with an art deco buffet and breakfront. It belongs to an antipasto plate with radishes, olives, celery, and *peperoncini*. It belongs with a grandmother, Mariuccia, who never once, not once, sat down to eat the meal with us, instead urging us onward to the second, third, and fourth courses with all the momentum and power of the locomotive whose smoke fed her boarder.

The other two tables, those of my grandmother Massima and my great-aunt, Teresa, are the other two points of the triangle, forming a plane where identity was the final prize in a tug of war where loyalties and allegiances were coaxed, then demanded, on the basis of broth and sauces.

Which do you prefer? Clear chicken broth? Chicken broth with a hint of beef? Beef consommé?

The loaded question? The Bolognese meat sauce or the meat sauce with tomatoes? Whether you like your *tortellacci* filled with spinach or swiss chard.

Each woman had special desserts, desserts that neither of the other two made. *Zia* Teresa made *torta mantovana,* a pound cake that called for almonds and ten eggs. She made *late portoghese,* a custard with glazed sugar that Hispanics call *flan.* She made *zupp'inglese,* literally, "English soup," a custard and sponge cake affair whose layers are

233

bonded together with sugar and whiskey. These dishes, each named for a place—Mantua, Portugal and England—belonged to a woman who, according to my father, prided herself on being the first woman on Ashland Avenue to serve guests celery stuffed with cream cheese. She cooked for fancy people, like the *maestro* Gennaro Papi, a conductor of the Chicago Symphony Orchestra. She picked up these recipes, where? Certainly not in Groppo—the town that means "lump"—where she grew up on *polenta* and *balucci*. She might have learned her fancy dishes when she went at the age of fifteen to work as a maid for the *signori* in Milano.

My *nonna* Massima's special claim included an orange cake, a semi-sweet cake which becomes more moist each day, a confection made of raisins and orange rinds, tart and sweet and topped with an adult glaze. She made, on occasion, a *torta* with prunes, an even more adult dessert. The zig-zagged edges of the lattice-work strands belonged as exclusively to my grandmother Massima as the pinking shears in her sewing drawer.

And if my *nonna* Massima's desserts were exact and hemmed neatly, my *nonna* Mariuccia's were casual and improvised. Her style was based on speed, as if how fast you moved in the kitchen showed how hard you worked, and how hard you worked, how good you were. Her dessert was *frappe*, rolled dough, cut, twisted in the middle, quickly fried in hot oil, then sprinkled with powdered sugar. Prune pies and layers of custard could not compete with confectionary sugar.

And then, there is the question of the holiday specialty, the treasure. Veal. It was treated with reverence. It was the sign of having achieved a good life.

Veal was prepared in three entirely different ways in my family. My *zia* Teresa cooked the cutlets in butter with only a hint of tomato paste. The cutlets were a honey color. My grandmother Mariuccia used more parsley and tomato, creating a sauce that was very dark red, almost brown. And my grandmother Massima added Marsala to her sauce, her sweet secret. Three dishes. Three different ways.

And how is it that these foods become the language of identity? How is it that the question is posed, the preferences asked of you? I am not entirely clear about the process. Perhaps as much as anything it was the rigidity with which these three strong women kept to their personal *cucina*, the steadfastness with which they stuck to certain types of noodles.

My *nonna* Mariuccia used rice-shaped noodles almost exclusively in her beef broth. For her *sugo*, a very red sauce with tomatoes, she used *rigatoni*, flattish, hollow noodles with ridges. And, as if the sauce and pasta were not enough to win us, she cut off cubes of butter that melted together with the sauce and cheese and noodles.

Never once, as far as I can recall, did my *nonna* Mariuccia opt for what I have always referred to as the "pillow noodles," the tiny little soup noodles of either square or round shape that always reminded me of throw pillows on a couch. These were in the repertoire of my grandmother Massima, the seamstress with the pinking shears. To Massima also belonged the bow-tie noodles with tiny zig-zag edges. These noodles were always in a broth that, while essentially chicken, was bolstered by a piece of beef.

I sensed somehow, even as a child, the solemnity of these divisions. Perhaps the message came to me most clearly when, once, I suggested to my mother that we buy "springs," coiled noodles that served as comedic props against the tongue when no adults were watching. My mother was in her mother's kitchen, and that kitchen consisted of spaghetti and mostaccioli. There was no room for the frivolity of springs.

That I came to associate certain foods with each grandparent might astonish them.

My grandfather Nello. Onions. Meat. Pork. Bacon. Mushrooms he collected at Exmoor Country Club where he worked as a groundskeeper. He was the Prince of *Tocchia,* which is the word in the dialect that means dunking a piece of vegetable or bread into a mixture of seasoned olive oil and vinegar. His vice was ketchup, which in his later years he used on everything. It was a smothering American habit of excess.

In his retirement, my grandfather Tony walked uptown, *in paese,* every day, buying one meal's worth of salami or mortadella and a loaf of Gonnella bread. He would sit at the end of the table, back to the door, with the mortadella cut into paper-thin pieces, crescent moons on unfolded butcher's paper, laid out as precisely as consecutive cards in a game of solitaire. There was always, to the side of his plate, a bowl of lettuce and tomatoes fixed in oil and vinegar, which he mixed himself because he did not trust my grandmother. He cut his pieces of bread three-quarters of an inch thick, methodically, with his pocket-knife, moving like he had all the time in the world.

These associations with food are among the earliest and most concrete building-blocks of kinship. And if a child learns by seeing a parent doing battle over tomatoes with another parent, one who loves the fruit and one who loathes it, does he make an impartial decision, or are his taste buds biased by bonds formed and forming? In my case, the impulse to like everything was basted frequently. It was a tangible response to praise and acceptance. "That's my girl, look at her eat those grilled onions." That was one impulse, an impulse to eat fearlessly.

Another impulse. To pause as I bring the spoon with broth to my
mouth, to breathe deeply on a winter evening and let the steam soothe
my nostrils while the windows fog up from the heat of the stove. To
eat solemnly and deliberately.

How will I choose to set my table? There are decisions to make. I
am committed to the Bolognese meat sauce. I prefer a piece of beef in
my broth to avoid the feathery taste. I use my aunt's *torta mantovana*
pan. But on this question of noodles? I am loyal to no one.

CHAPTER

14

The Burden of a Name

ALWAYS, AS LONG AS I can recall, there was the explaining of names.

The names of three grandparents did not translate into English. Giovanni may become John, Maria—Mary; but Massima, Mariuccia, and Nello are names forever formed in Italianate letters.

As a child in an American subdivision of colonial homes it was hard work for me to answer when playmates winced and said, "What are their names again?"

My other grandfather, Antonio, was called Tony, an easy name but one that sometimes became the topic of conversation. You see, my grandfather's first and last names rhymed: Tony Vanoni.

When you are claimed by different worlds, it is hard to find a name that will fit into both. My *nonna* Massima worked in a shop alongside American seamstresses. I remember sitting on the floor in my grandmother's kitchen while my aunt, then nineteen or twenty, tried out different names on my grandmother—as if she were suggesting a new hairstyle: "We'll call you Masie." This adaptation offended me. "Massima" may have been difficult, but "Masie" was ugly.

The names of my grandparents' world were confusing. They were part of the past, and I was a new guest at a dinner table where the conversation had originated decades before. They were names spoken frequently yet I was not acquainted with them. They were people, I was told as I listened, my feet not yet touching the floor, who were mine, who were me. They appeared to me only as a vague veil that surrounded me lightly but stretched to the very edges of my perception. How could I possibly be bonded to these people I knew only loosely, their names a mystery?

The names were ancient names. They were not the names given by American movie directors to Italian characters. They were old names, given by old mountain people to children who favored the modern world and faced it saddled with unfashionable names: my uncle Ber-

nardi, named Virgilio; his friend Massinelli, named Attilio. The husband
of my grandmother's cousin, Zagnoli, named Valerio. On my father's
side of the family, there was a great-great-aunt named Lucrezia, and
another named Estere. There was a great-great-uncle named Giacinto.
And on my mother's side, a great-great-aunt named Ravinia. I had a
great-great-grandmother named Prudenza, and a great-grandmother
named Cherubina.

Often, at the table, I had heard the name of Adelmo Bertucci. He
belonged to my grandfather Nello's clan. Adelmo, who was called
Delmo, lived in the yellow house and was married to Menga and played
the accordion. And, then, there was Elmer Bertucci who was golf
superintendent at Old Elm Country Club and gave people jobs. I had
been a guest at the table for twenty years before I realized that Delmo
and Elmer were the same person.

These are the tricks the ear plays when you are not fluent in the
language.

There was my grandmother's cousin, Delcisa, whose name to me
sounded as pungent and foreign as the pecorino cheese she oiled and
hung. She had a prominent, angular chin, and in my mind, her name,
"Delcisa," was derived from the words "chin" and "cheese." It was
only when I saw the remembrance card printed at her death that I
realized "Delcisa" was a shortened version of her given name, Maria
Adalgisa, a name free of harsh consonants.

Names may seem simple, as they were in the case of my grandfather
Nello's twin brothers. The babies, born first and second in the family,
were called Primo and Secondo. I have known of men named Terzo,
Quarto, Quinto, and Sesto—third, fourth, fifth, and sixth. Most names
are not so straightforward. Like all immigrants, the Italians of Highwood
belonged to different worlds, and their names signified a complicated
identity.

Domenico Linari quickly changed his name to Domenick, adding a
k—a graphic resolution of ambiguity. He said, "Domenico, seemed like
at the time, especially in the coal mine, nobody could spell it, nobody
knew what I was talking about. So I put Domenick with a k, and it
seemed like it worked."

Fanny Cassidy's husband was among the first Italians to join the
Highwood police force. A friend of her husband, an American who
was a lawyer and in the real estate business, had suggested the family
change the name: "He used to say, 'Oh, Cas-si-ta-ri, that's too long.
Change your name. Change your name. Make it Cassidy.' Then we
decided. Stupid. We decided to change and make it legal. Nobody was

never call him Cassitari. Even the Italians." Perhaps it better suited a
policeman in Highwood, still largely an Irish town, to be named Cassidy.

Mary Baldi, born in a small town in the Piemonte, came to the coal
town of Dalzell, Illinois. She was used to hearing American and she
didn't like her husband's name: "Oreste sounded like such a funny
name. Oreste. So I started calling him Rusty."

Italian names became Americanized. If the translation was not sa-
tisfatory, there was aural adaptation: Sante became "Sam," Domenico
became "Donald." And when the names were too difficult, they were
changed altogether. In the Lake Forest home where she worked as a
laundress, Eritrea Pasquesi was called "Dorothy."

The names of the past, of the language of birth, are not always so
easily shed. I have known women named Menga, which is the word
in the Modenese dialect for "Domenica." This same word means "Sunday." Both the woman and the sabbath are called Menga. And if the
woman is tiny, she is called Menghina.

Insults and inside jokes could sometimes be transported more easily
than trunks, and the nicknames of the dialect stuck. *Strappanecci* was
named after *necci*, pancakes made out of the flour of chestnuts. *Strappa*
means "snatches." So this man, who liked his chestnut-flour pancakes,
earned the name "he who snatches pancakes." And there was a family
in Italy who used to eat their gruel of chestnut flour plain, without
milk. When asked why she didn't give the children milk with the
porridge, the mother said, "Then the cats will die." So this family
became known as *i gatti*, "the cats," a name that followed them to
Highwood.

There was Faggiolo (string bean), Cavrin', (the little goat), Il Gallo
(the rooster). There was Il Mulo (the mule), who was a great, strong
man. And Perla (the little pearl), a name of irony assigned by a father
weary of his son's trouble-making: *"La mia Perlin'."*

Biases, tastes, hopes, religious and political sentiments are conferred
upon children through names. And in a new generation, if those sentiments are not shared, the names become archaic. Some children of
immigrants who saw their first operas in this country were given the
names of opera's most popular characters: Violetta, Enzo, Gilda. My
zia Teresa's sister-in-law named her boys Ferruccio, Osvaldo, and Tur-
rido. They shed these names and were called Bill, Tom, and Bob.

Eritrea Pasquesi tells of the names her father chose for his daughters.
He was a coal miner in Thurber, Texas, an anti-cleric and a free-thinker:
"We had very peculiar names. Svezia, which means 'Sweden.' Then,
my name, of course, Eritrea, which is in Abyssinia, and then my sister

Veneranda, which means 'venerated'—I guess for once that comes from the church. Because my father was an atheist. He named us all very funny names. And then my sister Ribella was the oldest." (*Ribelle* means "rebel.")

Did he name his daughter Eritrea out of a fierce nationalism, in support of Italy's belated attempt to become a colonial power? Or was it a joke, naming her after the disastrous Ethiopian military campaign of 1886? What would this man, who purposefully shunned the names of the saints, have said upon learning that two of his mightily named daughters had become known as "Dorothy" and "Swannie"?

My surname, itself, is a long story. Bernardi, contrary to the rules of naming progeny, was not my paternal grandfather's name. His was Piacentini.

My father, starting out in business in Chicago in the late 1950s, was given a piece of advice by a mentor, just as Fanny Cassidy's husband had been: Change your name.

And so, my father, an only child and only son, took up the difficult task of trading his father's name for another. The name Piacentini was so foreign, so intricate, that it would have been an insufficient gesture to merely drop the final vowel, following the immigrant's custom, a custom by which Lombardi became Lombard. Nor did he, as I have seen done, warble out a new name from the old, a phonetic rendering with no meaning. (If he had, would we have become the Pace family?)

No, my father did not acquiesce entirely to the brisk demands of the Chicago business world. He opted for a compromise. He renounced neither family, ethnic heritage, nor provincial origin. He took the name of his maternal grandmother.

The havoc wreaked by a son renouncing his father's name for the name of his mother's family must be a terrible thing to witness. The rage and confusion created in his parents' household I cannot imagine.

But in choosing the name of an uncle he admired, Bernardi, a man with a more accessible name, my father believed he had found an acceptable answer for a condition in which harmony was impossible. He chose a name he felt would allow him to carve an identity as an American businessman without sacrificing the link to his first community. Had he chosen the name Pace, however, I wonder if it would have been easier for my grandfather to accept.

A name is a mighty load we carry on backs. For those born with a good name, there is the responsibility of protecting it. Those born into a family with a name besmirched by an untidy event carry the burden of restoring—or denying—the name.

There is another meaning for the word "burden," however. In olden

times, in England, a burden was a melody, an accompaniment in the
bass voice. A burden was a refrain, the chorus. Not that we need,
necessarily, trumpets announcing our every consonant and vowel, it is
good nonetheless to see that each component is laden with meaning
tying us to places and people, going backward and forward. If our
names are a burden, perhaps it is best to see them as a recurring verse
that will carry us through.

And if it is not the name we would choose for ourselves, if the
burden is dissonant or somehow tangential to the chorus, so much the
better.

Belote in a Foreign Tongue

ON A FRIDAY NIGHT in Toulon at the dining room table of my father's cousin Alba, I watched a foursome play cards. They threw down cards swiftly, then efficiently swept them up. It moved too quickly. I was illiterate, unable to find common symbols and patterns. I was unable to decipher the trump and the values, much less the strategy. Then, as I frantically tried to follow the hand, the conversation turned to language.

My cousin's husband, Eugène, said, "It's the most unbelievable thing. In Highwood, near Chicago, you walk uptown, and it's filled with Italians. And when you listen to them, you hear that they're speaking the dialect of Alba's mother, from the mountains in Italy. The same. It's remarkable to go all that way to hear them all talking *modenese.*"

There I sat, listening to two men, one speaking the sing-song French of Provence, and the other, a giant man from Carcassone speaking in a rumbling, gutteral Mediterranean voice, discussing the Modenese dialect in the town of Highwood, Illinois, while I tried to interpret this new card game, *belote.*

It may have been the first time I thought about Highwood's language. I was frustrated and confused, taken aback by an outsider's attention to a birthright I had never thought to claim.

Highwood's language is assembled, in part, from the fragments of proper Italian with the wholesale import of certain Italian dialects. The language of the Italians of Highwood belongs to the kingdom of Italy, a country that was pieced together from a thousand separate duchies of dialect, where communication was impossible between the uneducated of one province and those of another, let alone with the rest of the world. The language of Highwood was born in a time before compulsory education, when a distance of twenty miles changed the name of things. Where, in Sant'Andreapelago, *musola,* means nothing, but in Lizzano in Belvedere, in the same mountains, on the other side of the provincial border, it means "whistle." Like these dialects, the language of Highwood is peculiar.

The language is comprised of only partially learned American-

English, where sentences contain part English, part dialect, part Italian. Mixed sentences, half-and-half, "af-ina-'af," *mezzo-mezzo*, where conjunctions, nouns, and verbs of disparate lineage are unassumingly summoned to attend the same sentence: "Now, *per esempio, cla guarzitta la, l'è* smart, *l'è* very smart," means, "Now, for example, that girl there is smart, very smart."

Italian words have been forgotten, perhaps never known, perhaps not yet invented when the person left Italy. So the Anglo noun stands unflinchingly in the Italo-American passage: "*C'era* linoleum, *non c'erano tapeti*—"There was linoleum, no carpets."

If one listens, the sound of Highwood's Italians, as of any culture with a distinct language, is not the same as its stereotype. Highwood's language does not sound like the Italian in the joke who goes around saying, "Hey, what's-a-matta-you?" any more than it sounds like advertisements for ragu-like-mamma-makes. Like an Italian obscenity learned by an American and replayed as the sign of knowing, these are facile scores and a false confirmation of sound.

This book is a translation. It is an interpretation. Scholars need the raw material, the actual voices and transcripts, and for this reason the tape recordings may be of more use to them than the book. Professionals dedicated to the evolution of language, to word order and etymology, cannot be satisfied with this treatment of language because it is not a precise analysis of components. But for those of us who will never speak or comprehend the language of Highwood, it is the translation that is important. My task, then, was to communicate to a reader who may understand no Italian, let alone the dialect of the *comune* of Pievepelago in the region of the Frignano in the province of Modena, the cadence and movement and spirit of the language.

In communicating the words of the immigrant in this book, I had to decide whether to print the exact transcript, faithfully recording each and every choice of word order. To have done this, I decided, would have made it impossible for a reader, and it would have made a mockery of those I interviewed.

At times, I edited out words, translating them into English. How, for example, could I expain the term *beché*—a hybrid of the word "because" and its Italian equivalent, *perché*. I wanted to include it but it came in the middle of a passage where a woman spoke movingly about her hardships. What were the options? To let the reader trip over an expression he could not possibly know? To undermine the speaker with a diversionary footnote? Or worse yet, to risk having the reader throw down the book without finishing the sentence?

Regardless of the care taken in editing, sound is irrevocably lost in the translation, remaining the privilege of those who have heard the language spoken. When some people say "it was," it is an expression melded with its Italian counterpart, *era*. It sounds like "ee-da." Or, the word "pretty" sounds closer to "poodi," as when the immigrant speaks of the Great Depression: "Ee-da poodi hard."

The geographic names of the North Shore formed a conspiracy of consonants for the immigrants. The word "north" is part of countless places, the *th* a messy construct that marks the foreigner: Nort' Shore, Nort' Chicago, Nort'brook. Even the name "Highwood" is a phonetic trap, where an *h* is aspirated, a *gh* silent, a *w* unheard of, and *oo* tricks a person who speaks a language in which every letter is pronounced as it is written.

The vocabulary related to work is integrally tied to the Chicago's affluent North Shore. There are the names for the affluent: *i ricchi*, rich people, big shot, *padrone, padrona*, businessman, millionaire, boss, head guy, big lady. They are called *signori*. And once, I heard my grandfather call them all *i capitalisti*.

There are other words related to work that represent an attempt to Italianize English words: *golfo* means golf, not gulf; *springolo*, for sprinkler; *scrubbare*, to scrub.

In 1932, Anthony M. Turano, who grew up in the mining town of Pueblo, Colorado, described the hybrid words of the Italian immigrant community there, many of which are the words of Highwood's Italians as well: *morgheggio* for mortgage (in Italy, it is *ipoteca*); *ghenga* for gang; *sciabola* for shovel (in Italian *sciabola* means "saber"). English verbs become adapted in order to sound Italian. The word "fight" becomes *faitare* (the infinitive), *faitato* (the past participle), and *faitava* (the past imperfect).

The immigrant's expressions also reflect the time at which he was introduced to American-English. Would an immigrant today incorporate into his vocabulary expressions like "monkey business" or "by gosh"?

The immigrants had their inside jokes at the expense of the host. Like my grandmother Mariuccia, who not without malice butchered the word "lawyers," calling them "liars." Or my grandfather Tony, who gave up his Chicago baseball team after the 1969 debacle, shaking his head over his poor *Gobbi*. His poor Cubs. His poor hunchbacks.

Language mirrors the immigrant's position in American society and the ethnic community. Whether one says, "*Quand iera piccol*," or "*Quando ero piccolo*," or "When I was just a kids" or "When I was a child," says much about the individual. Without a doubt, these immigrants were criticized by Americans as part of the great horde of uneducated who refused to learn English. The grandson of an immigrant criticized his grandmother, telling me with an edge in his voice: "She was here for sixty years. She never learned English. I think that's wrong. If you come to this country you should learn the language."

Those who attended English classes, those who arrived at younger ages, those who had a few more years of formal education in Italy were at an advantage in learning the language. You can hear this clearly in the tapes: a man who arrived at age fifteen, who had six years of schooling in Italy and attended a few months of language classes, speaks English better than a man who had three years of school in Italy and arrived in America at age thirty with a family.

Josephine Tagliani Fiore, who came as a child, recalled her first experience with education and language: "The teacher put me in front of a hole on the wall and she said, 'Now I want you to look in that hole. There's the devil in there. So you gotta be very good, otherwise the devil is going to get you.' How can a person, a young girl coming from Italy, never saw no teacher, never heard of any school, what would you think? I had no English, who's going to teach me in Italy, English? But to this day, I think that was wrong. And if you never have a pencil, never have a book, or paper, how can you learn?"

For many, ignorance in silence was more comfortable than public embarrassment. John Bagatti spoke about his brief experiences in night class: "We start, a bunch, pretty near the same level. Then somebody, they start laughing to one guy because they make mistake. They don't say right."

When I asked about language, my grandmother Massima said, in Italian: "Embarrassment about language I always had and I still have. It's a mistake not to go to school to learn like you should. Without it, it's an English that no one understands. When I came here, and those who came before me, there were hard times. Between the family and working there wasn't time. That's why many didn't learn. Maybe it wouldn't have been impossible, maybe it was in part laziness, but who had time? It was hard enough to make a living."

Domenick Linari was bolder in taking on a new language. He stepped out from the pack when he tried to organize a night school, as he related when talking about the coal mines. "When I came here, when I started to work and I couldn't understand the language, I wanted to learn so bad," he said. And when he tried to do this, the other miners thought him conceited.

My intention here is not to propose that the language of Highwood be championed like an endangered creature. I merely suggest that there is room to applaud the bold impulses that allow an individual to say, "I wanted to learn so bad," without condemning the vulnerabilities that made this community—and others—turn into itself.

The language heard from the crib is never drubbed out. As Italo Calvino has written: "Everything can change, but not the language that we carry inside us, like a world more exclusive and final than our mother's womb."

The combination of sounds in this book belongs exclusively to this community. It is based on imperfect remnants. It is an intersection of borrowed communications that will never be replicated. This confluence of sounds has a limited lifespan: one generation. The identity of the next generation, and the next generation, and the next and the next, will be separate; the language less fragmented, less varied, more precise.

Notes and Sources

WITH THE EXCEPTION of interviews with Teresa Saielli, my aunt, which were done several years before I began this project, the interviews in this book were conducted between 1984 and 1986. Everyone was interviewed at home, either in Highwood or Highland Park, except for Adelmo (Elmer) Bertucci, who was interviewed in a nursing home; Pia Gibertini, whom I interviewed in Tucson, Arizona, where she lives with her daughter and son-in-law; and Maria Manfredini, who was living in a nursing home in Princeton, Illinois. I interviewed most people once, and had second interviews with eight people, with each session ranging from two to four hours. Most conversations were in English; twelve were in Italian or in some combination of Italian and English. I then transcribed each of the interviews and edited the transcripts. The tapes remain in my possession.

I conducted each of the interviews except for the following: Joseph Muzzarelli and Judith Cassai were interviewed by Anthony Mansueto in 1980 as part of the Italians in Chicago Oral History Project, which was sponsored by the National Endowment for the Humanities and directed by Dominic Candeloro. Transcripts are housed at the Italian Cultural Center in Stone Park, Illinois. Lawrence Santi was interviewed in 1967 by Robert and Nancy Spoede and in 1980 by Richard Mason. Transcripts of both interviews are part of the Southwest Collection of Texas Tech University, Lubbock, Texas. Aldobrando Piacenza's papers, including a 1959 memoir written in Italian, are part of the collection of the Immigration History Research Center at the University of Minnesota in St. Paul. *La mia vita*, written by Sante Pasquesi in 1933, is housed at the Highwood Public Library, where there is also a typescript translation. All interviews are used with permission.

The process of selecting interview subjects has revealed to me that, nearly eighty years after the great wave of Italian immigration, *campanilismo* — the parochialism which makes one gravitate toward people from the same town—is alive and well (for better or worse). I first interviewed my great-aunt. Then I asked my grandmothers and parents for names. They made introductions for me. Then, those people suggested the names of other immigrants, and the circle widened. For all its widening, however, a quick glance at the roster will show that nearly all of those interviewed were Modenese, with the Bolognese a distant second. Without being aware of it, I had nicely demonstrated the pattern of emigration.

INTRODUCTION

An *aia* is a flat place, usually of stone, in front of the house where grain was threshed. In the dialect of the Frignano, this place is called an *ara*. In Italian *ara* means "altar" and is also a unit of land measurement.

For a discussion of Italian emigration statistics, see Robert F. Foerster, *The Italian Immigration of Our Times* (Cambridge: Harvard University Press, 1924), pp. 3-7.

Michael Ebner writes about Highwood in *Creating Chicago's North Shore: A Suburban History* (Chicago: University of Chicago Press, 1988), pp. 133-60.

For a discussion of Sarti's argument on "cosmopolitan villagers," see *Long Live the Strong* (Amherst: University of Massachusetts Press, 1985), pp. 115-36.

Accounts of Highwood's first Italian settlers are from family accounts in *Highwood, Illinois: 100 Years of Progress, 1887-1987*, a commemorative book which includes archival photographs and valuable documentation of Highwood's organizations and families. Other sources were my interviews with Gina DeBartolo and Adelmo Bertucci, and with Judith Mordini Cassai and Aldobrando Piacenza, cited above.

As this book goes to press, the federal government is preparing to close Fort Sheridan, and it is unclear which governmental body will acquire the valuable lakefront property, valued at as much as $300,000 an acre—or $209.4 million for the 698-acre area, by some estimates— according to a *Chicago Tribune* report of January 2, 1989.

Laborers from Highwood were employed when Albert Lasker built his palatial home and private golf course in Lake Forest. See John Gunther, *Taken at the Flood: The Story of Albert D. Lasker* (New York: Harper, 1960), pp. 174-76.

The Chicago Italian Chamber of Commerce *Bulletin* is part of the collection of the Immigration History Research Center, cited above.

CHAPTER 1

Since this first chapter is least tied to written sources, perhaps it is appropriate to begin a discussion of bibliography with works based upon the spoken word. Italo Calvino's *Italian Folktales* (New York: Harcourt Brace Jovanovich, 1980) is a work that does what most oral histories try to do: fill the reader's head with the sound of the language. Although not an oral history, another work dedicated to the spoken word and storytelling is John Berger's *Pig Earth* (New York: Pantheon, 1979). Studs Terkel's oral histories and John Egerton's portrait of a Kentucky family in *Generations* (Lexington: University Press of Kentucky, 1983) have been valuable models. Other works that helped shape this history are Danilo Dolci's *Sicilian Lives* (1981) and Ronald Blythe's *Akenfield: Portrait of an English Village* (1969), both published by Pantheon Books.

Oral histories have been written in many different styles. The following were very helpful to me: Ann Cornelisen, *Women of the Shadows: A Study of Wives and Mothers of Southern Italy* (New York: Vintage, 1977); Ann Banks, *First Person America* (New York: Vintage, 1980); Eva J. Salber, *Don't Send Me Flowers when I'm Dead: Voices of Rural Elderly* (Durham: Duke University Press, 1983); Jerome R. Mintz, *The Anarchists of Casas Viejas* (Chicago: University of Chicago Press, 1982); *Speaking for Ourselves: Women of the South*, ed. Maxine Alexander (New York: Pantheon, 1984); and Tamara K. Hareven and Randolph Langenbach, *Amoskeag: Life and Work in an American Factory City* (New York: Pantheon, 1978).

Delia H. Pugh's article, "House and Farm Names in North Wales," was published in *Names* 2, no. 1 (March, 1954): 28-30. Similar discussions include: Vivienne Dickson, "St. Helena Place-Names," *Names* 21, no. 4 (December 1973): 205-19; Gottfried Keller, "House Names in Goldach," *Names* 1, no. 3 (September 1953): 205-7; C. A. Weslager, "House Nicknames," *Names* 4, no. 2 (June 1956): 83-85.

CHAPTER 2

English-language studies about the Italians and immigrants of the Apennines of Modena, Bologna, and Tuscany and about those who came to the United States are rare, especially when compared with studies of other regions of Italy. For this reason, Roland Sarti's *Long Live the Strong* has been an invaluable resource. Sarti's final notes and bibliographic comments are a gold mine for those interested in an introduction to the regional studies about this area. See also his article

"Folk Drama and the Secularization of Rural Culture in the Italian Apennines," *Journal of Social History* 14 (Spring 1981): 465-79.

Several local histories of Modena were especially valuable, particularly Pietro Alberghi's *Quarant'anni di storia montanara* (Modena: Editrice Teic, 1980). This study will be useful to readers interested in immigration, especially Chapter 2, which is concerned with social and economic conditions prior to World War I. Most regional statistical data about population and agricultural production that appear in my book were taken from Sarti and Alberghi.

During the course of my reading I was also introduced to *La musola*, a periodical published in Lizzano and devoted to the folklore, language, and history of this region of Bologna.

Other local histories include: Aurelio Mordini and William Mordini, *Pievepelago: immagini del passato* (Modena: Ruggeri, 1986); Franco Mantovi and Graziano Manni, *Invitato al Frignano: L'Appennino Modenese* (Modena: Ruggeri, 1976); Antonio Galli, *Paesi e villaggi ai piedi del M. Cantiere: Carrellata storica su Barrigazzo, Serpiano, Castellino, La Santona, Piane di Mocogno, Selva dei Pini e La Fignola* (Avegno: AGIS); Galli, *Pievepelago: Carrellata Storica* (1974) and *Pievepelago durante la seconda guerra mondiale* (Pievepelago: Lo Scoltenna—Societa Letteraria del Frignano, 1971); Gino Boilini, *Sant'Andreapelago* (Modena: Teic, 1980); Mario Fante, *Una pieve, un popolo: Le visite pastorali nel territorio di Lizzano in Belvedere dal 1425 al 1912* (Lizzano in Belvedere: Gli scritturini della Musola, 1981).

In Italian, *nonno* and *nonna* mean "grandfather" and "grandmother"; however, among those from the Frignano, when affectionately referring to "father-in-law" or "mother-in-law," *nonno* and *nonna* often replace the terms *suocero* and *suocera*.

CHAPTER 3

My first discovery of Highwood in the academic literature was in the stacks of Memphis State University Library. The book, mustard yellow and oversized, cleared its throat: *L'immigration italienne dans le sud-est de la France*. I frantically flipped through it because for the first time I had in my hands a demographic study of emigration from the Apennine mountains of Modena, Bologna, and Tuscany. "Dans la province de Modene," I read, "les communes voisines de Fiumalbo, Pievepelago et Frassinoro se sont dirigées de 1890 á 1910 vers les Etats-Unis et leur petit colonie d'Highwood. . . ." (In the province of Modena, the neighboring towns of Fiumalbo, Pievepelago and Frassinoro were directed from 1890 to 1910 toward the United States and their small colony of Highwood.) This study by Anne-Marie Faidutti-Rudolph (Gap: Imprimerie Louis-Jean, 1964) was most helpful.

The citation from "Emigration and Its Dangers as Measured by the Clergy" that appears in this chapter is from Chapter 25 on emigration in Fanti's, *Una pieve, un popolo,* cited above.

Other useful studies of the emigration from Italy include: Grazia Dore, "Some Social and Historical Aspects of Italian Emigration to America," *Journal of Social History* 2 (Winter 1968): 95-122, and *La Democrazia italiana e l'emigrazione in America* (Brescia: Morcelliana, 1964), including bibliography, pp. 389-493; Francesco Cordasco, *Italian Mass Emigration: A Bibliographical Guide to the Bollettino dell'emigrazione 1901-1927* (Totowa, N.J.: Rowman and Littlefield, 1975); and Forester's *Italian Immigration of Our Times,* cited above.

Other articles relating to emigration discussed by narrators within this chapter include: G. Weber, "Il gran ducato di Lussemburgo e la immigrazione italiana," in *Emigrazione e Colonie* (1905), pp. 117-23; Enrico Chicco, "Tripoli e la colonia italiana," in *Emigrazione e Colonie* (1906), pp. 286-96; Giorgio Breen, "Le colonie italiane in Scozia," *Emigrazione e Colonie* (1903), pp. 190-92; C. Sardi, "I gelatieri italiani nelle Scozia," *Rivista Coloniale* (August-September, 1911): 284-92; Attilio Mori, "L'emigrazione dalla Toscana," *Bolletino dell'emigrazione,* no. 12 (1910): 2469-502; and Amy Bernardy, "L'emigrazione delle donne," *Bolletino dell'emigrazione,* no. 1 (1909): 69-87. Also helpful was an article referring specifically to the emigration from the Modenese Apennines, by G. Basso, "I cantoni francesi della Svizzera e le loro colonie," in *Emigrazione e Colonie* (1905): 117-23, especially page 55. The *Bolletino* and *Emigrazione e Colonie* are part of the collection of the Immigration History Center at the University of Minnesota.

For a discussion of the separation of men and women during emigration, see Robert F. Harney, "Men Without Women: Italian Migrants in Canada, 1885-1930," in *The Italian Immigrant Woman in North America,* ed. Betty Boyd Caroli, Proceedings of the American Italian Historical Association (Toronto: Multicultural History Society of Ontario, 1978).

For a discussion of the term *campagna* as used by emigrants, see Sarti, p. 86.

The term *scarplin'*, which means "stonecutter," is often used interchangeably with *muratore* to mean "stonemason."

For a discussion of the mudslide which destroyed Sant'Annapelago in 1896, see Sarti, page 107, and also the memoirs of Aldobrando Piacenza, pp. 3-4, as cited above.

CHAPTER 5

Detailed bibliographies of works concerning Italian immigration to the United States and studies of Italian Americans can be found in the following: Joseph Lopreato, *The Italian Americans* (New York: Random House, 1970); Alexander De Conde, *Half Bitter, Half Sweet* (New York: Knopf, 1972); Andrew Rolle, *The American Italians: Their History and Culture* (Belmont, Calif.: Wadsworth, 1972); Luciano J. Iorizzo and Salvatore Mondello, *The Italian-Americans* (New York: Twayne, 1971); Lydio F. Tomasi, ed., *Italian Americans: New Perspectives in Italian Emmigration and Ethnicity* (New York: Center for Migration Studies, 1985); Gary R. Mormino and George E. Pozzetta, *The Immigrant World of Ybor City* (Urbana: University of Illinois Press, 1987); and Virginia Yans-McLaughlin, *Family and Community, Italian Immigrants in Buffalo, 1880-1930* (Ithaca: Cornell University Press, 1977), and "A Flexible Tradition," *Journal of Social History* 7, no. 4 (Summer 1974): 430-45.

For the history of Italian immigrants in Chicago, see Humbert S. Nelli, *The Italians in Chicago: 1880-1930* (New York: Oxford University Press, 1970); Rudolph Vecoli, "Contadini in Chicago: A Critique of *The Uprooted*," *Journal of American History* 51 (1964): 404-17, and "Chicago's Italians Prior to World War I," Ph.D. diss., University of Wisconsin, 1962; Frank O. Beck, *The Italians in Chicago* (Chicago: Chicago Department of Public Welfare, 1919); Giovanni Schiavo, *The Italians in Chicago: A Study in Americanization* (Chicago: Italian American Publishing Co., 1928) and *The Italians in Missouri* (Chicago: Italian American Publishing Co., 1929).

For a history of Chicago, see Emmett Dedmon's *Fabulous Chicago* (New York: Atheneum, 1983). Also, Harold M. Mayer and Richard C. Wade, *Chicago: Growth of a Metropolis* (Chicago: University of Chicago Press, 1973); Studs Terkel, *Division Street* (New York: Pantheon, 1967) and *The WPA Guide to Illinois* (New York: Pantheon, 1983).

Local 39 of the Amalgamated Clothing Workers Union was founded in 1911, with strikes occurring in 1910, 1915, and 1919 in Chicago's garment industry. By 1919, 100 percent of the Chicago garment industry was organized. Also in 1919, Italian Local 270 was founded. For a discussion of immigrants and unionism in the Chicago garment industry, see Eugene Miller and Gianna Panofsky, "Radical Italian Unionism: Its Development and Decline in Chicago's Men's Garment Industry, 1910-30" (1981), on file at the Chicago Labor History Society.

For a discussion of Italian grocers in Memphis see my article, "Italian Grocers: A Look Back," *Mid South Magazine, Memphis Commercial Appeal*, July 13, 1986, pp. 15-17.

CHAPTER 6

The 1899 poster from miners in Carbon Hill to their hometowns in the Bolognese and Modenese Apennines is part of the permanent collection of the Center for Migration Studies in Staten Island, New York.

For an interesting discussion of the Iowa coal-mining industry, see Dorothy Schwieder's *Black Diamonds: Life and Work in Iowa's Coal Mining Communities, 1895-1925* (Ames: Iowa State University Press, 1983). This includes discussion of Italian immigrant coal-mining communities and emigration from Modena and Bologna, and the seasonal migration from coal communities to the Chicago area.

For an account of Italian immigrants in Texas, see Valentine Belfiglio, *The Italian Experience in Texas* (Austin: Eakin Press, 1983), which includes discussion of immigrant coal miners and emigration from Emilia-Romagna. Italian immigration to Thurber from Modena and Bologna is also noted in *Bollettino dell'emigrazione*, no. 18 (1909): 46-48, and *Bollettino dell'emigrazione*, no. 5 (1913): 25-26.

For a discussion of Italian immigrants in Colorado coal mines see, Giovanni Perelli, *Colorado and the Italians in Colorado* (Denver: 1922), and Philip F. Notarianni, "The Italian Involvement in the 1903-04 Coal Miner's Strike in Southern Colorado and Utah," in *Pane e Lavoro: The Italian American Working Class*, ed. George E. Pozzetta, Proceedings of American Italian Historical Association (Toronto: Multicultural History Society of Ontario, 1980).

My outline of the U.S. coal-mining industry was drawn largely from Philip Taft's *Organized Labor in American History* (New York: Harper and Row, 1964). See also Herbert G. Gutman, *Work, Culture and Society in Industrializing America* (New York: Knopf, 1976); Melvyn Dubofsky, *We Shall Be All: A History of the Industrial Workers of the World* (Chicago: Quadrangle, 1969); Edwin Fenton, "Italians in the Labor Movement, *Pennsylvania History* 26 (1959): 135; and Isaac Hourwich, *Immigration and Labor: The Aspects of European Immigration to the United States* (New York: G. P. Putnam, 1912).

For a discussion of Italian immigrants used as strike breakers in Pennsylvania coal mines, see Gutman, "The Buena Vista Affair, 1874-1875," *The Pennsylvania Magazine* (July 1964). For a discussion of radicalism in northern Illinois coal fields, see Gianna Sommi Panofsky, "A View of Two Major Centers of Italian Anarchism in the U.S.: Springfield and Chicago, Ill.," in *Italian Ethnics: Their Languages, Literature and Lives* (Staten Island, N.Y.: American Historical Association, 1989). See also Bruna Pieracci, "The Miners," in *The Immigrants Speak: Italian-*

Americans Tell Their Story, ed. Salvatore J. La Gumino (New York: Center for Migration Studies, 1979), pp. 33-47; Daniel Jensen, "Coal Towns in Egypt: Portrait of an Illinois Coal Mining Region, 1890-1930," Ph.D. diss., Northwestern University, 1973; and Dolores Manfredini, "The Italians Come to Herrin," *Journal of the Illinois State Historical Society* (December 1944): 317-19.

The publications of the Italian Chamber of Commerce are part of the permanent collection of the Immigration History Research Center at the University of Minnesota. A 1908 bulletin details distribution and population of Italian immigrants in Midwestern communities.

In this chapter, Eritrea Pasquesi mentions arranging flowers on the street. This is a tradition in Pievepelago in which flowers and flower petals are arranged in intricate designs on the pavement of the town's piazza.

It should be noted that Delma Muzzarelli's husband, Joe, is not the same person as the Joseph Muzzarelli whose interview appears in this book.

CHAPTER 7

Contemporary news accounts from the Italian-language newspapers *Il Proletario, La Parola dei Socialisti,* and *L'Italia* are published with permission of the Immigration History Research Center. The translations are my own.

Other contemporary accounts include: Ernest C. Bicknell, *The Story of Cherry: Its Mine, Its Disaster, the Relief of Its People* (Washington, D.C.: American Red Cross, 1911); F. P. Buck, *The Cherry Mine Disaster* (Chicago: M. A. Donahue, 1911); *Report on The Cherry Mine Disaster* (Springfield: State of Illinois Bureau of Labor Statistics, 1910).

"The Great Disaster of the Cherry Mine," translated by Mary Muzzarelli from Antenore Quartaroli's account of the disaster, was published in the *La Salle-Peru Daily News Tribune* on November 12-14, 1979. Other accounts include Betty Boyd Caroli, "Italians in the Cherry, Illinois, Mine Disaster," in *Pane e Lavoro;* Anton Demichelis, *Memorial of the Fiftieth Anniversary of the Cherry Mine Disaster"* (1959), and Steve Stout, *Black Damp* (Utica, Illinois: Utica House Publishing, 1980), a novel based on the event.

Sixty-four of the 259 victims of the Cherry mine disaster, nearly 25 percent, were of Italian origin. Twenty of the victims, or nearly 8 percent, had names of Highwood or of the Modenese-Bolognese Apennines. They are: Alfio Amedei, Gioacchino Benassi, Carlo Bernardini, Clemente Burchi, Candido Canovi, John Compasso, Angelo Costi, Luigi

Costi, Frank Dinelli, Tony Giacobazzi, John Guidarini, Francesco Lolli, Ilario Maestri, Archangelo Marchioni, Frank Marchioni, Joseph Nanni, Alberto Palmieri, Cesare Ricci, Costantino Tamarri, and Emilio Tonelli.

Copies of correspondence regarding the seventeen victims from Fiumalbo killed in the Dawson disaster were given to me by Franco Marchioni of Fiumalbo. The names of the victims are: Luigi Biondi, Domenico Brugioni, Federico Brugioni, Giovanni (Vanni) Brugioni, Lieto Brugioni, Giuseppe Laudurini, Ubaldo Marchetti, Giovanni Nizzi, Pellegrino Pagliai, Beniamino Santi, Carlo Santi, Domenico Santi, Geremia Santi, Luigi Santi, and three brothers—Angelo Santi, Egisto Santi, and Raimondo Santi. Other victims from nearby towns included Pacifico Santi and Giovanni Ugolini.

CHAPTER 8

An early draft of this chapter appears in Jerome Krase and William Egelman, eds., *The Melting Pot and Beyond: Italian Americans in the Year 2000* (Staten Island, N.Y.: American Italian Historical Association, 1987).

Highwood has always been dependent on the surrounding affluent communities. In many ways, the history of its water system is illustrative of the differences between Highwood and its neighbors. Although Highwood is a stone's throw from Lake Michigan, until as late as 1941 it had to purchase its water from Highland Park because all lakefront property was owned by either Highland Park or Fort Sheridan. In order to gain an easement to the lake, Highwood needed congressional approval. In his 1937 appeal to a congressional committee, Mayor Charles Portilia cited the needs of his working-class constituency: "Almost every man is a laborer who puts every penny into his home. It isn't fair that we should pay unreasonable rates for water." This is cited on page 101 of Marvyn Wittelle's *Twenty-eight Miles North* (Highwood, Ill.: Highwood History Foundation, 1953).

Twenty-eight Miles North, a local history of Highwood, provides an invaluable chronology of the town's political history. I am indebted to Marvyn Wittelle's study for this account of Highwood's waterworks system, as well as her account of Highland Park's declining to annex Highwood. Page 53 of her book gives population figures indicating that in 1901 there were only three Italians in Highwood out of a total population of 851.

Contemporary news accounts are from the *Highland Park Press,* which is on microfilm at the Highland Park public library. The quotation about the Old Elm Club is from January 9, 1913; the ad placed by greenhouse and landscape businesses is from September 4, 1913. Examples of ads placed by immigrant businessmen include Sante Tazioli's from the October 7, 1920, issue of the *Highland Park Press*; cement contractor P. Ugolini, from July 22, 1920; and Pasquesi Brothers Motor Express Company, from March 18, 1920. The Charles Fiore ad is from the March 11, 1920, issue of the *Highland Park Press*. For other Fiore ads see issues of April 1, 1920; March 10, 1921; and April 21, 1920.

The article on shortage of domestic help is quoted from May 20, 1920. The Fould's Macaroni help-wanted ad is from August 28, 1913, and the "Protestant girl" ad is from June 12, 1913, of the *Highland Park Press*. For an interesting account of a study by the local YWCA on the working conditions for women in Highland Park, see *Highland Park Press*, March 18, 1920.

"Moraine Notes," listing hotel's guests, is quoted from the June 2, 1921, issue of the *Highland Park Press*. In describing Highland Park as a summer resort for the affluent, a June 17, 1920, editorial of the *Highland Park Press* wrote of an "annual summer migration" in which city people paid "enormous prices for the privilege of spending the summer in Highland Park."

See the *Historical Encyclopedia of Illinois* (Chicago: Munsell, 1925) and *History of Lake County* (Philadelphia: R. S. Bates, 1912) for contemporary descriptions of Highwood and other North Shore communities.

For a history of Chicago's affluent northern suburbs see *Creating Chicago's North Shore*, by Michael Ebner, cited above. Information in this chapter about the founding dates of country clubs is taken from his book. See also: Susan S. Benjamin, ed., *An Architectural Album: Chicago's North Shore* (Evanston, Ill.: Junior League of Evanston, 1988); Philip Berger, ed., *Highland Park: American Suburb at Its Best* (Highland Park, Ill.: Highland Park Landmark Preservation Committee, 1982); and Edward Arpee, *Lake Forest, Illinois: History and Reminiscences* (Lake Forest, Ill.: Lake Forest/Lake Bluff Historical Society, 1979); *Highwood, Illinois: 100 Years of Progress, 1887-1987*, cited above. For an account of a suburban settlement see Dominic Candeloro, "Suburban Italians: Chicago Heights, 1890-1975," in *Ethnic Chicago*, ed. Peter d'A. Jones and Melvin G. Holli (Grand Rapids, Mich.: Eerdmans, 1981). This volume also includes Irving Cutler's "The Jews of Chicago: From Shtetl to Suburb," a study of the settlement of Jews on Chicago's North Shore.

Studies that discuss the transformation of domestic service include: Daniel E. Sutherland, *Americans and their Servants: Domestic Servants in the United States from 1800 to 1920* (Baton Rouge: Louisiana State University, 1981); Elizabeth H. Pleek, "A Mother's Wages: Income Earnings among Married Italian and Black Women, 1896-1911," in *The*

American Family in Social and Historical Perspective, ed. Michael Gordon (New York: St. Martin's, 1983); Mary Grove Smith, "Immigration as a Source of Supply for Domestic Workers," *Bulletin of Inter-Municipal Committee on Household Research* 2 (May 1906); and Ann Oakley, *The Sociology of Housework* (New York: Pantheon, 1974).

Eritrea Pasquesi's discussion of the A. B. Dick family in Lake Forest refers to A. B. Dick, Jr., son of the founder of the A. B. Dick Company.

Rosa Fiocchi refers to her husband, Caesar, as having worked in Lake Forest on the homes of W. Paul McBride, who served as mayor of Lake Forest and lived at 1390 N. Lake; the Henry K. Turnbull home, "Cotswold House," which was modeled after an English country estate; the Arthur Dixon home, 1015 N. Greenbay; the Edward Cudahy home, "Innisfail," 830 N. Greenbay, which was designed by architect David Adler and built in 1930. Lake Forest architects Stanley D. Anderson and James H. Ticknor practiced together and worked on many homes and public buildings, including Lake Forest High School. During the early years of the Depression, they designed homes for the newly developed area called Deerpath Hill Estates, located near the intersection of Deerpath and Waukegan roads. She also refers to the Dwight C. Orcutt home in Glencoe and the William Burry home in Lake Forest.

According to a discussion with Rev. Edward Garza of St. James Catholic Church in August 1988, about half of the Hispanics involved with the church are of Mexican heritage, most of them from the southern state of Guerrero. The other half of the parish's Hispanic population are from other Central American nations including Guatemala, El Salvador, and Nicaragua, and fled their homes seeking political asylum. Most of the first-generation immigrants work in low-paying jobs in landscaping, restaurants, dry cleaning, domestic occupations, or in light industry in the area. Landscaper Charles Fiore, Jr., in an interview for the Italians in Chicago Oral History Project, said that his family's landscaping business was the first to bring Mexican laborers to Highwood during the late 1940s (p. 45).

CHAPTER 9

For a history of opera in Chicago, see Ronald Davis, *Opera in Chicago: A Social and Cultural History, 1850-1965* (New York: Appleton-Century, 1966); John Hodge, "The Chicago Civic Opera Company, Its Rise and Fall," in the *Illinois State Historical Society Review* 55 (Spring 1962); and Fannia Weingartner, ed., *Ravinia, the Festival and Its Half Century* (Ravinia, Ill.: Ravinia Festival Association, 1985). The passage about Ravinia is from the *Highland Park Press,* June 2, 1921, page 1.

CHAPTER 10

Egidio Mocogni, born in 1890 in Sant'Annapelago, was the first Italian immigrant to serve as alderman in Highwood (1927-29). He became Highwood's first Italian mayor in 1933. In 1923, he and Angelo Menoni established the Menoni and Mocogni building materials business.

In 1906, immigrants from Pievepelago and Sant'Annapelago formed the *Società Modenese di Mutuo Soccorso*—the Modenese Society—a mutual aid organization. Carlo Carani served as its first president. The Italian Women's Prosperity Club, a social and philanthropic organization, was founded in 1929. Mary Somenzi was its first president. The Cuore Arte Club, another social organization, was founded in 1932. John Ugolini was its first president.

Italian-owned grocery stores in addition to those mentioned in this chapter include: Mike Angiuli's, A. Gandolfi's, Gandolfi and Giangiorgi, Pasquale Innocenzi's, and Frank Parenti's in Highwood. In Highland Park there was Lencioni's Grocery and Market, Piccietti Brothers', and Sunset Grocery, owned by the Cortesi family. This information is taken from the Highland Park and Highwood telephone directory, 1934-39.

CHAPTER 12

For a contrast to the starkness of economic conditions in Highwood during the Depression, see Frederick Mercer Van Sickle, "A Special Place: Lake Forest and the Great Depression, 1929-1940," *Illinois Historical Journal* (Summer 1986). His article is based largely on interviews with residents. See also Irving Bernstein, *The Lean Years* (Boston: Houghton Mifflin, 1960); and Studs Terkel, *Hard Times* (New York: Pantheon, 1970).

CHAPTER 13

Now that *tortellini* have made it as a frozen dinner entrée I feel compelled to set down some facts, at least as I learned them. In the Frignano region, *tortellini* refers to the navel-shaped noodles and they are served exclusively in broth; the filling is of meat and they are smaller than the noodle which is used in the pasta course. I never heard the word *tortelloni* until I visited Florence, where *tortelloni* are the larger navel-shaped noodles which are filled with either meat or a spinach and cheese mixture, and topped with either a ragù or cream sauce. That said, it should go in the record that in Highwood among families who originated in the Modenese and Bolognese Apennines, *tortelloni* are never called *tortelloni* but *tortellacci,* or *tord'lacci.* It has been my experience that these were always filled with a mixture of spinanch or swiss chard, ricotta, and a bit of cream cheese and a tinier bit of grated Parmesean. Never meat.

To recap on the chestnut question: *Balucci* are cooked in water; *mondine* are roasted, and *menni* are eaten as a soup with milk. Pancakes (crepes) made of chestnut flour are called *necci,* or by some, in other localities, *ciacci. Borlenghi* are pancakes made of wheat flour and eaten with lard and rosemary, or with cheese and prosciutto. *Crescentini* are biscuits eaten, like *borlenghi,* with lard and rosemary.

For a detailed discussion of *necci, ciacci, borlenghi, crescentine,* and other regional specialities, see Sandro Bellei and Ugo Preti, *Cosa bolle in pentola a Modena* (Modena: Modena Libri, 1979).

CHAPTER 14

The anecdotes about *i gatti* and *Strappanecci* were told to me by Philip Pasquesi. Nicknames abound in Highwood to such an extent that *Highwood, Illinois: 100 Years of Progress, 1887-1987,* cited above, devotes three pages to the nicknames of Highwood's residents. A list of nicknames also appears in the centennial commemorative publication of Spring Valley, Illinois.

EPILOGUE

This chapter was first published in *Italian Ethnics: Their Languages, Literature and Lives* (Staten Island, N.Y.: American Italian Historical Association, 1989).

The words used to illustrate the Frignano dialect version of "when I was little," (*"quand 'iera piccol"*) are taken from a poem entitled "L'Amdajna" (*La Medaglina*) by Giacomo Cortesi, from his collection of poetry, *La me Pieve* (1983).

In two volumes entitled *Le parole dell'alto Frignano* (1984 and 1986), Battista Minghelli discusses the etymology and origins of this dialect with learned glee and the irreverence of a *montanaro.* See, for example, his discussion of *faitare,* a monster of a word, whose use in the mountains he attributes to immigrants returning from the United States; see also his discussion of *metato,* and, *inculento,* the latter a term which I have always heard used in describing a person who is a pain in a certain anatomical region and which, as Professor Minghelli documents, is a derivative of the word *culo,* which is that certain anatomical region.

"The Speech of Little Italy," by Anthony M. Turano, was first published in the *American Mercury,* July, 1932. This article is reprinted in Wayne Moquin, ed., *A Documentary History of the Italian Americans* (New York: Praeger, 1974), pp. 363-65. See also Robert J. DiPietro, "The Need for a Language Component in the Study of Italian Americans," in *Perspectives in Italian Immigration and Ethnicity,* ed. S. M. Tomasi (New York: Center for Migration Studies, 1977).

Italo Calvino is quoted from "By Way of an Autobiography," in *The Uses of Literature* (New York: Harcourt Brace Jovanovich, 1986).

List of Narrators

261

Zeffero Pacini	(1888-1988)	Grammolazzo, Lucca
Eritrea Pasquesi	b. 1907	Thurber, Texas
Philip Pasquesi	(1901-89)	Cadagnolo, Modena
Sante Pasquesi	(1888-1956)	Cadagnolo, Modena
Mariuccia Piacentini	(1904-87)	Riolunato, Modena
Aldobrando Piacenza	(1888-1976)	Sant'Annapelago, Modena
Henry Piacenza	(1895-1985)	Sant'Annapelago, Modena
Teresa Ponsi	(1902-84)	Sant'Andreapelago, Modena
Viterbo Ponsi	b. 1895	Sant'Andreapelago, Modena
Teresa Saielli	(1894-1984)	Groppo, Modena
Lawrence Santi	(1893-1983)	Pievepelago, Modena
Teodoro Sassorossi	b. 1898	Pievepelago, Modena
Massima Vanoni	b. 1906	Sant'Andreapelago, Modena
Guy Viti	b. 1898	Guarcino, Frosinone

Index

Lucca, 15, 37
Lucca (province of), 24, 43, 261-62
Ludlow, Colo., 83
Lumber business, 177, 202
La Luna, 12
Lutheran Church, 197
Luxembourg, 1, 34, 43, 174

McBride home (Lake Forest, Ill.), 176, 257
McCormick, Cyrus, Jr., 3, 139, 145, 190
McCormick, Harold, 3, 55, 139, 142-43, 190
McCormick estates, 52, 55, 139, 142-43, 145, 190
McPherson Garage, 156
Maddalena (Sardinia), 40
Madonna of the Querciola, 4, 79
Madrid, Iowa, 83, 99, 102
Magnani, Robert, 209
Maids. See Domestic workers
Mandel brothers, 186
Manfredini, Maria (Ponsi), 134, 171, 172, 192, 247, 261
Maremma, 36, 59
Marengo, Ill., 209
Marble, 43
Mark, Ill., 4, 209
Market crash of 1929, 154, 210, 211, 227-28, 230-31
Marinello (Modena), 103
Markun, Mary (Linari), 84
Martinelli, Giovanni, 189-91
Maserno (Modena), 52, 80, 261
Masons, 114
Massa Carrara, 43, 59
Massinelli, Attilio, 238
Mavor Company, William (Chicago), 181
Mazzanti, Amedeo, 191-92
Mazzarossi, Cristina, 214
Mazzetta, Marsilla, 214
Mazzetta, Peter, 206
Mechanics, 3, 145-47, 152, 155-57, 202
Medale, 13
Melcher, Iowa, 88
Memphis, Tenn.: Italians in, 63, 252
Menni, 259
Menoni, Joe (Angelo), 101, 151, 184, 200, 258
Menoni and Mocogni Company, 151, 184, 200

Merceles, I. F., 142
Merchants, 1, 17, 37
Metato, 22, 36
Methodist Church (Highwood, Ill.), 197
Metropolitan Opera Company, 191
Mexicans: in Highwood. See Hispanics
Mezzanotte, 18
La mia vita, 36, 61, 70, 152, 247
Midway Coal Company (Missouri), 99
Midwife, 125
Milan, 38, 46
Minghelli, Romeo, 185
Minghelli (contractor), 39
Mingus, Tex., 109
Minnesota, 4, 63, 65, 84, 181
Minorini's (Teodoro) Bakery, 169, 195, 210
La miseria, 43, 202, 224, 227, 228. See also Chapters 2, 3, and 12
Missouri, 4, 90-94, 96-99, 261
Mocogni, Domenica (Polandri), 1, 5, 28, 34, 45, 228, 261
Mocogni, Egidio, 151, 184, 200, 258
Mocogni, Giosue, 29-30
Modena (province of), 2, 4, 6, 14-33, 34-50, 77-80, 90-92, 95-97, 101-3, 106, 109, 115, 133, 135, 261-62; dialect, 233, 239, 242-44, 259
Modenese Society, 214, 258
Modino (Modena), 18, 38, 70, 101
Mojica, Jose, 189-91
Mondine, 23, 259
Montana, 64
Montanari, Don Alfonso, 35
Montecreto (Modena), 12
Montefiorino (Modena), 19
Montesi (Modena), 80
Montgomery Ward and Company, 142
Moradina, 13
Moraine Hotel, 4, 61, 142, 151-54, 210
Morandi, John, 103
Mordini, Charlie, 197
Mordini, Enrico, 1
Mordini, Giulia (Bertucci), 213, 229, 261
Mordini family, 1, 197
Morelli, Cherubina, 17
Morra, 170, 220
Morton home (Lake Forest, Ill.), 178
Morton Wing (Art Institute of Chicago), 140-41
Motherwell (Scotland), 261

Note on the Author

ADRIA BERNARDI is a writer who has worked as a journalist in Chicago and Memphis. She is a graduate of Carleton College, Northfield, Minnesota, and earned a master's degree in Italian literature at the University of Chicago. She lives in Chicago with her husband, Jeffrey Stovall.